Godly and Righteous,
Peevish and Perverse

Godly and Righteous, Peevish and Perverse

Clergy and Religious in Literature and Letters:
an Anthology

Compiled by
Raymond Chapman

CANTERBURY
PRESS
Norwich

© in this compilation Raymond Chapman 2002

First published in 2002 by the Canterbury Press Norwich
(a publishing imprint of Hymns Ancient & Modern Limited,
a registered charity)
St Mary's Works, St Mary's Plain,
Norwich, Norfolk, NR3 3BH

www.scm-canterburypress.co.uk

British Library Cataloguing in Publication data

A catalogue record for this book is available
from the British Library

ISBN 1-85311-492-8

Typeset by Regent Typesetting, London
Printed in Great Britain by
Biddles Ltd, Guildford and King's Lynn

Contents

Introduction

No account of the English-speaking peoples, whether historical, sociological or cultural, would be complete without mention of the clergy. Many people may have been ignorant of theology, indifferent to ecclesiastical affairs, absent from public worship, but the clerical presence has been inescapable. Their profession, and the faith they have proclaimed, have aroused every emotion from reverence to contempt, but they have a way of appearing even at improbable moments in the literary as well as in the factual record. They have been praised, scorned, regarded with amusement or tolerant acceptance, but never ignored.

There have been times when the clergy, particularly those of the Established Church in Britain, have been positively unpopular. Such was the case during the agitation for the Reform Act of 1832 when all but two of the bishops in the House of Lords voted against parliamentary reform. Bad feeling about tithes and the levy of church rates often aroused anger against the parish clergy. But in Britain at least there has been little or no organized anti-clericalism to the degree that occurred on the Continent and became a factor in more than one political revolution. The position of the parish priest, changed but not abolished by the Reformation and temporarily usurped during the Commonwealth, shows a remarkable continuity over the centuries.

What the Reformation did bring, however, was a new diversity of clerical types. While the Roman Catholic priests were for a time suppressed and persecuted, and the religious orders were dissolved, the parish incumbent was now often a married man with a family, and with interests closely connected to those of the State. Increasingly, ministers of other denominations were ordained to cater for those who disliked the Establishment. As they and the Roman Catholic clergy gradually attained recognition and the right to their own places of worship, their number and influence grew and they in turn became subjects of public admiration or satire. The concept of a clerical profession was broadened, and the 'minister' was no longer only the incumbent of a Church of England parish.

The Church of England clergy were certainly in some ways a privileged class for hundreds of years. The privilege was by no means equally shared either socially or financially. There were pluralist incumbents of rich livings and prebends, some of them younger sons of the aristocracy who enjoyed large incomes and virtually unlimited leisure. There were others whose stipend was little more than a labourer's wages and who did work farmed out to them by their more affluent colleagues. There were parsons who dined and hunted with the squire and sat with him on the magistrates' bench, and whose children made fashionable marriages. There were curates who never rose to a parish of their own, whose daughters could hope for nothing better than the despised post of a governess. These discrepancies are not to be forgotten, and they are prominent in the pages that follow. The differences were most obvious in the rural parishes, where the parson was a central figure whose life and conduct were closely observed. Rich or poor, the parson might be the only educated man in a small village, the one to whom parishioners would turn for advice on more than spiritual matters. The Industrial Revolution brought a new phenomenon, the town slum parish, an unenviable task which was served by the most unfortunate or the most saintly of the clergy of all denominations.

If poverty was the lot of many Church of England priests, it was almost universal among other clergy. Even after the lifting of civil disabilities and restrictions on worship in the early nineteenth century, Roman Catholic priests and Nonconformist ministers often worked in the most deprived areas. For a long time they had little prestige or respect outside their own churches, yet they played an important part in social and political history as well as in spiritual care. Their achievements, and some of their faults, are remembered in these pages.

The insularity of Britain – both geographically and in mental attitude – meant that writers gave less attention to those who went overseas. As missionaries, explorers or service chaplains, many clergy did in fact leave their native land for a time or for life. They include some of the noblest and also some of the most eccentric, and they too are not forgotten.

In course of time, the little island contributed to the religious life of many countries. In the United States, and in the lands of the former British Empire, the development of churches to serve a growing population began from Britain. The Church of England created new dioceses overseas, eventually to became autonomous churches of the Anglican Communion. These have long since followed their own distinctive cultures, but the ghosts of the island past can still be discerned. Many clergy left to escape persecution and restraint from the same Established Church, to find freedom to worship in their own way. The churches which developed in opposition to the Establishment put down new roots elsewhere. It is reasonable to suggest that life in these countries today would be different if those early Christian settlements had not been made.

Clergy in the United States are represented in these pages, as well as American writers who have left their impressions of the clergy and churches in Britain. A shared heritage until the seventeenth century links both nations, and thereafter divergence does not completely erase likeness. There are, however, significant differences which appear in the work of American writers, both in fact and fiction. Notably, there has never been an established Church in the United States. The link between Church and State which prevailed in Britain for so many years is absent. The clerical teachers and lecturers who once dominated British education have no counterparts, and indeed the Constitution forbids religious teaching in the public schools (a title which, of course, has very different implications in the two countries).

Consequently, there is no heritage in the United Sates of resentment remaining from the memory of penal laws and limited privilege. All churches have had to make their own way without official favour or impediment. There is no lingering suggestion that the governing class – again a British rather than American concept – are likely to be members of a particular denomination. Much that is distinctive of Nonconformity in Britain is characteristic of all churches in the United States.

Until recently, Britain has had comparatively few permanent citizens whose origin is in other lands. The population of the United States has been enlarged by immigration for much longer, with the result that ministries to national and ethnic communities have developed to a greater extent. The older denominations, which were at the foundation of the American nation, have endured and flourished but have been accompanied by many new ones from abroad and perhaps even more of native growth. The American clergy have ministered to gathered rather than geographical congregations. None can claim even titular pastoral care for all the inhabitants of a given area. Even in the more organized and structured denominations, and certainly in the independent ones, the minister has needed to depend a good deal on personal charisma to win respect and authority. If some of the depictions seem to show excessive self-importance, and others to reveal troubling self-doubt, it is because both have been engendered by the system – or rather the lack of system as compared with the British situation. There have been no religious movements which have radically affected thought and practice, in the way that the Oxford Movement in England touched even those outside its immediate ambit. But there have been great and far-reaching religious revivals which have left their mark. These have depended largely on vigorous preaching, and it is 'the preacher' who typifies the United States' image of Christian ministry.

Deep respect and satirical contempt for the clergy are both expressed by American writers – and here the similarity between the two countries again proves to be greater than the differences. Today the clerical profile in most countries of the world is lower, blurred in a more heterogeneous society but by no means lost. There is less discernment of what the life of a priest or minister is really like, but perhaps there never was a time when those outside this or any profession really penetrated its nature. Any Anglican clergyman who is not obviously a bishop is universally known as a 'vicar', irrespective of more precise function. Roman Catholic priests are still 'priests' and other clergy are 'ministers' – a comprehensive word favoured for all denominations by funeral directors.

In Britain at least, it is the 'vicar' who is portrayed most often in the media. In the view of script-writers he, and increasingly she, seems to be mainly concerned with taking funerals and weddings, conducted in a dull and artificial voice. The rest of the time is given to 'preparing my sermon for Sunday', with occasional space for revealing a wide-eyed ignorance of the real world. In spite of dealing with every kind of human badness and sadness, the vicar remains easily shocked, especially by anything connected with sex – apparently synonymous in the clerical world with sin. 'Don't mention it in front of the vicar' – rather as if references to illness were regarded as out of place when there was a doctor in the room. But sometimes the clergy are allowed a more prominent role and there is still affection as well as entertainment value in *Father Ted, The Vicar of Dibley* and the various priests of *Ballykissangel*.

There is continuity as well as change, and the Church in any age can be best understood as part of a long evolution. This book does not set out to be a systematic history of the English-speaking churches. It has been put together by type and relationship rather than by chronology. Historical order is usually followed in individual chapters but sometimes gives way to sub-sections. I have tried to build up a picture of clerical life in its many aspects, and particularly its effects on the lay majority. As the story unfolds, it sometimes suggests that there are things which do not change with the years. Some of the men and women in these pages are well known, part of our reading memories. Others come from more obscure sources, to take their place in the roll of the past. Some have been, and will continue to be, loved; some disliked; many regarded with affectionate laughter. The best jokes are told by those who understand and are sympathetic to the subject at which they laugh.

For chapter headings I have drawn on the Book of Common Prayer, the principal source of public worship in English for hundreds of years. The choice is no derogation of the liturgies of other churches, or of those who prefer less structured services. It has been, and continues to be, the source of devotion and religious language for many who have not been members of the Church of England.

Some of our subjects are presented as brief character studies, others as part of a more developed situation. Some of these people are fictional, some are factual with perhaps a degree of embellishment. They live together in these pages: some as inhabitants of a past but still familiar landscape, some as participants in the present time. Clergy of the Church of England form the largest group numerically, not from any claim to superiority but because they have been the most fully and frequently recorded. Other churches are well represented and, in keeping with a more ecumenical age, they appear together, associated by character and not by denomination. There is space too for some who have not been formally ordained but have claims to be regarded as 'ministers and stewards' of the gospel. This is especially notable in the missionary field. The religious, the monks and friars and nuns, have had less literary attention, partly because their orders were for so long suppressed and partly because the nature of their calling kept them from public view – but they too are not absent.

Ordained women are, at least in the Anglican Communion, too recent a group to have attracted much description and comment yet. But clergy wives have, since the Reformation, had a very prominent place in both church and social life, and some of them are depicted here. Women in the religious life, and earlier female ministers, have not been forgotten.

If space were unlimited and copyright unrestricted, there are many more who could find a place here. In the work of more recent writers, there are some splendid eccentrics such as Rose Macaulay's Father Chantry-Pigg in *The Towers of Trebizond* who had retired from an Anglo-Catholic London parish and now 'devoted his life to conducting very High retreats and hunting for relics of saints, which he collected for the private oratory in his Dorset manor house'. Evelyn Waugh also specialized in clerical oddities, such as the returned missionary Mr Tendril in *A Handful of Dust* who was accustomed to preaching at a garrison chapel in India and never adapted his sermons for an English country congregation, so that they 'mostly conclude with some references to homes and dear ones far away', and Mr Prendergast in *Decline and Fall* who had been driven from parish ministry by doubts, not about specific doctines but because hs 'couldn't understand why God had made the world at all'.

Graham Greene specialized in unhappy, disillusioned priests, such as Father Rank in *The Heart of the Matter*, lonely in a West African mission, and the nameless 'whiskey priest' in *The Power and the Glory*, fleeing from Communist persecution. George Orwell gaves us Dorothy's stressed and bitter father in *A Clergyman's Daughter*, who hated harvest festivals (perhaps some more amiable clergy secretly share his feeling on the matter). Later in time, Lorna Sage wrote movingly in her autobiography *Bad Blood* about her grandfather who had many talents but whose 'past followed him like a long, glamorous, sinister shadow'. Joanna Trollope has created many clerical characters and has also brought a new voice to the clergy wife, as when Anna in *The Rector's Wife* cries out, 'I can't be an individual, only someone relative to Peter, to the parish, to the Church'.

Among clerical schoolmasters there are some additional good types, such as the Reverend John in Kipling's *Stalky and Co*, who is a great success with the boys but would certainly get into trouble today for sitting in one of their studies and smoking his pipe. There are also some very bad specimens, such as Joyce's Father Dolan in *A Portrait of the Artist as a Young Man* who announces his arrival in the classroom with 'Any boys want flogging here, Father Arnall? [. . .] Any lazy idle loafers that want flogging in this class?'

In the twentieth century, Hugh Walpole carried on the Trollopean tradition of novels with a full cast of clergy, notably in *The Cathedral.* Compton Mackenzie and Ernest Raymond recorded in fiction the Anglo-Catholic priests who were influential in the inter-war period. P. D. James continues to write from her intimate knowledge of the Church of England and its liturgy, most recently with a group of priests in a theological college in *Death in Holy Orders,* threatened by a tormented reforming Archdeacon, 'dark and bearded like an Old Testament prophet'.

If readers learn a little from these pages about their clergy, that will be good. If they find enjoyment, and come back again to revisit new friends, admire patterns of behaviour or remind themselves of some horrid warnings, that will be even better.

What we have in fact is a very motley collection of human beings sharing a common role and a common status. Here are the saintly and the venial, the pious and the worldly, some noisy, some reserved, some admirable and some a little absurd but, it is hoped, forming an essentially lovable company.

Editorial Notes

The authors' original spelling and punctuation have been retained, except where they were likely to cause difficulty or misunderstanding to the modern reader. The original use of capital letters within sentences, which may give a distinctive emphasis, has generally been retained.

[   ] denotes editorial additions or comments within extracts.
[…] denotes editorial omissions from the original text.
⟨ ⟩ denotes expansion of initials or abbreviations in the text.

Excessive use of dates has been avoided. Enough have been added to place each section in its historical perspective. I have not attempted to annotate every reference in the passages quoted, but have added a few explanations of points that might be obscure.

In the Sources section, a text's original date of publication is given first, where it differs from that of the edition quoted. Extracts from well-known poems and novels which have appeared in many editions are usually referenced only by title and chapter or lines.

Chapter 1

Godly, Righteous and Sober

One of the problems about being an ordained priest or minister is the general expectation that people in such a position will be 'good'. Personal problems, weariness, exasperation and the shared frailty of human nature have to be kept out of sight. It is in fact a stressful as well as a richly reward-ing vocation. Of course, suppression does not always work, and the clergy must be excused if they are not perfect people: they might be less useful to their flocks if they were. When one religious leader gets into trouble, the public reports are vivid and unforgiving. When thousands are doing their best, working with care and love in the way of life to which they have been called, very few take notice. They are no more specially virtuous than others, but faith and grace can do wonders with unpromising material. Neverthe-less, we all know some who put the rest of us to shame by their lives. As we shall meet in these pages a number of clergy who were less than perfect, let us begin with a few examples of virtue. When so many have been the victims of satire, humour or obloquy, it is pleasant to remember that the Church has not been served entirely by comic villains. Some of the descriptions may be a bit idealized, but they combine to give a generally happy picture of the Christian Church at large, through all the chances and changes of history and of the social position of the clergy themselves.

Let us begin at the beginning, with an idealized image of an Anglo-Saxon priest. Wordsworth was inspired by Bede's eulogy of the clergy and by the Romantic regard for life before the end of the Middle Ages.

How beautiful your presence, how benign,
Servants of God! Who not a thought will share
With the vain world; who, outwardly as bare
As winter trees, yield no fallacious sign
That the firm soul is clothed with fruit divine!

Such Priest, whose service worthy of his care
Has called him forth to breathe the common air
Might seem a stately image from its shrine
Descended – happy are the eyes that meet
The Apparition; evil thoughts are stayed
At his approach, and low-bowed necks entreat
A benediction from his voice or hand;
Whence grace, through which the heart can understand
And bows that bind the will, in silence made.

William Wordsworth, 'Primitive Saxon Clergy'[1]

*Chaucer was often critical of the Church, but among his pilgrims assembled
to set out for Canterbury he depicts a simple parish priest, idealized perhaps
but surely not without his real-life equals. This model priest displays the
qualities often regarded in later centuries as the clerical ideal: faithful visiting, no distinction in attitude to social rank, conscientious teaching and
material charity.*

There was a good man of religion
Who was the poor Parson of a town.
But he was rich in holy thought and work,
And also was a learned man, a clerk:
One who Christ's Gospel faithfully would preach
And with devotion would his people teach.
He was benign, extremely diligent,
Patient in every bad predicament –
Adversity was often on him laid.
He did not like to curse for tithes unpaid,
But rather would have given, without doubt,
To poor folk in his parish round about,
Both from church offerings and his private store,
For little wealth gave him enough, and more.
His parish wide, with houses far asunder –
But he'd not fail in either rain or thunder,
In sickness or distress, to visit duly
The farthest in his parish, high or lowly,
Going on foot, and in his hand a stave.

This fine example to his sheep he gave
That first he acted, afterwards he taught
In words which from the Gospel he had caught.
And he would add to them this figure too –
That if gold rusts, then what will iron do?
For if the priest is bad – the one we trust –
Small wonder if a common man should rust.
It is a scandal – let priests ponder deep –
A corrupt shepherd keeping spotless sheep.
The right example for a priest to give
Is purity, the way the sheep should live.
He did not rent his benefice for hire
And leave his sheep to wallow in the mire
While he ran off to London, to Saint Paul's,
To find himself a chantry there for souls,
Or in some Brotherhood to get enrolled.
He stayed at home and cared well for his fold,
So that no wolf should cause it to miscarry –
He was a shepherd, not a mercenary.
Holy and virtuous in every way,
But not despising those who went astray.
Not scornful or superior in speech,
Discreet and gentle when he went to teach.
By kindness to lead people towards heaven,
His duty was a good example given.
But as for those who would be obstinate,
Whether they were of high or low estate,
His reprimand would be both sharp and free.
There could not be a better priest than he.
The lore of Christ and his Apostles twelve
He taught, but first he followed it himself.

Geoffrey Chaucer, *The Canterbury Tales* [2]

Richard Hooker (c. 1554–1600) was one of the leading divines of the six-teenth century. His writings have been highly influential on Anglican thought. He was also a good parish priest.

He was diligent to enquire who of his Parish were sick, or any ways dis-tressed, and would often visit them, unsent for; supposing that the fittest time to discover to them those errors, to which health and prosperity had blinded them. And having by pious reasons and prayers moulded them into holy resolutions for the time to come, he would incline them to confession and bewailing their sins, with purpose to forsake them, and then to receive the Communion, both as a strengthening of those holy resolutions, and as a seal betwixt God and them of his mercies to their souls, in case that present sickness did put a period to their lives.

And as he was thus watchful and charitable to the sick, so he was as diligent to prevent law-suits; still urging his parishioners and neighbours to bear with each other's infirmities, and live in love, because, as St John says, 'He that lives in love, lives in God; for God is love.' And to maintain this holy fire of love constantly burning on the altar of a pure heart, his advice was to watch and pray, and always keep themselves fit to receive the Communion, and then to receive it often; for it was both a con-firming and strengthening of their graces. This was his advice; and at his entrance or departure out of any house, he would usually speak to the whole family, and bless them by name; insomuch, that as he seemed in his youth to be taught of God, so he seemed in this place to teach his precepts as Enoch did, by walking with him in all holiness and humility, making each day a step towards a blessed eternity. And though, in this weak and declining age of the world, such examples are become barren, and almost incredible; yet let his memory be blessed by this true recordation, because he that praises Richard Hooker, praises God who hath given such gifts to men; and let this humble and affectionate rela-tion of him become such a pattern, as may invite posterity to imitate these his virtues.

Isaac Walton, *The Life of Richard Hooker*[3]

George Herbert (1593–1633), known as a fine devotional poet, was Rector of Bemerton near Salisbury. He described the ideal country parson in A Priest to the Temple *and his personal sanctity was attested by many of his contemporaries.*

In another walk to Salisbury he saw a poor man with a poorer horse, that was fallen under his load: they were both in distress, and needed present help; which Mr Herbert perceiving, put off his canonical coat, and helped the poor man to unload, and after to load, his horse. The poor man blessed him for it, and he blessed the poor man; and was so like the good Samaritan, that he gave him money to refresh both himself and his horse; and told him, 'That if he loved himself he should be merciful to his beast.' Thus he left the poor man: and at his coming to his musical friends at Salisbury, they began to wonder that Mr George Herbert, which used to be so trim and clean, came into that company so soiled and discomposed: but he told them the occasion. And when one of the company told him, 'He had disparaged himself by so dirty an employ-ment', his answer was, 'That the thought of what he had done would prove music to him at midnight; and that the omission of it would have upbraided and made discord in his conscience, whensoever he should pass by that place: for if I be bound to pray for all that be in distress, I am sure that I am bound, so far as it is in my power, to practise what I pray for. And though I do not wish for the like occasion every day, yet let me tell you, I would not willingly pass one day of my life without comfort-ing a sad soul, or showing mercy; and I praise God for this occasion. And now let's tune our instruments.'

Thus, as our blessed Saviour, after his resurrection, did take occasion to interpret the Scripture to Cleopas, and that other disciple, which he met with and accompanied in their journey to Emmaus; so Mr Herbert, in his path toward heaven, did daily take any fair occasion to instruct the ignorant, or comfort any that were in affliction; and did always confirm his precepts by showing humility and mercy, and ministering grace to the hearers.

Isaac Walton, *The Life of George Herbert*[4]

George Herbert might qualify to be nominated as the ideal priest described by Thomas Ken (1637–1711). Bishop of Bath and Wells, Ken became one of the Non-Jurors who refused to take the oath of allegiance to William III. He was himself a saintly man, a writer of devotional works, poems and hymns.

Give me the priest these graces shall possess –
Of an ambassador the just address.
A father's tenderness, a shepherd's care,
A leader's courage, which the cross can bear;
A ruler's awe, a watchman's wakeful eye,
A pilot's skill, the helm in storms to ply;
A fisher's patience, and a labourer's toil,
A guide's dexterity to disembroil,
A prophet's inspiration from above,
A teacher's knowledge, and a Saviour's love.
Give me the priest, a light upon a hill,
Whose rays his whole circumference can fill;
In God's own word and sacred learning versed,
Deep in the study of the heart immersed;
Who in sick souls can the disease descry,
And wisely for restoratives apply;
To beatific pastures leads his sheep,
Watchful from hellish wolves his fold to keep;
Who seeks not a convenience but a cure,
Would rather souls than his own gain ensure.
Instructive in his visits and converse,
Strives everywhere salvation to disperse;
Of a mild, humble, and obliging heart,
Who with his all will to the needy part;
Distrustful of himself, in God confides,
Daily himself among his flock divides;
Of virtue uniform, and cheerful air,
Fixed meditation, and incessant prayer,
Affections mortified, well-guided zeal,
Of saving truth the relish wont to feel,
Whose province, heaven, all his endeavour shares,
Who mixes with no secular affairs,
Oft on his pastoral amount reflects,

By holiness, not riches, gains respects;
Who is all that he would have others be,
From wilful sin, though not from frailty, free;
Who still keeps Jesus in his heart and head,
Who strives in steps of our Arch-priest to tread,
Who can himself and all the world deny,
Lives pilgrim here, but denizen on high.[5]

The eighteenth century is often regarded as a bad period for religion, and especially for the Anglican Church. But it produced the Evangelical Revival, Methodism and the work of some remarkable devotional writers. This description of a country clergyman, even if idealized, shows that there were also good men among the more obscure. It celebrates virtues similar to those of Chaucer's Poor Parson, nearly four centuries earlier.

Near yonder copse, where once the garden smiled,
And still where many a garden flower grows wild;
There, where a few torn shrubs the place disclose,
The village preacher's modest mansion rose.
A man he was to all the country dear,
And passing rich with forty pounds a year;
Remote from towns he ran his godly race,
Nor e'er had changed, nor wished to change his place;
Unpractised he to fawn, or seek for power,
By doctrines fashioned to the varying hour;
Far other aims his heart had learned to prize,
More skilled to raise the wretched than to rise.
His house was known to all the vagrant train;
He chid their wanderings, but relieved their pain:
The long-remembered beggar was his guest,
Whose beard descending swept his aged breast;
The ruined spendthrift, now no longer proud,
Claimed kindred there, and had his claims allowed;
The broken soldier, kindly bade to stay,
Sat by the fire, and talked the night away,
Wept o'er his wounds, or, tales of sorrow done,
Shouldered his crutch and showed how fields were won.

Pleased with his guests, the good man learned to glow,
And quite forgot their vices in their woe;
Careless their merits or their faults to scan
His pity gave ere charity began.
Thus to relieve the wretched was his pride,
And e'en his failings leaned to Virtue's side;
But in his duty prompt at every call,
He watched and wept, he prayed and felt, for all;
And, as a bird each fond endearment tries
To tempt its new-fledged offspring to the skies,
He tried each art, reproved each dull delay,
Allured to brighter worlds, and led the way.
Beside the bed where parting life was laid,
And sorrow, guilt, and pain by turns dismayed,
The reverend champion stood. At his control
Despair and anguish fled the struggling soul;
Comfort came down the trembling wretch to raise,
And his last faltering accents whispered praise.
At church, with meek and unaffected grace,
His looks adorned the venerable place;
Truth from his lips prevailed with double sway,
And fools, who came to scoff, remained to pray.
The service past, around the pious man,
With steady zeal, each honest rustic ran;
Even children followed with endearing wile,
And plucked his gown, to share the good man's smile.
His ready smile a parent's warmth expressed;
Their welfare pleased him, and their cares distrest:
To them his heart, his love, his griefs were given,
But all his serious thoughts had rest in heaven.
As some tall cliff that lifts its awful form,
Swells from the vale, and midway leaves the storm,
Though round its breast the rolling clouds are spread,
Eternal sunshine settles on its head.

Oliver Goldsmith *The Deserted Village*[6]

George Arthur in Tom Brown's Schooldays *is certainly a schoolboy too good to be true, but the account of his deceased father who struggled in a poor Midland parish carries more conviction.*

Into such a parish and state of society, Arthur's father had been thrown at the age of twenty-five, a young married parson, full of faith, hope, and love. He had battled with it like a man, and had lots of fine Utopian ideas about the perfectibility of mankind, glorious humanity, and such like knocked out of his head; and a real wholesome Christian love for the poor struggling, sinning men, of whom he felt himself one and with and for whom he spent fortune, and strength, and life, driven into his heart. He had battled like a man, and gotten a man's reward. No silver teapots or salvers, with flowery inscriptions, setting forth his virtues and the appreciation of a genteel parish; no fat living or stall, for which he never looked, and didn't care; no sighs and praises of comfortable dowagers and well got-up young women, who worked him slippers, sugared his tea, and adored him as 'a devoted man'; but a manly respect, wrung from the unwilling souls of men who fancied his order their natural enemies; the fear and hatred of every one who was false or unjust in the district, were he master or man; and the blessed sight of women and children daily becoming more human and more homely, a comfort to themselves and to their husbands and fathers.

[*He dies during a typhus epidemic in which most of the other clergy decide to run away.*]

He was sensible to the last, and calm and happy, leaving his wife and children with fearless trust for a few years in the hands of the Lord and Friend who had lived and died for him, and for whom he, to the best of his power, had lived and died. His widow's mourning was deep and gentle; she was more affected by the request of the Committee of a Freethinking club, established in the town by some of the factory hands, (which he had striven against with might and main, and nearly suppressed), that some of their number might be allowed to help bear the coffin, than by anything else. Two of them were chosen, who, with six other labouring men, his own fellow-workmen and friends, bore him to his grave – a man who had fought the Lord's fight even unto the death.

Thomas Hughes, *Tom Brown's Schooldays*[7]

John Keble (1792–1866) was revered by the followers of the Oxford Movement, and respected even by its opponents. His Assize Sermon in 1833 is often regarded as the beginning of the Movement. He left Oxford to become a parish priest at Hursley, near Winchester. His early biographer, who knew him well, tells of his last years when many helpers were continuing his work.

Working by others, however, did not prevent him from occupying himself much in personal visitation; in this he was unwearied, in all weathers, at all hours; and sometimes to the injury of his own health. His was truly a ministry of consolation, and of cheering; he had consideration for all the special circumstances of each person under his charge. There was, for example, a poor cripple, deaf and dumb, whom he constantly found time to visit, because the man thought he could understand the motion of his lips; and he would hold conversations with him besides, by writing on a slate; then to amuse him in his solitary life, he would set him sums on the slate when he went away, and look them over at his next visit, and correct them.

He 'made friends', as one may say, with the inmates of the Workhouse, especially the old men, and was frequent in his visits there. He got them to the Daily Services, and, seating them on the front benches, addressed himself specially to them, as he read the second Lesson, reading slowly, and with pauses, almost as if he were alone with them, and were speaking to them. He was rewarded not seldom by finding how much they learned of the Gospels in this way. Indeed his manner of reading the Scriptures was remarkable: so simple, that your first impression of it was that it was the reading of a very intelligent and reverent child, yet so good, that he made you understand them more, I think, than any one else. At the same time he conveyed to you in some measure his own feeling of reverence.

J. T. Coleridge, *A Memoir of the Rev John Keble* [8]

Arthur Stanton (1839–1913) was one of many Victorian Anglo-Catholic priests who were distrusted by the Establishment and gained no preferment. He served as a curate in London at St Alban's, Holborn, throughout his ministry, famous as a preacher and confessor. Even allowing for the Victorian tendency to hero-worship, he was certainly an admirable priest. His sermons are still worth reading.

Stanton's ease with his neighbours in every walk of life, and his wonderful toleration in religion and in social intercourse, were rooted in his love for humankind. Seeing this world as a place of joyful pilgrimage, and missionary endeavour, the career he had chosen called forth for those whom he met day by day both sympathy and understanding, and the aid thus sought was never lacking. This is what was meant when people said Father Stanton was 'always a gentleman'. His sympathy and understanding, inspired by the sense of common kinship with all Christ's brethren – whether of the household of faith or not, and with all the children of a Heavenly Father – left no room for the vulgarity that fattens on the disparaging of neighbours, and finds an uncouth delight in making much of the faults of others, and noting their want of grace. Stanton perceived that manners and customs vary with races, nations, tribes, and families, and are not the same, and need not be the same, in all classes of society. Hence, he did not appear either shocked or hurt at what are called lapses of taste, because, in his case, these things really did not shock or hurt. Provost Ball has referred to this social catholicity of Stanton's: 'I have seen him in the company of the underbred, making himself quite at home with them, laughing at their jokes, adopting their phrases, and so forth, never, however, condoning the least approach to coarseness.' Many other friends of Stanton's have spoken in similar fashion of his comfortable habit of being at home with all sorts of queer neighbours. It was all on a par with his religious toleration. It wasn't that Stanton didn't value Catholic ritual that he could adapt himself to simple Protestant services, joining in a prayer-meeting, or listening to an Evangelical sermon in the barest or ugliest of non-Catholic places of worship. The unity of faith that was beneath externals was more to him than breaches of Church order. The latter might be regrettable, but the thing to rejoice over was the actual possibility of living in religious goodwill in spite of differences in church discipline.

Joseph Clayton, *Father Stanton*[9]

John Ellerton was Rector of St Mary's, Barnes, from 1876 to 1884. Re-
membered as a writer of hymns, he seems to have been a model parish priest.
Reminiscences of an incumbent by a former curate may be adulatory like
this one – but of course it could go the other way. The 'permanent and hand-
some structure' is the present parish church of St Michael's, Barnes, a part
of London which continues to be 'populous', if not 'important'.

The parish of Barnes, large, populous, and important, offered a noble
field for ministerial work, and into this the new rector threw himself with
unreserved devotion, giving all his powers of mind and body to the
welfare of those whom he had been called to serve. A very different congregation now listened to him from what he had been accustomed to
address in Cheshire, a congregation which had been taught to look for
teaching of the highest order from a pulpit long occupied by the eloquent
Henry Melvill, and after him by the scholarly Medd. As these pages are
designed to be but a sketch of Mr Ellerton's life, and by no means a full
biography, I say but little of his ministerial work at Barnes, where I had
the privilege of being associated with him as his curate, and dwell rather
upon the literary side of his industry. Suffice it to say, that every detail of
parochial work was thoroughly mastered. In one part of the parish a
room was opened for special services for the poor; in another an iron
church, since replaced by a permanent and handsome structure, was
erected. Whether it was the choir, the schools, district visitors, or confirmation classes, upon each in its turn he concentrated his whole mind,
spending and being spent in his Master's service, until his strength broke
down under the burden, and he was compelled to resign it to another.
Perhaps it was only the few who could appreciate his rare gifts of oratory,
his elegant scholarship; but all loved him, all, that is, whose hearts were
capable of responding to the reality of his sympathy, and the warmth of
his loving heart. One who knew him well wrote, on the occasion of his
death, 'That he was a man of deep learning and of varied and extended
reading, no educated listener could fail to discover, although his sermons
were remarkably free from parade of erudition or excess of ornament.
But it was not his mastery of English, his many-sided culture, and his
transparent sincerity that gave to his sermons the attractiveness to which
we refer. It was rather that rare and indefinable *something* which radiates
from poetic natures, and makes other hearts burn within them.'

Henry Housman, *John Ellerton*[10]

In a more rural setting, Angel Clare is walking with his clergyman father, who does not know of his interest in Tess, a distant descendant of the D'Urberville family.

Angel listened in a willing silence, as they jogged together through the shady lanes, to his father's account of his parish difficulties, and the coldness of brother clergymen whom he loved, because of his strict interpretations of the New Testament by the light of what they deemed a pernicious Calvinistic doctrine.

'Pernicious!' said Mr Clare, with genial scorn; and he proceeded to recount experiences which would show the absurdity of that idea. He told of wondrous conversions of evil livers of which he had been the instrument, not only amongst the poor, but amongst the rich and well-to-do; and he also candidly admitted many failures.

As an instance of the latter, he mentioned the case of a young upstart squire named d'Urberville, living some forty miles off, in the neighbourhood of Trantridge [...] After the death of the senior so-called d'Urberville the young man developed the most culpable passions, though he had a blind mother, whose condition should have made him know better. A knowledge of his career having come to the ears of Mr Clare, when he was in that part of the country preaching missionary sermons, he boldly took occasion to speak to the delinquent on his spiritual state. Though he was a stranger, occupying another's pulpit, he had felt this to be his duty, and took for his text the words from St Luke: 'Thou fool this night thy soul shall be required of thee!' The young man much resented this directness of attack, and in the war of words which followed when they met he did not scruple publicly to insult Mr Clare, without respect for his gray hairs. Angel flushed with distress.

'Dear Father,' he said sadly, 'I wish you would not expose yourself to such gratuitous pain from scoundrels!'

'Pain?' said his father, his rugged face shining in the ardour of self-abnegation. 'The only pain to me was pain on his account, poor, foolish young man. Do you suppose his incensed words could give me any pain, or even his blows? "Being reviled we bless; being persecuted we suffer it, being defamed we entreat; we are made as the filth of the world, and as the offscouring of all things unto this day." Those ancient and noble words to the Corinthians are strictly true at this present hour.'

'Not blows, father? He did not proceed to blows?'

'No, he did not. Though I have borne blows from men in a mad state of intoxication.'

'No!'

'A dozen times, my boy. What then? I have saved them from the guilt of murdering their own flesh and blood thereby; and they have lived to thank me, and praise God.'

'May this young man do the same!' said Angel fervently. 'But I fear otherwise, from what you say.'

'We'll hope, nevertheless,' said Mr Clare. 'And I continue to pray for him, though on this side of the grave we shall probably never meet again. But, after all, one of those poor words of mine may spring up in his heart as a good seed some day.'

Now, as always, Clare's father was sanguine as a child; and though the younger could not accept his parent's narrow dogma, he revered his practice and recognized the hero under the pietist.

Thomas Hardy, *Tess of the D'Urbervilles*[11]

Here is a country parson who is good, without seeming just a little too good to be true. Clergy in rural ministry today may wish that it was still possible to leave churches unlocked – but are thankful that churchwardens are less forceful in expressing their disapproval than when Hudson wrote in 1909.

To me the best thing in or of the village of Coombe was the vicar himself, my put-upon host, a man of so blithe a nature, so human and companionable, that when I, a perfect stranger without an introduction or any excuse for such intrusion, came down like a wolf on his luncheon-table, he received me as if I had been an old friend or one of his own kindred, and freely gave up his time to me for the rest of that day. To count his years he was old: he had been vicar of Coombe for half a century, but he was a young man still and had never had a day's illness in his life – he did not know what a headache was. He smoked with me, and to prove that he was not a total abstainer he drank my health in a glass of port wine – very good wine [...]

He took me to the church – one of the tiniest churches in the country, just the right size for a church in a tiny village, and assured me that he had never once locked the door in his fifty years – day and night it was open to anyone to enter. It was a refuge and shelter from the storm and the tempest, and many a poor homeless wretch had found a dry place to sleep in that church during the last half a century. This man's feeling of pity and tenderness for the very poor, even the outcast and tramp, was a passion. But how strange all this would sound in the ears of many country clergymen! How many have told me when I have gone to the parsonage to 'borrow the key' that it had been found necessary to keep the church door locked, to prevent damage, thefts, etc. 'Have *you* never had anything stolen?' I asked him. Yes, once, a great many years ago, the church plate had been taken away in the night. But it was recovered: the thief had taken it to the top of the hill and thrown it into the dew-pond there, no doubt intending to take it out and dispose of it at some more convenient time. But it was found, and had ever since then been kept safe at the vicarage. Nothing of value to tempt a man to steal was kept in the church.

He had never locked it, but once in fifty years it had been locked against him by the churchwardens. This happened in the days of the Joseph Arch agitation, when the agricultural labourer's condition was being hotly discussed throughout the country. The vicar's heart was stirred, for he knew better than most how hard these conditions were at Coombe and in the surrounding parishes. He took up the subject and preached on it in his own pulpit in a way that offended the landowners and alarmed the farmers in the district. The churchwardens, who were farmers, then locked him out of his church, and for two or three weeks there was no public worship in the parish of Coombe. Doubtless their action was applauded by all the substantial men in the neighbourhood; the others who lived in the cottages and were unsubstantial didn't matter. That storm blew over, but its consequences endured, one being that the inflammatory parson continued to be regarded with cold disapproval by the squires and their larger tenants. But the vicar himself was unrepentant and unashamed; on the contrary, he gloried in what he had said and done, and was proud to be able to relate that a quarter of a century later one of the two men who had taken that extreme course said to him, 'We locked you out of your own church, but years have brought me to another mind about that question. I see it in a different light now and know that you were right and we were wrong.'

W. H. Hudson, *Afoot in England*[12]

Stewart Headlam (1847–1924) was a controversial figure who aroused much hostility by his championing of unpopular causes. As a parish priest in Bethnal Green, East London, he campaigned on behalf of the poor and exploited. He was the prototype of Morell in Bernard Shaw's Candida. *He also worked to overcome the suspicion which still existed between the Church and the theatre. This extract describes the time when he was a curate in London's theatre district.*

Finally, at Drury Lane Stewart Headlam came into real touch with the theatre and with stage-players. He had, indeed, once on his way home from Cambridge, paid a furtive visit to the Alhambra, and at another time looked into a theatre for an hour in time to catch Adelaide Neilson in the balcony scene of 'Romeo and Juliet'. But now he began to make a practice of going to the theatre and the opera. He saw Irving's 'Hamlet' at the Lyceum and heard Titiens and other singers at Covent Garden in the sixpenny gallery. And in these days began his passion for the ballet and ballet-dancing which was to earn him Bishop Temple's reproof; the Alhambra was within easy reach. His interest in the theatre was partly the result of aesthetic appreciation, but partly arose from personal contact with its human instruments. Among the parishioners of St John's were some of the poorer members of the theatrical profession, including chorus girls and dancers. One evening Headlam recognised on the stage a couple of girls who were communicants, and he spoke of his discovery that they were dancers when he met them subsequently. They implored him not to let other church attendants know how they made their living, because if the nature of their work were once known they would be cold-shouldered in the church.

This little incident made a great impression on the young curate. It determined him to see more of the art these victims of prejudice practised, and to frequent the theatre generally more. It stirred up in him the fount of indignant pity which always welled up and broke his crust of reserve at any signs of injustice. It was the inspiration of his future Church and Stage Guild scheme, and it led him to make serious study of the technique of the ballet which culminated in the issue of that book of his or, rather, reprint entitled 'The Art of Dancing.' His whole career might have been different, his quarrel with his Bishops might never have reached an acute stage, had he not met those two dancing girls and listened to their story.

F. G. Bettany, Stewart Headlam[13]

Ministers in the Church of Scotland were often poorly paid and working in parishes where the majority of the people were even poorer. Gavin Dishart, a very young new minister, is preparing to take over from the retiring one, Mr Carfrae. If the older man is narrow in some of his views, he also reveals a saintly care for his flock.

Gavin only saw a very frail old minister who shook as he walked, as if his feet were striking stones. He was to depart on the morrow to the place of his birth, but he came to the manse to wish his successor God-speed.

'May you never lose sight of God, Mr Dishart,' the old man said in the parlour. Then he added, as if he had asked too much, 'May you never turn from Him as I often did when I was a lad like you.'

As this aged minister, with the beautiful face that God gives to all who love Him and follow his commandments, spoke of his youth, he looked wistfully around the faded parlour.

'It is like a dream,' he said. 'The first time I entered this room the thought passed through me that I would cut down that cherry-tree, because it kept out the light, but, you see, it outlives me. I grew old while looking for the axe. Only yesterday I was the young minister, Mr Dishart, and to-morrow you will be the old one, bidding good-bye to your successor.'

His eyes came back to Gavin's eager face. 'You are very young, Mr Dishart?'

'Nearly twenty-one.'

'Twenty-one! Ah, my dear sir, you do not know how pathetic that sounds to me. Twenty-one! We are children for the second time at twenty-one, and again when we are grey and put all our burden on the Lord. The young talk generously of relieving the old of their burdens, but the anxious heart is to the old when they see a load on the back of the young. Let me tell you, Mr Dishart, that I would condone many things in one-and-twenty now that I dealt harshly with at middle age. God Himself, I think, is very willing to give one-and-twenty a second chance.'

'I am afraid,' Gavin said anxiously, 'that I look even younger.'

'I think,' Mr Carfrae answered smiling, 'that your heart is as fresh as your face; and that is well. The useless men are those who never change with the years. Many views that I held to in my youth and long afterwards are a pain to me now, and I am carrying away from Thrums memories of errors into which I fell at every stage of my ministry. When you are older you will know that life is a long lesson in humility.'

He paused. 'I hope,' he said nervously, 'that you don't sing the Paraphrases?'

Mr Carfrae had not grown out of all his prejudices, you see; indeed, if Gavin had been less bigoted than he on this question they might have parted stiffly. The old minister would rather have remained to die in his pulpit than surrender it to one who read his sermons. Others may blame him for this, but I must say here plainly that I never hear a minister reading without wishing to send him back to college.

'I cannot deny,' Mr Carfrae said, 'that I broke down more than once to-day. This forenoon I was in Tillyloss, for the last time, and it so happens that there is scarcely a house in it in which I have not had a marriage or prayed over a coffin. Ah, sir, these are the scenes that make the minister more than all his sermons. You must join the family, Mr Dishart, or you are only a minister once a week. And remember this, if your call is from above it is a call to stay. Many such partings in a lifetime as I have had today would be too heartrending.'

James Barrie, *The Little Minister*[14]

The Anglican Church in Ireland was associated with the 'Ascendancy' and was often resented for its apparently privileged status. But many of its clergy were both devoted and underprivileged. George Birmingham (Canon J. O. Hannay) records his memories of the Revd Harold Burnaby.

I do not know what Harold said to those parishioners of his when he got to their homes, or what he did. But I think that he somehow brought them the most precious of all gifts, 'the Bread of Life.' Those people loved him. I like to think of him, too, as I once saw him at Christmas time, a curiously unconventional Santa Claus. He walked all day to reach two widely separated cottages in which there were children. He had his pockets full of all sorts of queer things for the delight of children: pigs made of sugar, with pink eyes, short thick legs, and little bits of cotton for tails – brittle creatures which Harold was very much afraid of breaking as he walked; little mice which ran round and round in wire cages when you turned a handle; shiny balls which were very awkward to carry; and other things. Town children, even the poorest, would have scorned the toys. They did not cost more than a penny each. But 'the minister's' coming was eagerly looked for at Christmas time in these far-away cottages. I think there would be great disappointment if he forgot to bring his toys. But he never does forget.

These people of his always speak of him as 'the minister' just as their Roman Catholic neighbours do. I think he likes the title. He always considers himself as 'one that serveth', and prefers to be thought a minister rather than an elder, ruler, priest. He is, and always has been, very literally the servant of those around him. It is not only his own people, those who accept his ministrations in church and listen to his preaching, who come to him with troublesome requests. He writes letter after letter for some unfortunate claimant of an Old Age Pension who has no evidence of the date of his birth. He searches patiently among his far-off acquaintances and finds situations for boys and girls. People of all kinds who want things done for them have a way of calling on 'the minister' – and it is quite astonishing how few people in the West of Ireland seem able to do anything for themselves [...] He has had love enough, work enough, faith enough; and he once told me that it is those things which really matter, not the other things which most of us try to get. He may be right.

George A. Birmingham, *Irishmen All*[15]

For the sake of ecumenical harmony, here is a poem about an Irish Roman Catholic priest by William Percy French (1854–1920): sentimental perhaps, but a strong proof of the affection in which the memory of a good priest can be held.

Father Cornelius O'Callaghan,
To most of us Father Con –
To all of us quite the kindliest man,
That ever the sun shone on.
I mind me when I was a bit of a lad,
He stood with me out in the cold
While I told him a curious dream I'd had,
Of findin' a crock of gold.

O Father O'Callaghan!
When will the dream come true?
O Father O'Callaghan,
If anyone knows 'tis you!
And Father O'Callaghan stroked me pate,
Sez he, 'The story is old –
Every one that can work and wait
Will find his crock of gold.'

Rosie Mulvany was bright as a bird,
I loved her, she didn't object,
But somehow I never could bring out the word,
That Rose had a right to expect.
I'd dream of her nightly, I'd dream she said 'Yes',
Be daylight me courage was gone,
I was wore to a shadow, so in my distress,
I went and I saw Father Con.

O Father O'Callaghan,
Will the dream come true?
O Father O'Callaghan,
What is a boy to do?
And Father O'Callaghan said, 'See here,
You must call in your Sunday clothes.
Say to her this, "Will you marry me dear?"
You can leave the rest to Rose.'

We talk'd one night of the glorious days,
Whern Ireland led the van,
With scholars as thick as the stars in the sky
And work for every man.
' 'Twill come again,' said Father Con,
And his fertile fancy paints
The glorious day when the sun shines on
A new Isle of the Saints.

O Father O'Callaghan,
When will the dream come true?
O Father O'Callaghan,
If anyone knows, 'tis you.

And Father O'Callaghan raised his head,
And smiled his humorsome smile,
'When ev'ry man learns to rule himself
'Twill then be a saintly isle.'

Father O'Callaghan's dead and gone,
This many and many a day –
But we haven't forgot you Father Con
And it keeps us from goin' astray.
And so at the last great earthquake shock,
When the trumpet's soundin' clear,
He'll guide to their God the faithful flock
That knew him and loved him here.

O Father O'Callaghan,
When will the dream come true?
O Father O'Callaghan,
If anyone knows 'tis you!
And Father O'Callaghan says no word
For he's sleepin' softly yet,
And when the archangel's voice is heard,
We know that he won't forget.

Percy French, 'Father O'Callaghan'[16]

Returning to an earlier century, here is the pattern of a model clergyman as set out by Richard Baxter (1615–91). Ordained as an Anglican priest, he became opposed to episcopacy and turned to the Puritan cause. He was always a wise and moderating influence. At the Savoy Conference in 1661 he presented some 'Exceptions' to the Book of Common Prayer, only a few of which were accepted. This passage is a powerful and perhaps somewhat uncomfortable challenge to clergy of all denominations.

That man that is not himself taken up with the predominant love of God and is not himself devoted to Him; and doth not devote to him all that he hath or can do; that man that is not addicted to pleasing God, and making Him the centre of all his actions, and living to Him as his God and happiness; that is, that man that is not a sincere Christian himself, is utterly unfit to be a pastor of a Church. And if we be not in a case of desperate necessity, the Church should not admit such, so far as they discover them! A man that is not heartily devoted to God, and attached to His service and honour, will never set heartily about the pastoral work, for no man can be sincere in the means, that is not so in his intentions of the end. A man must heartily love God above all before he can heartily serve Him before all.

No man is fit to be a minister of Christ that is not of a public spirit as to the Church, and delighteth not in its beauty, and longeth not for its felicity; as the good of the commonwealth must be the end of the magistrate, so must the felicity of the Church be the end of the pastors of it. So that we must rejoice in its welfare and be willing to spend and be spent for its sake.

No man is fit to be a pastor of a Church that doth not set his heart on the life to come, and regard the matters of everlasting life, above all the matters of this present life, and that is not sensible in some measure how much the inestimable riches of glory are to be preferred to the trifles of this world.

Richard Baxter, *The Reformed Pastor*[17]

Chapter 2

Erred and Strayed

The higher public expectations attached to the clergy may cause their faults to be magnified. They have been targets for satire, good-humoured or bitter, moral censure and downright abuse. There are many motives behind attacks on the clergy: envy, snobbery, bad conscience and a failure to get one's own way are among them. But much of the adverse comment has come from faithful people genuinely distressed by the faults of their clergy. 'Speaking the truth in love' is a phrase that is too often a prelude to one Christian being unpleasant about another Christian, but it is sometimes proper and necessary. When all excuses have been made, we have to accept that many clergy have not lived up to the highest principles of their calling, and that failure has been as continual and endemic as saintliness. The New Testament, and the early history of the Christian Church, have their darker moments. It does no good to the true faith to pretend that things have been otherwise. Let us read about some of these clergy, not with a feeling of superiority or condemnation, but with sadness mingled with sympathy – and perhaps even with a little amusement in some of the less venal cases. Any who are disappointed in their spiritual leaders may study this assembly of bad types and feel that things could be even worse than they are.

Milton took a poor view of the Anglican clergy of his day, especially the bishops. In the elegy for his friend Edward King, he makes a strong and comprehensive indictment. His choice of St Peter, complete with keys, for his mouthpiece is perhaps a little surprising for a Puritan. What exactly he meant by the 'two-handed engine' is uncertain, but he was clearly expecting summary punishment for clerical offences. It is not everyone who can make poetry out of invective.

Last came, and last did go,
The Pilot of the Galilean lake;

Two massy keys he bore of metals twain
(The golden opes, the iron shuts amain).
He shook his mitred locks, and stern bespake:
'How well could I have spared for thee, young swain,
Enow of such as for their bellies' sake.
Creep and intrude and climb into the fold!
Of other care they little reckoning make
Than how to scramble at the shearers' feast,
And shove away the worthy bidden guest.
Blind mouths! that scarce themselves know how to hold
A sheep-hook, or have learned aught else the least
That to the faithful herdman's art belongs!
What reeks it them? What need they? They are sped;
And when they list, their lean and flashy songs
Grate on their scrannel pipes of wretched straw;
The hungry sheep look up, and are not fed,
But swoln with wind, and the rank mist they draw,
Rot inwardly, and foul contagion spread;
Besides what the grim wolf with privy paw
Daily devours apace, and nothing said;
But that two-handed engine at the door
Stands ready to smite once, and smite no more.'

John Milton, *Lycidas*[1]

While Milton took a poor view of the Established Church, his contemporary Samuel Butler (1613–80) was equally scathing about the Presbyterians. In the time of the Restoration of both Church and Monarchy, he expressed what many had felt about the puritanical religion of the Commonwealth period. His foolish knight Hudibras falls in with this attitude, lay supporters of which were as earnest as the clergy who led them. Butler well hits off the negative aspects of the Puritan divines but gives no credit to their more positive virtues of faith.

Great piety consists in pride;
To rule is to be sanctified:
To domineer, and to control
Both o'er the body and the soul,

Is the most perfect discipline
Of church-rule, and by right divine.
Bel and the Dragon's chaplains were
More moderate than these by far:
For they, poor knaves, were glad to cheat,
To get their wives and children meat;
But these will not be fobbed off so,
They must have wealth and power too,
Or else with blood and desolation,
They'll tear it out o' th' heart o' th' nation,
Sure these themselves from primitive
And heathen priesthood do derive,
When butchers were the only clerks,
Elders and presbyters of kirks;
Whose directory was to kill;
And some believe it is so still.
The only difference is, that then
They slaughtered only beasts, now men.
For then to sacrifice a bullock,
Or, now and then, a child to Moloch,
They count a vile abomination,
But not to slaughter a whole nation.
Presbytery does but translate
The papacy to a free state,
A commonwealth of popery,
Where every village is a see
As well as Rome, and must maintain
A tithe-pig metropolitan;
Where every presbyter and deacon
Commands the keys for cheese and bacon.
And every hamlet's governed
By's holiness, the church's head,
More haughty and severe in 's place,
Than Gregory and Boniface.

Samuel Butler, *Hudibras*[2]

The Vicar of Bray has become a stock name for a person who changes sides for personal advantage. One historian offers a different origin for the phrase, dubious but amusing, and a legendary sixteenth-century vicar to embody it.

This especially hateful class of priests [in the sixteenth century] consisted of men who, after changing their religion from prudential motives, were not content to live quietly with their neighbours, but, partly from a desire to justify their conduct to their own consciences, partly from an ambition to convince the worldly of the sincerity of their latest conversion, but chiefly from a base design to win professional advancement by noisy zeal, became angry disputants in behalf of their newly adopted tenets, and bitter maligners of those outward conformists whom they suspected of secret attachment to prohibited opinions. In King Edward's time these men railed with equal rancour and insolence at the creatures of papal bigotry; after Mary's accession they became malicious informers against peaceful folk who seldom attended mass and were suspected of inclinations to Lollardy; under Elizabeth they raised their harsh voices with characteristic spitefulness against Catholic recusants and Puritan precisians. For these men, odious in the extreme to moderate people of all parties, popular satire invented a nickname that bids fair to live so long as the English tongue endures. It was seen that they were men of no charity, no manly feeling, no truthfulness, no real religion, but they could *bray*. Their bray was audible in every part of the kingdom, it was uttered now on this side, now on that, as interest dictated. To their incessant braying they were indebted for notoriety, influence, preferment. They brayed themselves from miserable curacies into rich livings; they brayed themselves into deaneries and episcopal thrones. For each of these men, whatever his rank in the sacerdotal class, what nickname could be more exact and pungent than – Vicar of Bray? Only the other day, lashing the malice and uncharitableness and arrogance of a sanctimonious sectarian, Tom Hood [1799–1845] compared the object of his invective to a noisy jackass, who had 'not got no milk but he could bray.' In the same spirit of healthy loathing and fierce disdain, the satirist of the sixteenth century designated the vindictive turncoats and shouters of the pulpit 'Vicars of Bray.' The offender might hold no actual vicarage; he might be a mere stipendiary lecturer; he might be rector, archdeacon, a dean, or even a prelate, but if he exhibited the qualities of virulent turncoat, he was called a Vicar of Bray.

The term became proverbial, and when the proverb had survived the odious class for whose special infamy it was invented – when the original delinquents had passed out of the world and popular memory – the nickname gave rise to a mythical story of a certain vicar of the parish of Bray, in the county of Berkshire and the diocese of Oxford, who was supposed to have distinguished himself in the reigns of Henry the Eighth, Edward the Sixth, Mary, and Elizabeth, by figuring successively as a Papist, a Protestant, a Papist once more, and yet again a Protestant. Fuller gravely tells his readers that this particular vicar of Bray – who thus distinguished himself by merely doing exactly what thousands of English clergymen did in the same reigns – was Simon Aleyn, canon of Windsor, who held the vicarage of Bray in Berkshire from 1540 to 1588; and that this same vicar Aleyn, on being taunted with his continual changes of religion, answered his assailant with facile effrontery that, though a turncoat in creeds, he had stuck to his one grand principle, which was 'to live and die the Vicar of Bray'.

J. C. Jeafferson, *A Book about the Clergy*[3]

This popular song, of unknown authorship but allegedly composed by an army officer in the reign of George I, is set in the period from Charles II to George I. It may be remarked that a parson who wanted to keep his benefice rather than seek preferment had only to remain quiet and did not need to make a show of his politics. But the tradition is entrenched and perhaps the actual words of the song are less well known today. Some readers may have slight textual variants.

In good King Charles's golden days,
When loyalty had no harm meant,
A zealous High Churchman was I,
And so I got preferment.
To teach my flock I never miss'd,
Kings were by God appointed,
And they are damned who dare resist,
Or touch the Lord's anointed.

Chorus
And this is law I will maintain,
Until my dying day, sir,
That whatsoever king shall reign,
I'll be the Vicar of Bray, sir.

When Royal James obtained the throne,
And Popery grew in fashion,
The penal laws I hooted down,
And read the Declaration;
The Church of Rome I found would fit
Full well my constitution;
And I had been a Jesuit,
But for the Revolution.

When William, our deliverer, came
To heal the nation's grievance,
Then I turned cat-in-pan again,
And swore to him allegiance.
Old principles I did revoke,
Set conscience at a distance;
Passive obedience was a joke,
A jest was non-resistance.

When glorious Anne became our Queen,
The Church of England's glory,
Another face of things was seen,
And I became a Tory;
Occasional conformists base –
I damned such moderation,
And thought the Church in danger was
By such prevarication.

When George in pudding-time came o'er,
And moderate men looked big, sir,
My principles I changed once more,
And so became a Whig, sir.
And thus preferment I procured

From our Faith's great Defender,
And almost every day abjured
The Pope and the Pretender.

The illustrious House of Hanover
And Protestant Succession,
By these I lustily will swear,
While they can keep possession.
For in my faith and loyalty
I never once will falter,
But George my king shall ever be –
Except the times do alter.

Anonymous

William Cowper, son of a clergyman and himself a hymnwriter, had great
affection for his clerical friends but took a poor view of those who brought
the cloth into disrepute. He tells of the venal side of the eighteenth-century
clergy, an image which at one time became a stereotype, but which was far
from the whole story.

I venerate the man whose heart is warm,
Whose hands are pure, whose doctrine and whose life
Coincident, exhibit lucid proof
That he is honest in the sacred cause.
To such I render, more than mere respect,
Whose actions say that they respect themselves.
But, loose in morals, and in manners vain,
In conversation frivolous, in dress
Extreme, at once rapacious and profuse,
Frequent in park, with lady at his side,
Ambling and prattling scandal as he goes,
But rare at home, and never at his books,
Or with his pen, save when he scrawls a card,
Constant at routs, familiar with a round
Of ladyships, a stranger to the poor;
Ambitious of preferment for its gold,
And well prepared by ignorance and sloth,
By infidelity and love of world,

To make God's work a sinecure; a slave
To his own pleasures and his patron's pride:
From such apostles, O ye mitred heads,
Preserve the Church! and lay not careless hands
On skulls that cannot teach, and will not learn.

William Cowper, *The Task*[3]

Mr Collins is perhaps one of the best-known and least-liked of fictional clergymen. He represents the worst abuses of patronage at a time when presentation to a rich living could depend on winning the favour of a lay patron. Jane Austen dissects him with her usual irony.

Mr Collins was not a sensible man, and the deficiency of nature had been but little assisted by education or society; the greatest part of his life having been spent under the guidance of an illiterate and miserly father; and though he belonged to one of the universities, he had merely kept the necessary terms, without forming at it any useful acquaintance. The subjection in which his father had brought him up, had given him originally great humility of manner, but it was now a good deal counteracted by the self-conceit of a weak head, living in retirement, and the consequential feelings of early and unexpected prosperity. A fortunate chance had recommended him to Lady Catherine de Bourgh when the living of Hunsford was vacant; and the respect which he felt for her high rank, and his veneration for her as his patroness, mingling with a very good opinion of himself, of his authority as a clergyman, and his rights as a rector, made him altogether a mixture of pride and obsequiousness, self-importance and humility.

[*Later, he is allowed to complete the portrait by speaking for himself. He intervenes in the musical entertainment at a party.*]

'If I,' said Mr Collins, 'were so fortunate as to be able to sing, I should have great pleasure, I am sure, in obliging the company with an air; for I consider music as a very innocent diversion, and perfectly compatible with the profession of a clergyman. I do not mean however to assert that we can be justified in devoting too much of our time to music, for there are certainly other things to be attended to. The rector of a parish has much to do. In the first place, he must make such an agreement for tithes as may be beneficial to himself and not offensive to his patron. He must write his own sermons; and the time that remains will not be too much for his parish duties, and the care and improvement of his dwelling, which he cannot be excused from making as comfortable as possible. And I do not think it of light importance that he should have attentive and conciliatory manners towards everybody, especially towards those to whom he owes his preferment. I cannot acquit him of that duty; nor could I think well of the man who should omit an occasion of testifying his respect towards any body connected with the family.'

And with a bow to Mr Darcy, he concluded his speech, which had been spoken so loud as to be heard by half the room. Many stared. Many smiled; but no one looked more amused than Mr Bennet himself, while his wife seriously commended Mr Collins for having spoken so sensibly, and observed in a half-whisper to Lady Lucas, that he was a remarkably clever, good kind of young man.

Jane Austen, *Pride and Prejudice*[4]

A fitting companion for Mr Collins a generation later is Mr Slope, the chaplain of Bishop Proudie of Barchester. Trollope's vigorous moral and physical description of him deserves full quotation, as a portrait of a clerical type and also as a commentary on Victorian religious controversies.

He is possessed of more than average abilities, and is of good courage. Though he can stoop to fawn, and stoop low indeed, if need be, he has still within him the power to assume the tyrant; and with the power he has certainly the wish. His acquirements are not of the highest order, but such as they are they are completely under control, and he knows the use of them. He is gifted with a certain kind of pulpit eloquence, not likely indeed to be persuasive with men, but powerful with the softer sex. In his sermons he deals greatly in denunciations, excites the minds of his weaker hearers with a not unpleasant terror, and leaves an impression on their minds that all mankind are in a perilous state, and all womankind too, except those who attend regularly to the evening lectures in Baker Street. His looks and tones are extremely severe, so much so that one cannot but fancy that he regards the greater part of the world as being infinitely too bad for his care. As he walks through the streets, his very face denotes his horror of the world's wickedness; and there is always an anathema lurking in the corner of his eye.

In doctrine, he, like his patron, is tolerant of dissent, if so strict a mind can be called tolerant of anything. With Wesleyan-Methodists he has something in common, but his soul trembles in agony at the iniquities of the Puseyites. His aversion is carried to things outward as well as inward. His gall rises at a new church with a high-pitched roof; a full-breasted black silk waistcoat is with him a symbol of Satan; and a profane jest-book would not, in his view, more foully desecrate the church seat of a Christian, than a book of prayer printed with red letters, and ornamented with a cross on the back. Most active clergymen have their hobby, and Sunday observances are his. Sunday, however, is a word which never pollutes his mouth – it is always 'the Sabbath.' The 'desecration of the Sabbath,' as he delights to call it, is to him meat and drink: he thrives upon that as policemen do on the general evil habits of the community. It is the loved subject of all his evening discourses, the source of all his eloquence, the secret of all his power over the female heart. To him the revelation of God appears only in that one law given for Jewish observance. To him the mercies of our Saviour speak in vain, to him in vain has been preached that sermon which fell from divine lips on the mountain – 'Blessed are the meek, for they shall inherit the earth . . . Blessed are the merciful for they shall obtain mercy.' To him the New Testament is comparatively of little moment, for from it can he draw no fresh authority for that dominion which he loves to exercise over at least a seventh part of man's allotted time here below.

Mr Slope is tall, and not ill made. His feet and hands are large, as has ever been the case with all his family, but he has a broad chest and wide shoulders to carry off these excrescences, and on the whole his figure is good. His countenance, however, is not specially prepossessing. His hair is lank, and of a dull pale reddish hue. It is always formed into three straight lumpy masses, each brushed with admirable precision, and cemented with much grease; two of them adhere closely to the sides of his face, and the other lies at right angles above them. He wears no whiskers, and is always punctiliously shaven. His face is nearly of the same colour as his hair, though perhaps a little redder: it is not unlike beef – beef, however, one would say, 'of a bad quality'. His forehead is capacious and high, but square and heavy, and unpleasantly shining. His mouth is large, though his lips are thin and bloodless; and his big, prominent, pale brown eyes inspire anything but confidence. His nose, however, is his redeeming feature: it is pronounced, straight, and well-formed; though I myself should have liked it better did it not possess a somewhat spongy, porous appearance, as though it had been cleverly formed out of a red coloured cork.

I never could endure to shake hands with Mr Slope. A cold clammy perspiration always exudes from him, the small drops are ever to be seen standing on his brow, and his friendly grasp is unpleasant.

Anthony Trollope, *Barchester Towers*[5]

Not only those ambitious for preferment in the Church of England have been unworthy of their calling. Mr Stiggins, the minister of the 'Ebenezer Chapel', exploits the hospitality of the pious women in his flock and stimulates his exhortations with drink. Dickens cauterizes him with his usual vigour, but perhaps Stiggins and those like him were as much to be pitied as reviled while they tried to keep up a position for which they were not fitted.

He was a prim-faced, red-nosed man, with a long thin countenance and a semi-rattlesnake sort of eye – rather sharp, but decidedly bad. He wore very short trousers, and black-cotton stockings, which, like the rest of his apparel, were particularly rusty. His looks were starched, but his white neckerchief was not; and its long limp ends straggled over his closely-buttoned waistcoat in a very uncouth and unpicturesque fashion. A pair of old, worn, beaver gloves, a broad-brimmed hat, and a faded green umbrella, with plenty of whalebone sticking through the bottom, as if to counterbalance the want of a handle at the top, lay on a chair beside him; and being disposed in a very tidy and careful manner, seemed to imply that the red-nosed man, whoever he was, had no intention of going away in a hurry.

To do the red-nosed man justice, he would have been very far from wise if he had entertained any such intention, for, to judge from all appearances, he must have been possessed of a most desirable circle of acquaintance, if he could have reasonably expected to be more comfortable anywhere else. The fire was blazing brightly, under the influence of the bellows, and the kettle was singing gaily, under the influence of both. A small tray of tea-things was arranged on the table; a plate of hot buttered toast was gently simmering before the fire, and the red-nosed man himself was busily engaged in converting a large slice of bread, into the same agreeable edible, through the instrumentality of a long brass toasting-fork. Beside him, stood a glass of reeking hot pineapple rum and water, with a slice of lemon in it, and every time the red-nosed man stopped to bring the round of bread to his eye, with the view of ascertaining how it got on, he imbibed a drop or two of the hot pineapple rum and water.

[*On another occasion Stiggins delivers an impromptu sermon, directed particularly at the sceptical Sam Weller. Dickens takes the opportunity to add some of his favourite moral sentiments, which perhaps have never lacked legitimate targets.*]

Mr Stiggins, getting on his legs as well as he could, proceeded to deliver an edifying discourse for the benefit of the company, but more especially of Mr Samuel, whom he adjured, in moving terms, to be upon his guard in that sink of iniquity into which he was cast; to abstain from all hypocrisy and pride of heart; and to take in all things exact pattern and copy by him (Stiggins), in which case he might calculate on arriving sooner or later at the comfortable conclusion, that, like him, he was a most estimable and blameless character, and that all his acquaintance and friends were hopelessly abandoned and profligate wretches; which consideration, he said, could not but afford him the liveliest satisfaction. He furthermore conjured him to avoid, above all things, the vice of intoxication, which he likened unto the filthy habits of swine, and to those poisonous and baleful drugs which being chewed in the mouth are said to filch away the memory. At this point of his discourse the reverend and red-nosed gentleman became singularly incoherent, and staggering to and fro in the excitement of his eloquence, was fain to catch at the back of a chair to preserve his perpendicular.

Mr Stiggins did not desire his hearers to be upon their guard against those false prophets and wretched mockers of religion, who, without sense to expound its first doctrines, or hearts to feel its first principles, are more dangerous members of society than the common criminal; imposing as they necessarily do upon the weakest and worst inform-ed natures, casting scorn and contempt on what should be held most sacred, and bringing into partial disrepute large bodies of virtuous and well-conducted persons of many excellent sects and persuasions; but as he leant over the back of the chair for a considerable time, and closing one eye, winked a good deal with the other, it is presumed that he thought it all, but kept it to himself.

Charles Dickens, *The Pickwick Papers*[6]

The early Romantic reading of the Brontë sisters sometimes betrayed them into exaggeration in the portrayal of characters. Mr Brocklehurst has something of the Gothic ogre in the eyes of little Jane Eyre. Nevertheless, he is a searing reminder of the many clergy who have emphasized the judgemental side of Christian belief to the exclusion of love and mercy. Coupled with the idea that children were naturally inclined to be bad, it has caused much innocent suffering in the name of Christianity. Already in disgrace with Mrs Read, her guardian, Jane is brought into the presence of the clergyman who runs a school to which she is to be sent. Charlotte's personal memories of Carus-Wilson and his school at Cowan Bridge greatly influenced her depiction of Brocklehurst's character.

The handle turned, the door unclosed, and passing through and curtseying low, I looked up at – a black pillar! – such, at least, appeared to me, at first sight, the straight, narrow, sable-clad shape standing erect on the rug: the grim face at the top was like a carved mask, placed above the shaft by way of capital.

Mrs Reed occupied her usual seat by the fireside; she made a signal to me to approach; I did so, and she introduced me to the stony stranger with the words: 'This is the little girl respecting whom I applied to you.'

He, for it was a man, turned his head slowly towards where I stood, and having examined me with the two inquisitive-looking grey eyes which twinkled under a pair of bushy brows, said solemnly, and in a bass voice, 'Her size is small: what is her age?'

'Ten years.'

'So much?' was the doubtful answer; and he prolonged his scrutiny for some minutes. Presently he addressed me –

'Your name, little girl?'

'Jane Eyre, sir.'

In uttering these words I looked up: he seemed to me a tall gentleman; but then I was very little; his features were large, and they and all the lines of his frame were equally harsh and prim.

'Well, Jane Eyre, and are you a good child?'

Impossible to reply to this in the affirmative: my little world held a contrary opinion: I was silent. Mrs Reed answered for me by an expressive shake of the head, adding soon, 'Perhaps the less said on that subject the better, Mr Brocklehurst.'

'Sorry indeed to hear it! She and I must have some talk;' and bending from the perpendicular, he installed his person in the armchair opposite Mrs Reed's. 'Come here,' he said.

I stepped across the rug; he placed me square and straight before him. What a face he had, now that it was almost on a level with mine! What a great nose! and what a mouth! and what large prominent teeth!

'No sight so sad as that of a naughty child,' he began, 'especially a naughty little girl. Do you know where the wicked go after death?'

'They go to hell,' was my ready and orthodox answer.

'And what is hell? Can you tell me that?'

'A pit full of fire.'

'And should you like to fall into that pit, and to be burning there for ever?'

'No, sir.'

'What must you do to avoid it?'

I deliberated a moment; my answer, when it did come, was objectionable: 'I must keep in good health, and not die.'

'How can you keep in good health? Children younger than you die daily. I buried a little child of five years old only a day or two since – a good little child, whose soul is now in heaven. It is to be feared the same could not be said of you were you to be called hence.'

Not being in a condition to remove his doubt, I only cast my eyes down on the two large feet planted on the rug, and sighed, wishing myself far enough away.

'I hope that sigh is from the heart, and that you repent of ever having been the occasion of discomfort to your excellent benefactress.'

'Benefactress! benefactress!' said I inwardly: 'they all call Mrs Reed my benefactress; if so, a benefactress is a disagreeable thing.'

'Do you say your prayers night and morning?' continued my interrogator.

'Yes, sir.'

'Do you read your Bible?'

'Sometimes.'

'With pleasure? Are you fond of it?'

'I like Revelations, and the book of Daniel, and Genesis and Samuel, and a little bit of Exodus, and some parts of Kings and Chronicles, and Job and Jonah.'

'And the Psalms? I hope you like them?'

'No, sir.'

'No? oh, shocking! I have a little boy, younger than you, who knows six Psalms by heart: and when you ask him which he would rather have, a gingerbread nut to eat or a verse of a Psalm to learn, he says: "Oh! the verse of a Psalm! angels sing Psalms", says he, "I wish to be a little angel here below;" he then gets two nuts in recompense for his infant piety.'

'Psalms are not interesting,' I remarked.

'That proves you have a wicked heart; and you must pray to God to change it: to give you a new and clean one: to take away your heart of stone and give you a heart of flesh.'

Charlotte Brontë, *Jane Eyre*[7]

Anthony Trollope's mother was herself a novelist, with an eye for clerical failings equal to that of her son. Her portrayal of Cartwright was thought to be based on Cunningham, the Vicar of Harrow where the family lived for a time, though she later denied this. Cartwright marries a rich widow, and is manipulative in his dealings with people. This passage shows how much power could be misused by parish clergy – not confined to the 'evangelical divines' towards whom Mrs Trollope had an antipathy.

Among the many highly-valued comforts and privileges which Mr Cartwright's exclusive possession of the library afforded him, that of receiving in solitary state and privacy the family letter-bag, was not the one least valued. It may, I believe, be laid down as a pretty general rule, that those persons who conceive, or profess it to be their duty, to dive into the hearts and consciences of their fellow-creatures, and to regulate the very thoughts and feelings of all the unfortunate people within their reach, are not very scrupulous as to the methods used to obtain that inward knowledge. Mr Cartwright, according to the usual custom of evangelical divines, had his village matron, ostensibly only a merchant of apples, gingerbread and lollypops, but entrusted with as many secret missions of inquiry as the most jealous pontiff ever committed to a faithful and favoured nuncio on quitting the gates of Rome. She could tell, and was not ill paid for that precious knowledge, how often Betty Jackson went to buy baccy; and how many times in the day Sally Wright looked over her shoulder at the passers-by while walking out with her master's children; and how many pots of porter were carried to one house, and how many times the ladies walked forth from another; besides innumerable other facts and anecdotes, which, though apparently not of sufficient importance to record, were nevertheless of great value to the vicar and to his curate, as themes to lecture upon in private, and preach upon in public.

Sources of information such as these had never been overlooked or neglected by Mr Cartwright at any period of his ministry; but hitherto he had held them to be important rather to the general welfare of the Christian world than to his own family: no sooner, however, did he find himself placed in the responsible position of master of a large household than, besides taking the butler into a sort of evangelical partnership for the discovery of petty offences, and having moreover an elected stable-boy, who made a daily report of all that he saw and heard, and a little more, he determined that all letters addressed to any of the family should pass through his hand; and in like manner, that all those put into the letter-box in the hall, of which he kept the key himself, should be submitted to the same species of religious examination before they were deposited in the post-bag.

In the execution of this part of his duty Mr Cartwright displayed, to himself at least, considerable mechanical skill – for the letters were excellently well resealed – and likewise great equanimity of temper; for, scanty as the family correspondence proved to be, he chanced to fall upon some few passages which might have shaken the philosophy of a mind less admirably regulated.

Frances Trollope, *The Vicar of Wrexhill*[8]

There were parsons who took advantage of the security of their freehold to indulge in hunting and other pastimes. Not all were as bad as Parson Chowne, as described by some of his flock to the narrator at an inn.

For this man was a man, as we say. No other man must have a will that stood across the path of his. If he heard of any one unwilling to give way to him, he would not go to bed until he had taken that arrogance out of him. Many people, and even some of ten times his own fortune, had done their best, one after the other, not to be beaten by him. All of them found, one after another, that they could not do it, and that their only chance of comfort was to knock under to Parson Chowne. And even after that had been done, he was not always satisfied, but let them know

The service was performed by a snuffling well-fed vicar, who had a snug dwelling near the church. He was a privileged guest at all the tables of the neighbourhood, and had been the keenest fox-hunter in the country; until age and good living had disabled him from doing anything more than ride to see the hounds throw off, and make one at the hunting dinner.

Under the ministry of such a pastor, I found it impossible to get into the train of thought suitable to the time and place: so, having like many other feeble Christians, compromised with my conscience, by laying the sin of my own delinquency at another person's threshold, I occupied myself by making observations on my neighbours.

Washington Irving, *The Sketch Book*[11]

The hunting parson is usually considered typical of the eighteenth and nineteenth centuries, but he had earlier antecedents. Robert Herrick (1591–1674), himself a clergyman, is epigrammatic about one of them.

Old Parson Beane hunts six days of the week,
And on the seventh he has notes to seek;
Six days he holloas so much breath away
That on the seventh he cannot preach nor pray.

Robert Herrick, 'Upon Parson Beane'[12]

Let us be ecumenical in blame as well as in praise. Lest it should be thought that any denomination has been unfairly prominent in this recital of bad clergy, here is a blanket condemnation by John Greenleaf Whittier. It was occasioned by a pro-slavery meeting in Charleston, South Carolina, in 1835 which 'the clergy of all denominations attended in a body, lending their sanction to the proceedings'. Whittier, a Quaker, was a powerful advocate of abolition and this is a scathing indictment. The sincerity and seriousness of the attack may excuse the plethora of exclamation marks.

Just God! – and these are they
Who minister at Thine altar, God of Right!
Men who their hands with prayer and blessing lay
On Israel's Ark of light!

What! preach and kidnap men?
Give thanks – and rob Thy own afflicted poor?
Talk of Thy glorious liberty, and then
　　Bolt hard the captive's door?

What! servants of Thy own
Merciful Son, who came to seek and save
The homeless and the outcast – fettering down
　　The tasked and plundered slave!

Pilate and Herod, friends!
Chief priests and rulers, as of old, combine!
Just God and holy! is that church, which lends
　　Strength to the spoiler, Thine?

Paid hypocrites, who turn
Judgment aside, and rob the Holy Book
Of those high words of truth which search and burn
　　In warning and rebuke.

Feed fat, ye locusts, feed!
And, in your tasseled pulpits, thank the Lord
That, from the toiling bondman's utter need,
　　Ye pile your own full board.

How long, O Lord! how long
Shall such a priesthood barter truth away,
And, in Thy name, for robbery and wrong
　　At Thy own altars pray?

Is not Thy hand stretched forth
Visibly in the heavens, to awe and smite?
Shall not the living God of all the earth,
　　And heaven above, do right?

Woe, then, to all who grind
Their brethren of a common Father down!
To all who plunder from the immortal mind
　　Its bright and glorious crown!

Woe to the priesthood! woe
To those whose hire is with the price of blood –
Perverting, darkening, changing, as they go,
 The searching truths of God!

 Their glory and their might
Shall perish; and their very names shall be
Vile before all the people, in the light
 Of a world's liberty.

 Oh! speed the moment on
When Wrong shall cease – and Liberty, and Love,
And Truth, and Right, throughout the earth be known
 As in their home above.

J. G. Whittier, 'Clerical Oppression'[13]

Chapter 3

Divers Orders

The New Testament assures us that 'If a man desire the office of a bishop, he desireth a good work' (1 Timothy 3:1). The churches which have maintained the episcopal order have generally regarded it as being essential to ecclesiastical structure, whereas those that have repudiated it have tended to see it as a corrupt assertion of prelacy. There have certainly been considerable changes and developments since the days of the early Church. In the Middle Ages, and for some time later, dioceses were large and it was not always possible for the bishop to visit all his parishes. He became a remote figure, in some cases more often to be found at his palace in the capital city when he was taking his legislative role as one of the Lords Spiritual. Services of Confirmation became infrequent and were consequently unedifyingly large and disordered. There were many good and faithful bishops, and their task was gradually eased by the creation of new dioceses and the appointment of area or suffragan bishops to assist them. Happily, the issue is less bitterly divisive today and bishops are as enthusiastic for ecumenical relations as are those known as the 'inferior clergy'. The office is indeed a 'good work' as the Epistle says, but it brings heavy responsibilities and stresses, as administrative and financial problems must concern the chief pastor of a diocese. Through the ages the bishop has had a special place in the clerical record, whether the account is respectful, affectionate or hostile.

Bishops have never been free from criticism, from inside or outside the Church, not least in our own day, though they have seldom been criticized for being too lenient. Baldwin became Archbishop of Canterbury in 1184 and later went on the Third Crusade. His establishment of the supremacy of Canterbury over the Church in Wales may not endear him to Welsh readers, but Gerald, known as 'the Welshman', thought highly of him, with one reservation.

He was a man of a dark complexion, of an open and venerable countenance, of a moderate stature, a good person, and rather inclined to be thin than corpulent. He was a modest and grave man, of so great abstinence and continence, that ill report scarcely ever presumed to say any thing against him; a man of few words; slow to anger, temperate and moderate in all his passions and affections; swift to hear, slow to speak; he was from an early age well instructed in literature, and bearing the yoke of the Lord from his youth, by the purity of his morals became a distinguished luminary to the people; wherefore voluntarily resigning the honour of the archdeacon, which he had canonically obtained, and despising the pomps and vanities of the world, he assumed with holy devotion the habit of the Cistercian order; and as he had been formerly more than a monk in his manners, within the space of a year he was appointed abbot, and in a few years afterwards preferred first to a bishopric, and then to an archbishopric; and having been found faithful in a little, had authority given him over much. But, as Cicero says, 'Nature had made nothing entirely perfect'; when he came into power, not laying aside that sweet innate benignity which he had always shown when a private man, sustaining his people with his staff rather than chastising them with rods, feeding them as it were with the milk of a mother, and not making use of the scourges of the father, he incurred public scandal for his remissness. So great was his lenity that he put an end to all pastoral rigour; and was a better monk than abbot, a better bishop than archbishop. Hence pope Urban addressed him: 'Urban, servant of the servants of God, to the most fervent monk, to the warm abbot, to the lukewarm bishop, to the remiss archbishop, health, etc.'

Geraldus Cambrensis, *Itinerary through Wales*[1]

Thomas Becket has come to be a revered archetypal defender of Church privileges against the State. The favourable image has been enhanced by T. S. Eliot's brilliant portrayal in Murder in the Cathedral. *The following extracts from a work by John Morris relate the beginning of his dispute with Henry II, to whom he has just quoted the words of St Peter, 'We ought to obey God rather than men'.*

Then said the king, 'I do not want you to preach me a sermon just at present. Are you not the son of one of my rustics?' St Thomas answered,

'In truth I am not sprung of royal race; no more was blessed Peter, the prince of the apostles, on whom the Lord deigned to confer the keys of heaven, and the headship of the universal Church.' 'It is true,' said the king; 'but he died for his Lord.' The Primate replied, 'I too will die for my Lord, when the time comes.' Henry retorted, 'You trust too much to your elevation.' 'I trust,' he answered, 'in the Lord; for cursed is he that putteth his trust in man. I am ready for your honour and good pleasure, saving my order; as of old, so also now. But on the matters relating to your honour and the good of your soul you should have consulted me, whom you have always found faithful and useful in your counsels, and not those who have raised this flame against me, though I have never injured them. You will not deny, I think, that I was faithful to you when I was in sacred orders; much more, then, ought you to expect to find me faithful when raised to the priesthood.' The king continued to urge that the saving clause should be omitted; and the Saint refusing, they parted.

[*Becket is, of course, most famous for his martyrdom in Canterbury Cathedral. Even after his death, he had a surprise for his friends.*]

They buried him in the cowl, as well as his hair-shirt, which, to their astonishment, extended to the knees. This was covered with linen, and so made that it could be readily undone, to enable him to receive the discipline. The stripes which he had received on the morning of his martyrdom were clearly visible. This hair-shirt was alive with vermin, the torment of which must have made his life a martyrdom. In the breast of the hair-shirt was the letter he had received on Sunday, warning him of his coming fate. He was vested in the vestments in which he had been consecrated; a simple superhumeral or amice, the alb, chrismatic, mitre, stole, and maniple: all these he had preserved, for this purpose; he had also the tunicle, dalmatic, chasuble, the pall with its pins, gloves, ring, sandals, and pastoral staff. The chalice as usual was placed with him in a new marble coffin in the crypt, before the two altars of St John the Baptist and St Augustine, the Apostle of England. The doors were then securely fastened, and the vessel containing the blood and brain was placed outside. The crypt remained closed until the Easter following. If any one was admitted, it was secretly done: but the miracles becoming exceedingly frequent [...] and their fame very widely spread, so that the memorable places were much visited, the crypt was thrown open at the urgent petition of the people, on the second of

April, being the Friday in Easter week. Miracles followed in still greater numbers.

John Morris, *The Life and Martyrdom of Saint Thomas Becket*[2]

Thomas Wolsey (c. 1474–1530) has come to be regarded as a type of the cleric with a thirst for worldly power. His rise from humble origins to be a Cardinal, Archbishop of York and Chancellor of England ended in a fall from favour, and death on his way to London to face a charge of high treason. Shakespeare gives him a more sympathetic hearing as he takes leave of his aide Thomas Cromwell. The Renaissance view that ambition was a fault, not only for the clergy, is emphasized. (Critics differ about the extent of John Fletcher's hand in the play, but I think that this scene is by Shakespeare.)

Cromwell, I did not think to shed a tear
In all my miseries; but thou hast forced me,
Out of thy honest truth, to play the woman.
Let's dry our eyes; and thus far hear me, Cromwell,
And when I am forgotten, as I shall be,
And sleep in dull cold marble, where no mention
Of me more must be heard of, say I taught thee –
Say Wolsey, that once trod the ways of glory,
And sounded all the depths and shoals of honour,
Found thee a way, out of his wreck, to rise in –
A sure and safe one, though thy master missed it.
Mark but my fall and that that ruined me.
Cromwell, I charge thee, fling away ambition:
By that sin fell the angels. How can man then,
The image of his Maker, hope to win by it?
Love thyself last; cherish those hearts that hate thee;
Corruption wins not more than honesty.
Still in thy right hand carry gentle peace
To silence envious tongues. Be just, and fear not;
Let all the ends thou aim'st at be thy country's,
Thy God's, and truth's; then, if thou fall'st, O Cromwell,
Thou fall'st a blessed martyr!
Serve the King, and prithee lead me in.

There take an inventory of all I have
To the last penny; 'Tis the King's. My robe,
And my integrity to heaven, is all
I dare now call mine own. O Cromwell, Cromwell!
Had I but served my God with half the zeal
I served my King, he would not in mine age
Have left me naked to mine enemies.

William Shakespeare, *King Henry VIII*[3]

Matthew Parker (1504–75) was the first Archbishop of Canterbury in the restored Church of England under Queen Elizabeth I. A nineteenth-century biographer gives a judicious and generally favourable summing-up. The attacks on Parker from both sides remind us that being a bishop is not always easy and that being Archbishop of Canterbury is particularly exacting. The anecdote of the Queen's reception of his wife may be compared with her general injunction on clerical marriages (see p. 135). Here again, a lack of ambition is seen as a virtue.

In March, 1575, the queen visited him at Canterbury, when she was entertained at a cost of about £2000, a sum nearly equal to the income of his see. She frequently dined with him at Lambeth, and on one such occasion is said to have insulted Mrs Parker, though we hope for her credit as a lady the story is not true, by an indecorous jibe at the status of the wives of the clergy. 'Madam I may not call you,' she addressed her hostess as she took leave of her, 'and Mistress I am ashamed to call you, so as I know not what to call you, but yet I do thank you.'

Archbishop Parker died at Lambeth on May 17, 1575, and was buried with great pomp in his chapel, but in the time of the Civil War his tomb was broken open, and his remains thrust into a hole. They were afterwards recovered by his successor, Sancroft, and suitably re-interred.

Though he was not, perhaps, a great archbishop, yet his attainments and character, and the great services he rendered to religion and the Church of England, remove him far from mediocrity. Humble, modest, learned, and pious, he was always inclined to moderation, which was ill understood by the extremists of either party; the queen finding fault with him for being 'too soft and easy' in his treatment of the nonconformists, while they railed upon him as a persecutor and a papist: yet that part of his public conduct for which he has been so severely censured was due to his conscientious conviction of the extent of the royal authority, and of the importance of maintaining order in the Church.

His devotion to the queen was certainly very great, yet it was not servile, proceeding neither from ambition nor fear, from the first of which faults his sincere desire to escape the primacy acquits him. That he was constitutionally diffident, if not timid, we have from his own pen, that records his 'natural viciosity of overmuch shamefastness,' but in the cause of duty he was brave enough, and could, and did, face the royal lioness herself. 'I will not be abashed,' he wrote, after a stormy interview with Elizabeth, 'to say to my prince that I think in conscience, in answering to my charging. As this other day I was well chidden at my prince's hand; but with one ear I heard her hard words, and with the other, and in my conscience and heart, I heard God.'

His faithful rebukes to his old friend, the Lord Keeper Bacon, for his alienation of Church property, well illustrates his moral courage; for few things are more painful to sensitive natures than to reprove one's friends, especially those to whom we lie under great obligations. As a public character he was a great encourager of learning, and also of art, for the promotion of which his purse was always open. In private life he was faultless, a loving husband, a tender and affectionate parent, an attached and constant friend, a just and kind master.

F. O. White, *Lives of the Elizabethan Bishops*[4]

Alexander Pope (1688–1744) was the most waspish and incisive of English satirists, but he was wholly laudatory in his epitaph for John Hough, Bishop successively of Oxford, Lichfield and Worcester, who died aged ninety-three in 1743.

A Bishop, by his neighbours hated,
Has cause to wish himself translated;
But why should Hough desire translation,
Loved and esteemed by all the nation?
Yet if it be the old man's case,
I'll lay my life I know his place:
'Tis where God sent some that adore him,
And whither Enoch went before him.

Alexander Pope, 'Bishop Hough'[5]

Bishops do not always win unqualified approval from those known as the
'inferior clergy'. William Cole confided to his diary in 1766 his opinion
of Bishop John Green of Lincoln, adding for good measure John Gordon,
Archdeacon of Buckingham, whose Visitation he had recently endured. His
liberal use of capital letters may reflect his indignation.

This priggish Archdeacon, at his late Visitation at Newport-Pagnal on 17
June 1766, was pleased to display his Oratory in a Charge to the Clergy,
prefacing it with a notorious Mistake, in telling us, what made every one
stare & amazed, That his Appointment to that Office was peculiarly
happy, in that he was promoted by a B⟨isho⟩p who had the Hearts of his
Clergy, & that however unworthy he might be himself for such a Dignity
in the Church, yet his being sent among us by such a Diocesan, he was
sure his Failings would be overlooked on the Account of his Patron. &
that he thought it the wisest way to rest his Merits there – these were his
very Expressions – than to plead any Desert in himself. He then proceeded to tell us an old Story of the antient Office of an Archdeacon
seeming full of himself, & to abuse the old Clergy for their Ignorance,
which used to be corrected by his Predecessor's Learning. But now, he
added most fulsomely, the inferior Clergy were so learned as to be able
to instruct their Archdeacon: he then proceeded to give a sort of Lecture
on Elocution, & seemed to hint a Prosecution of such Lectures, as more
than ordinarily useful to the Clergy, & there ended, most quaintly, (in
the State of the Church-Wardens' Presentments, to which he alluded),
that he was very glad to find, as he hoped he always should do, That All
was well. What he had said relating to the B⟨isho⟩p's being esteemed by
the Clergy was so false & fulsome, as nothing could be more so. If he had
said so of his Predecessor, the late worthy B⟨isho⟩p of Salisbury, it would
have been true & just: whose gentlemanly Behaviour had gained him the
universal Love & Esteem of his Clergy: whereas the clownish Carriage, &
want of Behaviour & Manners in the present B⟨isho⟩p was so notorious
at his last Visitation, that every one was scandalized at it, & among all my
Acquaintance I never heard him mentioned but with the utmost
Disrespect: & by no one more than by Dr Forester himself about 2 years
ago. Indeed the B⟨isho⟩p's ungain, awkward, splay-footed Carriage &
Yorkshire Dialect is a full Indication of his humble Education & mean
Extraction. Mrs Dowbiggin's Father, his Lordship's Brother, being a
Miller at Beverley. I do not mean this as any Reflection on his Lordship:

if I did, I should bespatter my own Self, whose Father was no other than a substantial Farmer: all I mean is, that a Person of such Extraction & Accomplishments, when they forget themselves & their former Acquaintance on gaining Titles and Preferments, are sure to be remembered for their Forgetfulness.

The Blecheley Diary of the Rev. William Cole[6]

In 1816 another clerical diarist takes the death of John Randolph (Bishop of London from 1809 to 1813) as a point from which to moralize about the vanity of human wishes, and has little respect for his successor. This was William Howley who later became Archbishop of Canterbury and presided at the coronation of Queen Victoria. William Jones was Rector of Broxbourne in Hertfordshire. His opening sentence refers to Shakespeare's line, 'Man, proud man, drest in a little brief authority' (Measure for Measure, II.ii.120).

The 'authority' with which Dr R⟨andolph⟩ was 'dressed' as Bishop of London was not *little* – but it was *brief*. He did not long enjoy it. He has ceased to be an object of envy; but I humbly trust that he is infinitely happier than he could be in the midst of the highest earthly honours!

The Royal Preacher says, 'A living dog is better than a dead lion;' – & who is not ready to say that a living curate is better than a dead Bishop, or even Archbishop; 'for to him' (the curate) 'that is joined to all the living there is hope' of obtaining what is called – or, rather, what is often miscalled – 'a living'!

'London-House' in St James's Square, & the delightful Palace at Fulham, have long ago welcomed Dr Howley, the present Bishop, as they had done his predecessors; & abundance of flatterers, doubtless buzzed about him with compliments of congratulation. How long Dr H⟨owley⟩ may continue, Heaven only knows; but there seems to be little or nothing of him; he has not any substance; to look at that part of his Lordship which, in human bodies, is, generally, somewhat rotund – he seems as if, though a Bishop, 'he never dined'! – he is of a *thread-paper form*.

[...] As some pure, prim, faded females, with all the airs of antiquated virginity, have been heard to say, 'I might have been married – if it had not been for &c, &c' – so, on the death of this or that Bishop, some parsons, ashamed of being unwedded to a benefice, have pretended to have been on, & very near the top of the Bishop's list of preferment.

The Diary of the Revd William Jones[7]

Sydney Smith (1771–1845) held country livings before becoming a canon of St Paul's Cathedral, London. He is remembered for his incisive wit, much of it displayed in contributions to the Edinburgh Review, *of which he was one of the founders in 1802. He campaigned for many reforming causes, including those within the Church. He warns of the dangers which may attend a new bishop. The Targum of Onkelos is a third-century Aramaic version of the Pentateuch.*

A good and honest bishop (I thank God there are many who deserve that character!) ought to suspect himself, and carefully to watch his own heart. He is all of a sudden elevated from being a tutor, dining at an early hour with his pupil, (and occasionally, it is believed, on cold meat,) to be a spiritual Lord; he is dressed in a magnificent dress, decorated with a title, flattered by Chaplains, and surrounded by little people looking up for the things which he has to give away; and this often happens to a man who has had no opportunities of seeing the world, whose parents were in very humble life, and who has given up all his thoughts to the frogs of Aristophanes and the Targum of Onkelos. How is it possible that such a man should not lose his head? that he should not swell? that he should not be guilty of a thousand follies, and worry and tease to death (before he recovers his common sense) a hundred men as good, and as wise, and as able as himself? *but then* […] How can a bishop marry? How can he flirt? The most he can say is, 'I will see you in the vestry after service.'

The Wit and Wisdom of the Rev. Sydney Smith[8]

Nicholas Wiseman became Archbishop of Westminster when the Roman Catholic hierarchy was restored in England in 1850. Browning had him in mind when he wrote this verse monologue of a bishop being interviewed by a journalist. The presentation says much about the disturbed state of religious thought at the time, but little about the real Wiseman, and is to be taken as an imaginary portrait. Friedrich Schelling (1775–1854) was a

German thinker who tried to reconcile Christian belief with an almost
pantheistic philosophy of Nature.

Our interest's on the dangerous edge of things.
The honest thief, the tender murderer,
The superstitious atheist, demirep
That loves and saves her soul in new French books –
We watch while these in equilibrium keep
The giddy line midway: one step aside,
They're classed and done with: I, then, keep the line
Before your sages – just the men to shrink
From the gross weights, coarse scales and labels broad
You offer their refinement. Fool or knave?
Why needs a bishop be a fool or knave
When there's a thousand diamond weights between?
So, I enlist them. Your picked twelve, you'll find,
Profess themselves indignant, scandalized
At thus being held unable to explain
How a superior man who disbelieves
May not believe as well: that's Schelling's way!
It's through my coming in the tail of time,
Nicking the minute with a happy tact.
Had I been born three hundred years ago
They'd say, 'What's strange? Blougram of course believes;'
And, seventy years since, 'disbelieves of course.'
But now, 'He may believe; and yet, and yet
How can he?' All eyes turn with interest.
Whereas, step off the line on either side –
You, for example, clever to a fault,
The rough and ready men who write apace,
Read somewhat seldomer, think perhaps even less –
You disbelieve! Who wonders and who cares?
Lord So-and-so – his coat bedropped with wax,
All Peter's chains about his waist, his back
Brave with the needlework of Noodledom –
Believes! Again, who wonders and who cares?
But I, the man of sense and learning too,
The able to think yet act, the this, the that,

I, to believe at this late time of day!
Enough; you see, I need not fear contempt.

Robert Browning, 'Bishop Blougram's Apology'[9]

Wiseman was succeeded as Archbishop of Westminster by Henry Manning, who did much to raise esteem for the Roman Catholic Church in England by his social concern, particularly by his mediation in the London Dock Strike of 1889. He was made a cardinal in 1875. His later years are described by Lytton Strachey with his usual irony: not an entirely fair picture but evocative.

Manning was now an old man, and his outward form had assumed that appearance of austere asceticism which is, perhaps, the one thing immediately suggested by his name to the ordinary Englishman. The spare and stately form, the head, massive, emaciated, terrible, with the great nose, the glittering eyes, and the mouth drawn back and compressed into the grim rigidities of age, self-mortification, and authority – such is the vision that still lingers in the public mind – the vision which, actual and palpable like some embodied memory of the Middle Ages, used to pass and repass, less than a generation since, through the streets of London. For the activities of this extraordinary figure were great and varied. He ruled his diocese with the despotic zeal of a born administrator. He threw himself into social work of every kind; he organised charities, he lectured on temperance. He delivered innumerable sermons; he produced an unending series of devotional books. And he brooked no brother near the throne: Newman languished in Birmingham; and even the Jesuits trembled and obeyed.

Nor was it only among his own community that his energy and his experience found scope. He gradually came to play an important part in public affairs, upon questions of labour, poverty, and education. He sat on Royal Commissions, and corresponded with Cabinet Ministers. At last no philanthropic meeting at the Guildhall was considered complete without the presence of Cardinal Manning. A special degree of precedence was accorded to him. Though the rank of a Cardinal-Archbishop is officially unknown in England, his name appeared in public documents – as a token, it must be supposed, of personal consideration – above the names of peers and bishops, and immediately below that of the Prince of Wales.

In his private life he was secluded. The ambiguities of his social position and his desire to maintain intact the peculiar eminence of his office combined to hold him aloof from the ordinary gatherings of society, though on the rare occasions of his appearance among fashionable and exalted persons he carried all before him. His favourite haunt was the Athenaeum Club, where he sat scanning the newspapers, or conversing with the old friends of former days.

Lytton Strachey, *Eminent Victorians*[10]

A less famous Victorian bishop, Durnford of Chichester, is praised by a priest serving in his diocese in 1890. Durnford was a scholar and a conscientious man, who supported the greater emphasis on frequent confirmations which was one of the results of the Oxford Movement. The last paragraph reveals that he was also firm about the laws of the parish church and the perennial problem of faculties.

Dr Gilbert was succeeded by Bishop Durnford, who had been for thirty-five years Rector of Middleton, in Lancashire. When he first came his ideas evidently were for carrying on the administration of his office as he would have done in a thickly populated district like that from which he had come. But he quickly learnt to accommodate himself to circumstances, and has proved an excellent Diocesan. He has continued – notwithstanding his great age – most indefatigable in work, ever ready to preach at the reopening of a church after restoration, himself to induct a new incumbent. He has greatly increased his number of Confirmations and in the various towns has held Confirmations annually. He has instituted annual Diocesan Conferences, and never (unless absolutely obliged) absents himself from any Diocesan meeting, and thus gets through an amount of work which few men, ten or fifteen years his junior, are physically able to perform [...]

I never met with anyone better acquainted with parochial business, and I have heard that when he was in the large parish of Middleton he made a first-rate chairman. He is also a good botanist and archaeologist. Once when I was with him at Alfriston he had no hesitation in pronouncing the Star Inn to be of the period of Richard II, and gave his reasons for so doing.

The first time I met him was a few months after his Consecration, at a Confirmation at Firle in 1871. The then vicar, Mr Smith, was too ill to venture out, so I acted as cicerone to the Bishop. On going into Firle Church his quick eye immediately caught sight of a mural tablet of very recent date. He asked by whose authority it was put up, and said that he wished it to be generally known that nothing of the kind was to be erected or done without applying to him for a faculty, and then added, 'And if they do apply I shall not grant it'.

E. B. Ellman, *Recollections of a Sussex Parson*[11]

As the bishops seem to be criticized even more than the lower clergy, it is right that a tribute to an exemplary bishop should be included. Arthur Winnington-Ingram was Bishop of London from 1901 to 1939. This description was written during his episcopate.

He is a great bishop, in the sense that he is a great Christian. His heart is filled with the love of his fellow men, but most of all with love of the poor. From the days when he left Lichfield and came to the Oxford House Settlement in the East End, he has given himself to the cause of the disinherited and the miserable. Slumming to him has been no idle diversion. It has been his vocation, his life. Into it he has poured all the wealth of a boundless joy, of a nature all sunshine and generous emotion. He as much as any man of our time has realised that if you would reach the souls of men you must first care for their bodies, heal their sores, lessen their miseries. Of this primitive law of the faith, he has carried a cup of cold water to the lips of the dying girl in the garret, laboured to drain the morass of the slum, lived his days and nights among the forsaken and the hopeless. And then, his heart full of the goodness of the poor rather than of contempt of their squalor, he has gone down to Oxford to call others into the same harvest field. 'It was an address he gave when I was an undergraduate,' said a friend of mine to me, 'that brought me here ten years ago to live in the slums. I thank God for it.' Or he has gone out into Victoria Park to meet the atheists face to face; answer their pet posers with ready wit, and win their hearts by his genial comradeship. He is not a humorist, but he has the gift of inexhaustible good-humour. 'I enjoy,' he says, 'every minute of my work, every minute.'

A. G. Gardiner, *Prophets, Priests and Kings*[12]

The author of this moral tale seems to be unknown, though it has appeared in both oral and written form. It is a pleasant fantasy which suggests that there are humble bishops and charity is sometimes materially rewarded.

The bishop glanced through his window pane
On a world of sleet, and wind, and rain,
When a dreary figure met his eyes
That made the bishop soliloquize.

And as the bishop gloomily thought
He ordered pen and ink to be brought,
Then 'Providence Watches' he plainly wrote
And pinned the remark to a ten bob note.

Seizing his hat from his lordly rack
And wrapping his cloak around his back,
Across the road the bishop ran
And gave the note to the shabby man.

That afternoon was the bishop's 'at home'
When everyone gathered beneath his dome,
Curate and canon from far and near
Came to partake of the bishop's cheer.

There in the good old bishop's hall
Stood a stranger lean and tall.
'Your winnings, my lord,' he cried. 'Well done.
"Providence Watches", at ten to one.'

It is to be noted on Sunday next
The bishop skilfully chose his text,
And from the pulpit earnestly told
Of the fertile seed that returned tenfold.

Anonymous

Chapter 4

To Instruct the People

For centuries education above the lowest level was chiefly in the hands of the clergy. The ancient universities of Oxford and Cambridge were religious foundations. The Fellows of their colleges were obliged to be in holy orders until well into the nineteenth century, and to be celibate unless they were Heads of Houses. Teaching was almost the only profession open to a clergyman of the Church of England who was not engaged in parish work. Some clergy taught in the public schools and there were many famous – and a few infamous – clerical headmasters. Others ran their own private schools to meet the growing middle-class demand for education. All these types are recorded in this chapter. The earliest attempts to provide free schooling were nearly all sponsored by the various denominations, sometimes in rivalry with each other, and later in dispute with the new State system. The question of what are now sometimes called 'faith schools' has not gone away, and continues to cause controversy about admissions quotas and religious teaching. In the United States, religious teaching and worship has been forbidden in the public schools – a title with a different meaning from the British one. As in the parishes, the clerical educators included the good, the bad and the indifferent. Being a member of two professions at the same time, both of them open to public scrutiny and expected to reach high personal standards, has not always been easy. The combination is less common today, though the role of the school and university chaplains is important.

Nicholas Udall (1504–56) is known by students of English literature as the author of the early comedy Ralph Roister Doister. *He was the headmaster successively of Eton and Westminster. Thomas Tusser, the Tudor writer on agriculture, recalled his own unpleasant experience at Eton.*

From Paul's I went, to Eton sent,
To learn straightways the Latin phrase,

Where fifty-three stripes given to me,
   At once I had
For fault but small, or none at all.
See, Udall, see the mercy of thee,
   To me, poor lad.

Thomas Tusser, 'The Author's Life'[1]

This description of a college Fellow unwillingly teaching while waiting for a comfortable benefice, was probably true of many celibate dons at Oxford and Cambridge in holy orders in the seventeenth century and later. They could not marry unless they left the university for a parish, although the heads of colleges were exempt from this provision.

He is a pedant in show, though his title be tutor; and his *pupils*, in broader phrase, are *schoolboys*. On these he spends the false gallop of his tongue; and with senseless discourse tows them along, not out of ignorance. He shews them the rind, conceals the sap: by this means he keeps them the longer, himself the better. He hath learnt to cough, and spit, and blow his nose at every period, to recover his memory; and studies chiefly to set his eyes and beard to a new form of learning. His religion lies in wait for the inclination of his patron; neither ebbs nor flows, but just standing water, between Protestant and Puritan. His dreams are of plurality of benefices and non-residency; and when he rises, acts a long grace to his looking glass. Against he comes to be some great man's chaplain, he hath a habit of boldness, though a very coward [...] He hath less use than possession of books. He is not so proud, but he will call the meanest author by his name, nor so unskilled in the heraldry of a study, but he knows each man's place. So ends that fellowship, and begins another.

Thomas Overbury, *Miscellaneous Works*[2]

In contrast to the reluctant college tutor, there were many parish clergy, not only in Britain, who supplemented their income by taking private pupils. James Fenimore Cooper (1789–1851) writes of an English clergyman settled in North America in the eighteenth century, who acts as tutor to the narrator, a boy whose family could not afford to send him to England for his

*education. It is certainly not the only example of a complacent British asser-
tion of superiority over the American system. The names of the colleges thus
scorned make even more ironical reading in view of their development to the
present day.*

I was taught enough Latin and Greek to enter college, by the Rev Thomas
Worden, an English divine, who was rector of St Jude's, the parish to
which our family properly belonged. This gentleman was esteemed a
good scholar, and was very popular among the gentry of the county,
attending all the dinners, clubs, races, balls, and other diversions that
were given by them, within ten miles of his residence. His sermons were
pithy and short; and he always spoke of your half-hour preachers, as
illiterate prosers, who did not know how to condense their thoughts.
Twenty minutes were his gauge, though I remember to have heard my
father say, he had known him to preach all of twenty-two. When he
compressed down to fourteen, my grandfather invariably protested he
was delighted.

I remained with Mr Worden until I could translate the two first
Aeneids, and the whole of the Gospel of St Matthew, pretty readily; and
then my father and grandfather, the last in particular, for the old gentleman had a great idea of learning, began to turn over in their minds, the
college to which I ought to be sent. We had the choice of two, in both of
which the learned languages and the sciences were taught to a degree,
and in a perfection, that is surprising for a new country. These colleges
are Yale, at New Haven, in Connecticut, and Nassau Hall, which was
then at Newark, New Jersey, after having been a short time at Eliza-
bethstown, but which has since been established at Princeton. Mr
Worden laughed at both; said that neither had as much learning as a
second-rate English grammar school, and that a lower-form boy, at Eton
or Westminster, could take a master's degree at either and pass for a
prodigy into the bargain.

J. F. Cooper, *Satanstoe*[3]

*When Edward Gibbon (1737–94) went to Oxford at the age of fifteen, he was
not impressed by the clerical Fellows of Magdalen College. Did his later contempt for the Christian Church, as expressed in his* Decline and Fall of the
Roman Empire, *begin then?*

The fellows or monks of my time were decent easy men, who supinely enjoyed the gifts of the founder; their days were filled by a series of uniform employments; the chapel and the hall, the coffee-house and the common room, till they retired, weary and well satisfied, to a long slumber. From the toil of reading, or thinking, or writing, they had absolved their conscience; and the first shoots of learning and ingenuity withered on the ground, without yielding any fruits to the owners or the public. As a gentleman-commoner, I was admitted to the society of the fellows, and fondly expected that some questions of literature would be the amusing and instructive topics of their discourse. Their conversation stagnated in a round of college business, Tory politics, personal anecdotes, and private scandal: their dull and deep potations excused the brisk intemperance of youth: and their constitutional toasts were not expressive of the most lively loyalty for the house of Hanover [...]

The first tutor into whose hands I was resigned appears to have been one of the best of the tribe: Dr Waldegrave was a learned and pious man, of a mild disposition, strict morals, and abstemious life, who seldom mingled in the politics or the jollity of the college. But his knowledge of the world was confined to the University; his learning was of the last, rather than of the present age; his temper was indolent; his faculties, which were not of the first rate, had been relaxed by the climate, and he was satisfied, like his fellows, with the slight and superficial discharge of an important trust. As soon as my tutor had sounded the insufficiency of his disciple in school-learning, he proposed that we should read every morning from ten to eleven the comedies of Terence. The sum of my improvement in the University of Oxford is confined to three or four Latin plays, and even the study of an elegant classic, which might have been illustrated by a comparison of ancient and modern classic, was reduced to a dry and literal interpretation of the author's text.

Edward Gibbon, *Autobiography*[4]

Some years later, Charles Lamb sat under a similar cleric in the less comfortable conditions of school.

The Upper and Lower Grammar Schools were held in the same room; and an imaginary line only divided their bounds. Their character was as different as that of the inhabitants on the two sides of the Pyrenees. The

Rev. James Boyer was the Upper Master, but the Rev. Matthew Field presided over that portion of the apartment of which I had the good fortune to be a member [...]

Matthew Field belonged to that class of modest divines who affect to mix in equal proportion the *gentleman*, the *scholar*, and the *Christian*; but, I know not how, the first ingredient is generally found to be the predominating dose in the composition. He was engaged in gay parties, or with his courtly bow at some episcopal levée, when he should have been attending upon us. He had for many years the classical charge of a hundred children, during the four or five first years of their education; and his very highest form seldom proceeded further than two or three of the Introductory fables of Phaedrus. How things were suffered to go on thus, I cannot guess. Boyer, who was the proper person to have remedied these abuses, always affected, perhaps felt, a delicacy in interfering in a province not strictly his own. I have not been without my suspicions, that he was not altogether displeased at the contrast we presented to his end of the school. We were a sort of Helots to his young Spartans. He would sometimes, with ironic deference, send to borrow a rod of the Under Master, and then, with sardonic grin, observe to one of his upper boys, 'how neat and fresh the twigs looked'. While his pale students were battering their brains over Xenophon and Plato, with a silence as deep as that enjoined by the Samite, we were enjoying ourselves at our ease in our little Goshen. We saw a little into the secrets of his discipline, and the prospect did but the more reconcile us to our lot. His thunders rolled innocuous for us; his storms came near, but never touched us; contrary to Gideon's miracle, while all round were drenched, our fleece was dry. His boys turned out the better scholars, we, I suspect, have the advantage in temper. His pupils cannot speak of him without something of terror allaying their gratitude; the remembrance of Field comes back with all the soothing images of indolence, and summer slumbers, and work like play, and innocent idleness, and Elysian exemptions, and life itself a 'playing holiday'.

Charles Lamb, 'Christ's Hospital Five and Thirty Years Ago'[5]

Martin Joseph Routh (1755–1854) was the President of Magdalen College, Oxford for sixty-three years until his death at the age of ninety-nine. A scholar and a High Churchman, he influenced the men of the Oxford Movement. He made a lasting impression on J. W. Burgon, later Dean of Chichester, who is remembered for one line in his Newdigate Prize Poem on Petra, 'A rose-red city, half as old as time'. Routh's parting advice to Burgon remains as wisdom for all researchers and writers.

Availing myself of a pause after he had inquired after my intended pursuits, I leaned forward (for he was more than slightly deaf) and remarked that perhaps he would allow me to ask him a question. 'Eh, sir?' 'I thought that perhaps you would allow me to ask a question about Divinity, sir.' He told me to go on. I explained that I desired a few words of counsel, if he would condescend to give them – some directions as to the best way of pursuing the study which he had himself cultivated with such signal success. Aware that my request was almost as vague as the subject was vast, and full of genuine consideration for the aged oracle, I enlarged for a minute on the matter, chiefly in order to give him time to adjust his thoughts before making reply. He inquired what I had read. 'Pearson and Eusebius, carefully.'

The gravity which by this time his features had assumed was very striking. He lay back in his chair. His head sank forward on his chest, and he looked like one absorbed in thought. 'Yes – I think, sir' (said he after a long pause, which, besides raising my curiosity, rather alarmed me by the contrast it presented to his recent animated manner) 'I think, sir, were I you, sir – that I would – first of all – read the – the Gospel according to St Matthew.' Here he paused. 'And after I had read the Gospel according to St Matthew – I would – were I you, sir – go on to read – the Gospel according to St Mark.' I looked at him anxiously to see whether he was serious. One glance was enough. He was giving me (but at a very slow rate) the outline of my future course. 'I think, sir, when I had read the Gospel according to St Mark, I would go on, sir – yes I would go on to – to the – the Gospel – according to – St Luke, sir.' (Another pause, as if the reverend speaker were reconsidering the matter.) 'Well, sir, and when I had read those three gospels, sir, were I in your place, I would go on – yes, I would certainly go on to read the Gospel according to St John.'

For an instant I had felt an inclination to laugh. But by this time a very different set of feelings came over me. Here was a theologian of ninety-one, who, after surveying the entire field of sacred science, had come back to the point he had started from; and had nothing better to advise me to read than the Gospel! A full year elapsed before I ventured to repeat the intrusion. I ventured to address him somewhat as follows: 'Mr President, give me leave to ask you a question I have sometimes asked of aged persons, but never of any so aged or so learned as yourself.' He looked so kindly at me that I thought I might go on. 'Every studious man, in the course of a long and thoughtful life, has had occasion to experience the special value of some axiom or precept. Would you mind giving me the benefit of such a word of advice?' He bade me explain, evidently to gain time. I quoted an instance. He nodded and looked thoughtful. Presently he brightened up and said, 'I think, sir, since you care for the advice of an old man, sir, you will find it a very good practice' (here he looked me in the face) *'always to verify your references, sir!'*

J. W. Burgon in the *Quarterly Review*[6]

The enforced celibacy of college Fellows did not always make them as accessible and urbane as Routh. William Whewell (1794–1866) was a brilliant man, one of the leading Victorian geologists, but when he became Master of Trinity College, Cambridge, he was not entirely a social success.

He was impatient and he was overbearing; or he was thought to be so, which, so far as his success as a Master went, came to the same thing. He had lived so long as a bachelor among bachelors – giving and receiving thrusts in argument, like a pugilist in a fair fight – that he had become somewhat pachydermatous. It is probable, too, that he was quite ignorant of the weight of his own blows. He forgot those he received, and expected his antagonist to have an equally short memory. Again, the high view which he took of his position as Master laid him open to the charge of arrogance. We believe the true explanation to be that he was too conscientious, if such a phrase be admissible; too inflexible in exacting from others the same strict obedience to College rules which he imposed upon himself. There are two ways, however, of doing most things; and he was unlucky in nearly always choosing the wrong one. For instance, his hospitality was boundless; whenever strangers came to Cambridge, they were entertained at Trinity Lodge; and, besides, there were weekly parties at which the residents were received. The rooms are spacious, and the welcome was intended to be a warm one; but the parties were not successful. Even at those social gatherings he never forgot that he was Master; compelling all his guests to come in their gowns, and those who came only after dinner to wear them during the entire evening. Then an idea became current that no undergraduate might sit down. So far as this notion was not wholly erroneous, it was based on the evident fact that the great drawing-room, large as it is, could not contain more than a very limited number of guests, supposing them all to sit; and that the undergraduates were obviously those who ought to stand.

J. W. Clark, *Old Friends at Cambridge*[7]

Even after the end of the clerical monopoly in education, many still regarded the clergyman as a superior breed of teacher. The prosperous miller Mr Tulliver accepts the opinion of a friend that 'all the best schoolmasters are of the clergy. The schoolmasters who are not clergymen are a very low set of men generally', and sends his son to a school run by a clergyman. But Mr Stelling is not one of those committed to teaching as a vocation; it is a useful source of income while he develops the other potentialities of his order. J-B. Masillon and Louis Bourdaloue were celebrated French preachers of the seventeenth and eighteenth centuries.

Mr Stelling was a well-sized, broad-chested man, not yet thirty, with flaxen hair standing erect, and large lightish-grey eyes, which were always very wide open; he had a sonorous bass voice, and an air of defiant self-confidence inclining to brazenness. He had entered on his career with great vigour, and intended to make a considerable impression on his fellow men. The Rev. Walter Stelling was not a man who would remain among the 'inferior clergy' all his life. He had a true British determination to push his way in the world. As a schoolmaster, in the first place; for there were capital masterships of grammar-schools to be had, and Mr Stelling meant to have one of them. But as a preacher also, for he meant always to preach in a striking manner, so as to have his congregation swelled by admirers from neighbouring parishes, and to produce a great sensation whenever he took occasional duty for a brother clergyman of minor gifts. The style of preaching he had chosen was the extemporaneous, which was held little short of the miraculous in rural parishes like King's Lorton. Some passages of Massillon and Bourdaloue, which he knew by heart, were really very effective when rolled out in Mr Stelling's deepest tones; but as comparatively feeble appeals of his own were delivered in the same loud and impressive manner, they were often thought quite as striking by his hearers. Mr Stelling's doctrine was of no particular school; if anything, it had a tinge of evangelicalism, for that was 'the telling thing' just then in the diocese to which King's Lorton belonged. In short, Mr Stelling was a man who meant to rise in his profession, and rise by merit, clearly, since he had no interest beyond what might be promised by a problematic relationship to a great lawyer who had not yet become Lord Chancellor. A clergyman who has such vigorous intentions naturally gets a little into debt at starting; it is not to be expected that he will live in the meagre style of a man who means to be a poor curate all his life, and if the few hundreds Mr Timpson advanced towards his daughter's fortune did not suffice for the purchase of handsome furniture, together with a stock of wine, a grand piano, and the laying out of a superior flower-garden, it followed in the most rigorous manner, either that these things must be procured by some other means, or else that the Rev. Mr Stelling must do without them – which last alternative would be an absurd procrastination of the fruits of success, where success was certain. Mr Stelling was so broad-chested and resolute that he felt equal to anything; he would become celebrated by shaking the consciences of his hearers, and he would by-and-by edit a Greek play, and invent several new readings. He had not yet selected the play, for having been married little more than two years, his leisure time had been much occupied with attentions to Mrs Stelling; but he had told that fine woman what he meant to do some day, and she felt great confidence in her husband, as a man who understood everything of that sort.

George Eliot, *The Mill on the Floss*[8]

Not all the clerical teachers were like Mr Stelling. Thomas Arnold (1785–1842) is the most famous Victorian headmaster, whose real achievements at Rugby School have been made more widely known by his appearance in fiction. A fierce opponent of the Oxford Movement and particularly of Newman, he devoted his greatest energy to his school. One of his former pupils wrote his life. Here he recalls Arnold's combination of educational and priestly work.

The Communion was celebrated four times a year. At first some of the Sixth Form boys alone were in the habit of attending; but he took pains to invite to it boys in all parts of the school, who had any serious thoughts, so that the number out of two hundred and ninety or three hundred boys, was occasionally a hundred, and never less than seventy. To individual boys he rarely spoke on the subject, from the fear of its becoming a matter of form or favour; but in his sermons he dwelt upon it much, and would afterwards speak with deep emotion of the pleasure and hope which a larger attendance than usual would give him. It was impossible to hear these exhortations or to see him administer it, without being struck by the strong and manifold interest, which it awakened in him; and at Rugby it was of course more than usually touching to him from its peculiar relation to the school. When he spoke of it in his sermons, it was evident that amongst all the feelings which it excited in himself, and which he wished to impart to others, none was so prominent as the sense that it was a communion not only with God, but with one another, and that the thoughts thus roused should act as a direct and especial counterpoise to that false communion and false companionship, which, as binding one another not to good but to evil, he believed to be the great source of mischief in the school at large. And when, especially to the very young boys, who sometimes partook of the Communion, he bent himself down with looks of fatherly tenderness, and glistening eyes, and trembling voice, in the administration of the elements, it was felt, perhaps, more distinctly than at any other time, how great was the sympathy which he felt with the earliest advances to good in every individual boy.

That part of the Chapel service, however, which, at least to the world at large, is most connected with him, as being the most frequent and most personal of his ministrations, was his preaching. Sermons had occasionally been preached by the Headmaster of this and other public schools to their scholars before his coming to Rugby; but (in some cases from the peculiar constitution or arrangement of the school) it had never before been considered an essential part of the Headmaster's office. The first half-year he confined himself to delivering short addresses, of about five minutes' length, to the boys of his own house.

But from the second half-year he began to preach frequently; and from the autumn of 1831, when he took the chaplaincy which had then become vacant, he preached almost every Sunday of the school year to the end of his life.

A. P. Stanley, *The Life and Correspondence of Thomas Arnold*[9]

Stanley also tells us that Arnold was no opponent of corporal punishment. Another ex-pupil, an equally fervent admirer, recalls Arnold in a less gentle mood. Tom Brown has already been in trouble for playing games during lessons.

The only occasions on which they cared about the matter, were the monthly examinations, when the Doctor came round to examine their form, for one long awful hour, in the work which they had done in the preceding month. The second monthly examination came round soon after Tom's fall, and it was with anything but lively anticipations that he and the other lower-fourth boys came into prayers on the morning of the examination-day.

Prayers and calling-over seemed twice as short as usual, and before they could get construes of a tithe of the hard passages marked in the margin of their books, they were all seated round, and the Doctor was standing in the middle, talking in whispers to the master. Tom couldn't hear a word which passed, and never lifted his *eyes* from his book; but he knew by a sort of magnetic instinct that the Doctor's under-lip was coming out, and his eye beginning to burn, and his gown getting gathered up more and more tightly in his left hand. The suspense was agonising, and Tom knew that he was sure on such occasions to make an example of the School-house boys. 'If he would only begin' thought Tom, 'I shouldn't mind.'

At last the whispering ceased, and the name which was called out was not Brown. He looked up for a moment, but the Doctor's face was too awful; Tom wouldn't have met his eye for all he was worth, and buried himself in his book again.

Thomas Hughes, *Tom Brown's Schooldays*[10]

Edward Thring became headmaster of Uppingham after a college fellow-ship and a curacy. Like the more famous Arnold, he was passionately concerned for the Christian quality of the public school system. This description is a reminder that there were men of high ideals who could find in teaching a true expression of their priesthood.

He wished to establish a school based on true principles. But in his mind these principles themselves rested upon and grew out of what can only be described as a passionate conviction that education was, in a special sense, a work for God. No one can gauge Edward Thring's work and character unless he understands the supreme influence of this belief on his life. From the time when he came to Uppingham a young and perhaps over-confident enthusiast, through years of work and weariness, of mingled success and disappointment, to the day thirty-four years later when, suddenly stricken, he turned away a dying man from the altar of his noble chapel with the words of the communion service upon his lips, this thought that he was doing a work for God, and under His immediate eye, never forsook him. In every crisis of an anxious life it was the central and sustaining thought which gave new courage. It was marked by the fixed habit of always devoting a moment to private prayer before leaving his study to go to his first morning class. It shone out in the morning Scripture lessons to his sixth form, recalled by many a pupil as memorable in the awakening they gave to higher views of Christian life. It appears on every page of the Diary, written almost daily for well-nigh thirty years of his school career. Here every note of true work accomplished, every step in school progress has, in Greek, or Latin, or English, its brief ascription of praise to God, as to every beginning of work he gave its dedication of prayer. Not only did the thought run through his school sermons, as might have been expected, but it also gave a solemn earnestness to his ordinary talk on school questions. This feeling, indeed, that in training young lives he was doing a special and direct work for God dominated his own life and all his views of school life. It gave him his starting-point for practical work.

'Thring was the most Christian man of this generation', was a remark made to me in the House of Commons soon after his death by a well-known public man. One was curious to know the genesis of a thought that seemed to savour of exaggeration. 'Because', he went on to explain, 'he was the first man in England to assert openly that in the economy of

God's world a dull boy had as much right to have his power, such as it is, fully trained as a boy of talent, and that no school did honest work which did not recognise this truth as the basis of its working arrangements.' This was in effect the essential element in his school beliefs.

George R. Parkin, *Edward Thring: Life, Diary and Letters*[11]

E. W. Benson became Archbishop of Canterbury in 1883, after a distin-guished career which began when he was appointed Headmaster of Wellington, a new public school founded in 1859 with the patronage of the Prince Consort as Chairman of the governors. While we properly regret that schoolchildren today do not get enough religion in their education, it is possible to have too much of even the very best things, as Benson's son recalls.

My father, who had hewn Wellington out of the heather, left it in 1873 a full and prosperous public school. The pioneer work was over: he had launched this ship, he had steered it safely past innumerable shoals, he had coaxed it along through contrary cross-currents of the Prince Consort, and now it was sailing brave and free on the high seas. His boyish devotion to the Church, its organization and its place in the life of England, was still a passion with him, but his exclusive view of the benefits of prayer, as shown in his oratory with the booby-trap on the door to catch trespassers, had given place to the widest catholicism, and the schedule of devotional activities for the day of rest at Wellington, not forbidden to boys but compulsory on them, was really prodigious. There was chapel at nine in the morning, after which Bible verses were learned by heart and repeated to form-masters at ten. There was chapel again at a quarter to twelve, and after dinner, at half-past one, there was more Bible-study, followed by a Bible-class in school at half-past three. A third chapel service was held at half-past six, and there were prayers in the dormitories at nine. No secular books could be taken out of school library that day, but a special section of it, furnished with devotional and religious volumes, was open for those who wanted them. It was not indeed to be wondered at that the Prince Consort had asked my father to consider 'Whether there may not be too much excessive employment in Religious Education in the present system of the College'. But he did not think so: a day spent like that was festival to him.

E. F. Benson, *As We Were*[12]

Chapter 5

Then Shall Follow the Sermon

The sermon, often stigmatized as long and boring, is nevertheless at the centre of many people's idea of public worship, and continues to flourish even in an age of many public media. Homilies have been given in churches since the beginning of Christianity: some of the greatest works of the early Fathers of the Church were presented in that form. The speech of St Peter in Acts 2:14–36 is the first recorded instance of following the example of Jesus in giving instruction to a gathered company. In the Middle Ages, sermons were sometimes preached in the vernacular language while the rest of the service was in Latin. The Reformation, with its emphasis on the Ministry of the Word, gave an even more important place to the sermon, often delivered at great length and sometimes to large crowds in the open air. Churches and chapels were planned in a way which gave prominence to the pulpit rather than the altar. Some of the finest English prose went into sermons: Andrewes, Donne, Taylor and others have become as much a part of literary as of ecclesiastical history. In the eighteenth century, John Wesley was the most famous of a line of Nonconformist divines whose preaching extended through the Victorian period, when Newman and others of a different persuasion were equally eloquent in the pulpit. The name 'preacher' is sometimes used to identify a priest or minister, particularly in the United States. Here is a selection of preachers of various qualities, and from several denominations, not forgetting some of the reactions of the laity who have been on the receiving end.

John Earle (?1601–65), Bishop of Worcester and of Salisbury, wrote a collection of short character sketches of various contemporary types. It is to be hoped that this one, allowing for changes in the fashion of clothing, does not come too close to any young curate or minister of the present day. Cardinal

Robert Bellarmine (1542–1621) was a powerful defender of the Roman Catholic Church of his time.

A young raw preacher is a Bird not yet fledged, that hath hopped out of his nest to be chirping on a hedge, and will be straggling abroad at what peril soever. His backwardness in the University hath set him thus forward; for had he not truanted there, he had not been so hasty a Divine. His small standing and time hath made him a proficient only in boldness, out of which and his table-book he is furnished for a preacher. His collections of study are the notes of sermons, which taken up at St Mary's he utters in the country. And if he write brachigraphy [*short-hand*], his stock is so much the better. His writing is more than his reading; for he reads only what he gets without book. Thus accomplished he comes down to his friends, and his first salutation is grace and peace out of the pulpit. His prayer is conceited, and no man remembers his College more at large. The pace of his sermon is a full career, and he runs wildly over hill and dale till the clock stop him. The labour of it is chiefly in his lungs; and the only thing he has made of it himself is the faces. He takes on against the Pope without mercy, and has a jest still in lavender for Bellarmine; yet he preaches heresy, if it comes in his way, though with a mind I must needs say very orthodox. His action is all passion, and his speech interjections. He has an excellent facility in bemoaning the people, and spits with a very good grace. His style is compounded of some twenty several men's, only his body imitates some one extraordinary. He will not draw his handkercher out of his place, nor blow his nose without discretion. His commendation is, that he never looks upon book; and indeed, he was never used to it. He preaches but once a year, though twice on Sunday; for the stuff is still the same, only the dressing a little altered. He has more tricks with a sermon than a tailor with an old cloak, to turn it, and piece it, and at last quite disguise it with a new preface. If he have waded farther in his profession, and would shew reading of his own, his authors are postils [*Bible commentaries*], and his School-divinity a catechism. His fashion and demure habit gets him in with some Town-precisian and makes him a guest on Friday nights. You shall know him by his narrow velvet cape and serge facing, and his ruff, next his hair the shortest thing about him. The companion of his walk is some zealous tradesman, whom he astonisheth with strange points, which they both understand alike. His friends and much painfulness may prefer him to thirty pounds a year, and by this means, to a chamber-maid; with whom we leave him now in the bonds of wedlock. Next Sunday you shall have him again.

John Earle, *Microcosmographie*[1]

Preaching sermons already published by others would be frowned on today, but at one time it was not only tolerated but positively encouraged. Sir Roger de Coverley explains how he made sure of a good sermon from his domestic chaplain.

'At his first settling with me. I made him a present of all the good sermons which have been printed in English, and only begged of him that every Sunday he would pronounce one of them in the pulpit. Accordingly, he has digested them into such a series, that they follow one another naturally, and make a continued system of practical divinity.'

As Sir Roger was going on in his story, the gentleman we were talking of came up to us; and upon the Knight's asking him who preached to-morrow (for it was Saturday night) told us, the Bishop of St Asaph in the morning, and Dr South in the afternoon. He then shewed us his list of preachers for the whole year, where I saw with a great deal of pleasure Archbishop Tillotson, Bishop Saunderson, Dr Barrow, Dr Calamy, with several living authors who have published discourses of practical divinity. I no sooner saw this venerable man in the pulpit, but I very much approved of my friend's insisting upon the qualifications of a good aspect and a clear voice; for I was so charmed with the gracefulness of his figure and delivery, as well as with the discourses he pronounced, that I think I never passed any time more to my satisfaction. A sermon repeated after this manner, is like the composition of a poet in the mouth of a graceful actor.

I could heartily wish that more of our country-clergy would follow this example; and, instead of wasting their spirits in laborious composi-tions of their own, would endeavour after a handsome elocution, and all those other talents that are proper to enforce what has been penned by greater masters. This would not only be more easy to themselves, but more edifying to the people.

Joseph Addison in *The Spectator*[2]

Two eighteenth-century clergymen have met at an inn and their conversa-
tion soon moves to matters which exclude the laymen who are present.
Volumes of sermons do not figure prominently in publishers' lists today,
though at one time a collection of sermons could be a useful addition to the
stipend. There does, however, seem to be a market for sermon outlines, so
perhaps some of the anxieties expressed in the eighteenth century are not
altogether irrelevant.

They had not been long together before they entered into a discourse on
small tithes, which continued a full hour, without the doctor or the
exciseman's having one opportunity to offer a word.

It was then proposed to begin a general conversation, and the exciseman opened on foreign affairs; but a word unluckily dropping from
one of them introduced a dissertation on the hardships suffered by the
inferior clergy; which, after a long duration, concluded with bringing the
nine volumes of sermons on the carpet. Barnabas greatly discouraged
poor Adams; he said, 'The age was so wicked, that nobody read sermons:
would you think it, Mr Adams?' said he, 'I once intended to print
a volume of sermons myself, and they had the approbation of two
or three bishops; but what do you think a bookseller offered me?'
'Twelve guineas perhaps,' cried Adams. 'Not twelve pence, I assure
you,' answered Barnabas: 'nay, the dog refused me a Concordance in
exchange. At last I offered to give him the printing them, for the sake of
dedicating them to that very gentleman who just now drove his own
coach into the inn; and, I assure you, he had the impudence to refuse my
offer; by which means I lost a good living, that was afterwards given away
in exchange for a pointer, to one who – but I will not say anything against
the cloth. So you may guess, Mr Adams, what you are to expect; for if
sermons would have gone down, I believe – I will not be vain; but to be
concise with you, three bishops said they were the best that ever were
writ: but indeed there are a pretty moderate number printed already,·
and not all sold yet.'

'Pray, sir,' said Adams, 'to what do you think the numbers may
amount?' – 'Sir,' answered Barnabas, 'a bookseller told me, he believed
five thousand volumes at least.' 'Five thousand?' quoth the surgeon:
'What can they be writ upon? I remember when I was a boy, I used to
read one Tillotson's sermons, and, I am sure, if a man practised half so
much as is in one of those sermons he will go to heaven.' – 'Doctor,' cries

Barnabas, 'you have a profane way of talking, for which I must reprove you. A man can never have his duty too freely inculcated into him. And as for Tillotson, to be sure he was a good writer, and said things very well; but comparisons are odious; another man may write as well as he – I believe there are some of my sermons,' – and then he applied the candle to his pipe. – 'And I believe there are some of my discourses,' cries Adams, 'which the bishop would not think totally unworthy of being printed; and I have been informed I might procure a very large sum (indeed an immense one) on them.' 'I doubt that,' answered Barnabas: 'however, if you desire to make some money of them, perhaps you may sell them by advertising the manuscript sermons of a clergyman lately deceased, all warranted originals, and never printed. And now I think of it, I should be obliged to you, if there be ever a funeral one among them, to lend it to me; for I am this very day to preach a funeral sermon, for which I have not penned a line, though I am to have a double price.' – Adams answered, 'He had but one, which he feared would not serve his purpose, being sacred to the memory of a magistrate, who had exerted himself very singularly in the preservation of the morality of his neighbours, insomuch that he had neither alehouse nor lewd woman in the parish where he lived.' 'No,' replied Barnabas, 'that will not do quite so well, for the deceased upon whose virtues I am to harangue, was a little too much addicted to liquor, and publicly kept a mistress. I believe I must take a common sermon, and trust to my memory to introduce something handsome on him.'

Henry Fielding, *The Adventures of Joseph Andrews*[3]

While clergy of the Established Church might find preaching sometimes a chore and sometimes profitable, it is worth remembering that for members of other confessions it could lead to persecution. The suffering and the courage of a dissenting minister in the early years of the Restoration after the English Civil War are recorded by a sympathetic chronicler. It is an experience echoed in many other reports, though whether the moral anecdote at the end is strictly true or not we shall never know.

Mr Palmer, a certain nonconformist preacher, was taken at his own house in Nottingham, by the mayor of the town, for preaching upon the Lord's day, and some others with him and put into the town's gaol, where they continued about two or three months. There being a grated window in the prison, which was almost even with the ground, and looked into the street, all people coming by might see these poor people, kept in a damp, ill-favoured room, where they patiently exhorted and cheered one another. One Lord's day, after sermon time, the prisoners were singing a psalm, and the people as they passed up and down, when they came to the prison, stood still, till there were a great many gathered about the window at which Mr Palmer was preaching; whereupon the mayor, one Toplady, who had formerly been a parliament officer, but was now a renegade, came violently with his officers, and beat the people, and thrust some into prison that were but passing the street, kicked and pinched the men's wives in his rage, and was but the more exasperated, when some of them told him, how ill his fury became him who had once been one of them. The next day, or a few days after, having given order that the prisoners should every Lord's day after be locked in the coal-house, he went to London and made information, I heard on oath, to the council, that a thousand of the country came into the town armed, and marched to the prison window to hear the prisoner preach; whereupon he procured an order for a troop of horse to be sent down to quarter at Nottingham to keep the fanatics in awe. But one who had a relation to the town, being then at court, and knowing this to be false, certified to the contrary and prevented the troop. After the mayor came down, he was one night taken with a vomiting of blood, and being ill, called his man and his maid, who also at the same time fell & bleeding, and were all ready to be choked in their own blood, which at last stopping, they came to assist him; but after that he never lifted up his head, but languished for a few months and died.

Lucy Hutchinson, *Memoirs of the Life of Colonel Hutchinson*[4]

Sermons which question the ultimate destiny of members of the congregation are not usually popular. Alexander Pope wrote satirically of the fashionable chapel where 'To rest the cushion and soft Dean invite,/ Who never mentions Hell to ears polite.' But satire can be overtaken by fact: an eighteenth-century clergyman in Ireland had the courage to defend his sermon. The trouble starts when he criticizes a book recommended by the wife of his Bishop.

In the morning, an Archdeacon, by the lady's directions, came to Skelton's room to sound him on the book, and asked him carelessly if he had read any of it? Yes, he told him, he had looked into it here and there. He then asked him how he liked it? He said but indifferently, for he thought there was a great deal of nonsense in it. This brought on a sort of a scuffle between them. At last Skelton said he would lay him a wager, open the book at any page he pleased, and he would show him nonsense in it before he read to the bottom. The Archdeacon agreed and while he was reading the page, Skelton stopped him now and then, and said, 'That's nonsense'; 'Yes it is', he owned; and thus he was forced to acknowledge there was nonsense in every page of it. The Bishop's lady when she heard how contemptibly he spoke of the book which she so highly esteemed could scarce keep her temper; especially as she was accustomed to be flattered in her notions by the clergy, who would never oppose her. She therefore resolved to affront Mr Skelton in an open company, supposing a poor Curate like him dare not say a word. Accordingly, after dinner, before the Bishop and a large company of clergy and others, she said to him, 'Mr Skelton, I heard you preached in St James's chapel when you were in London'. 'Yes Madam, I did.' 'Well sir a lady, a friend of mine who heard you, told me you preached very absurdly, talking of hell's fire and such coarse subjects as are never introduced in so polite a place'.

'Pray, Madam, who is this lady, a friend of yours that makes these remarks on my preaching?'

'Such a lady, Sir,' she answered, naming her.

'Oh!' he said, 'she has a good right not to like sermons about hell's fire, for she is whore to the Archbishop of York, all London knows it'.

Samuel Burdy, The Life of Philip Skelton[5]

Parson Yorick, as created by Laurence Sterne, would have a deserved place in a later chapter of eccentrics. His habitual treatment of his sermon papers may be an interesting variant on normal clerical practice. The first sentence will have general agreement, and the idea of an infinite adaptability of text and sermon may be pleasing. For the rest, Sternes' idiosyncratic spelling and punctuation add to the oddity of Yorick's comments on his own work.

It was Yorick's custom, which I suppose a general one with those of his profession, on the first leaf of every sermon which he composed, to chronicle down the time, the place, and the occasion of its being preached: to this, he was ever wont to add some short comment or stricture upon the sermon itself, – seldom, indeed, much to its credit. For instance, 'This sermon upon the Jewish dispensation – I don't like it at all; – though I own there is a world of water-landish knowledge in it; – but 'tis all tritical, and most tritically put together. –This is but a flimsy kind of composition. What was in my head when I made it?'

N.B. 'The excellency of this text is that it will suit any sermon; – and of this sermon, that it will suit any text.'

'For this sermon I shall be hanged, – for I have stolen the greatest part of it. Doctor Paidagunes found me out. Set a thief to catch a thief.'

On the back of half a dozen I find written, So, *so* – and no more; – and upon a couple, *moderato*; by which, as far as one may gather from Alteiri's Italian Dictionary – but mostly from the authority of a piece of green whipcord, which seemed to have been the unravelling of Yorick's whip-lash, with which he has left us the two sermons marked *Moderato*, and the half dozen of *So so*, tied fast together in one bundle by themselves, one may safely suppose he meant pretty nearly the same thing.

There is but one difficulty in the way of this conjecture, which is this, that the *moderatos* are five times bigger than the *so sos*: – show ten times more knowledge of the human heart; – have seventy times more wit and spirit in them; – (and, to rise properly in my climax) – discover a thousand times more genius; – and, to crown all, are infinitely more entertaining than those tied up with them – for which reason, whenever Yorick's *dramatic* sermons are offered to the world, though I shall admit but one out of the whole number of the *so sos*, I shall, nevertheless, adventure to point the two *moderatos* without any sort of scruple.

What Yorick could mean by the words *lentamente*, – *tenuté*, – *grave*, and sometimes *adagio*, – as applied to theological compositions, and with which he has characterised some of these sermons, I dare not venture to guess. I am more puzzled still upon finding *a l'octavo alta!* upon one; – *Con strepito* upon the back of another. – *Scicilliana* upon a third; – *Alla capella* upon a fourth; – *Con l'arco* upon this; – *Senza l'arco* upon that. – All I know is that they are musical terms, and have a meaning; – and, as he was a musical man, I will make no doubt but that, by some quaint application of such metaphors to the compositions in hand, they impressed very distinct ideas of their several characters upon his fancy, – whatever they may do upon that of others.

Laurence Sterne, *The Life and Opinions of Tristram Shandy, Gentleman*[6]

George Whitefield (1714–70) was an early follower of Wesley, though his strong Calvinist opinions later caused them to draw apart. He was a powerful and influential preacher. The writer of this memoir was an actor, and perhaps more observant of Whitefield's mannerisms than of his message. He refers to Bayes, a character in The Rehearsal *by Sheridan, and to Squintum, a satirical depiction of Whitefield in Foote's play* The Minor. *He spells the name 'Whitfield'.*

His dialect was very particular – *Lurd* instead of Lord, *Gud* instead of God – as, *O Lurd*.

I remember a text of his was – *May we all work the harder.* 'There was a poor woman, and she was a long time before she was converted: she was three-score years and ten – yes she was – she was three-score years and ten. "Sir" says she to the good man that converted her, "sir", says she, "I am three-score years and ten, I have been a long time about it: but sir", says she, "I will work the harder; yes, sir", says she, "I will work the harder!" And O! may you all, like that dear good woman, work the harder!'

Then followed a groan of applause; for he had, like Mr Bayes, a selected number in his pit that understood their cues, and were sure to applaud, and the rest of the house followed of course.

Then Whitfield, looking round the rails of his little desk below, 'What, you young ones! Why, you are some of you twelve, some fourteen, and some sixteen years of age, yet you do not think of going to hell? What!' exclaimed Whitfield, 'twelve or fourteen years of age, and not think of going to hell! O ye little brats you!'

And at that instant the old women groaned, and, like fell Charybdis, murmured hoarse applause; and Whitfield shook his head, and growled in his white wig, exactly like my performance of Squintum, as I actually practised it from the serious comical discourse I am now relating.

Whitfield then proceeded thus. – 'You go to plays! and what do you see here? Why, if you will not tell me, I will tell you what you see there! – When you see the players on the stage, you see the devil's children grinning at you; and when you go to the playhouse, I suppose you go in ruffles – I wonder whether St Paul wore ruffles? No; there were no ruffles in those days. I am told,' continued he archly, 'that people say I bawl. – Well, I allow it, I do bawl, and I will bawl – I will not be a velvet-mouthed preacher, I will not speak the word of Gud in a sleepy manner, like your church preachers.'

Tate Wilkinson, *Memoirs of his own Life*[7]

The early Methodists were among the first to have women preachers. Despite opposition from the Establishment, many of them were very effective in informal preaching in the open air. Dinah Morris, based on George Eliot's Methodist aunt, is a fine example. The novel is set towards the end of the eighteenth century.

She spoke slowly, though quite fluently, often pausing after a question, or before any transition of ideas. There was no change of attitude, no gesture; the effect of her speech was produced entirely by the inflections of her voice, and when she came to the question, 'Will God take care of us when we die?' she uttered it in such a tone of plaintive appeal that the tears came into some of the hardest eyes. The stranger had ceased to doubt, as he had done at the first glance, that she could fix the attention of her rougher hearers, but still he wondered whether she could have that power of rousing their more violent emotions, which must surely be a necessary seal of her vocation as a Methodist preacher, until she came to the words, 'Lost! – Sinners!' when there was a great change in her voice and manner. She had made a long pause before the exclamation, and the pause seemed to be filled by agitating thoughts that showed themselves in her features. Her pale face became paler; the circles under her eyes deepened, as they did when tears half-gather without falling; and the mild loving eyes took an expression of appalled pity, as if she had suddenly discerned a destroying angel hovering over the heads of the people. Her voice became deep and muffled, but there was still no ges-ture. Nothing could be less like the ordinary type of the Ranter than Dinah. She was not preaching as she heard others preach, but speaking directly from her own emotions and under the inspiration of her own simple faith.

But now she had entered into a new current of feeling. Her manner became less calm, her utterance more rapid and agitated, as she tried to bring home to the people their guilt, their wilful darkness, their state of disobedience to God, as she dwelt on the hatefulness of sin, the Divine holiness, and the sufferings of the Saviour, by which a way had been opened for their salvation. At last it seemed as if, in her yearning desire to reclaim the lost sheep, she could not be satisfied by addressing her hearers as a body. She appealed first to one and then to another, beseeching them with tears to turn to God while there was yet time; painting to them the desolation of their souls, lost in sin, feeding on the husks of this miserable world, far away from God their Father, and then the love of the Saviour, who was waiting and watching for their return.

George Eliot, *Adam Bede*[8]

Edward Irving was a minister of the Church of Scotland who, moved by his reading of the Book of Revelation, came to London and founded what he claimed to be the Catholic Apostolic Church. He added angels and apostles to the regular threefold order of bishops, priests and deacons. For a time he attracted a considerable following at his church in Hatton Garden. The Irvingites, as they came to be known, built a number of churches, some on a grand scale. The movement gradually died out in the twentieth century. Hazlitt suggests that Irving's popular sermons were not entirely theological.

Conceive a rough, ugly, shock-headed Scotchman, standing up in a Caledonian Chapel, and dealing 'damnation round the land' in a broad northern dialect, and with a harsh, screaking voice, what ear polite, what smile serene would have hailed the barbarous prodigy, or not consigned him to utter neglect and derision? But the Rev. Edward Irving, with all his native wildness, 'hath a smooth aspect framed to make women' saints; his very unusual size and height are carried off and moulded into elegance by the most admirable symmetry of form and ease of gesture; his sable locks, his clear iron-grey complexion, and firm-set features, turn the raw, uncouth Scotchman into the likeness of a noble Italian picture; and even his distortion of sight only redeems the otherwise 'faultless monster' within the bounds of humanity, and, when admiration is exhausted and curiosity ceases, excites a new interest by leading to the idle question whether it is an advantage to the preacher or not. Farther, give him all his actual and remarkable advantages of body and mind, let him be as tall, as strait, as dark and clear of skin, as much at his ease, as silver-tongued, as eloquent and as argumentative as he is, yet with all these, and without a little charlatanry to set them off he had been nothing. He might, keeping within the rigid line of his duty and professed calling, have preached on for ever; he might have divided the old-fashioned doctrines of election, grace, reprobation, predestination, into his sixteenth, seventeenth, and eighteenth heads, and his *lastly* have been looked for as a 'consummation devoutly to be wished'; he might have defied the devil and all his works, and by the help of a loud voice and strong-set person [...] have increased his own congregation, and been quoted among the godly as a powerful preacher of the word; but in addition to this, he went out of his way to attack Jeremy Bentham, and the town was up in arms. The thing was new. He thus wiped the stain of musty ignorance and formal bigotry out of his style. Mr Irving must have something superior in him, to look over the shining close-packed heads of his congregation to have a hit at the *Great Jurisconsult* in his study. He next, ere the report of the former blow had subsided, made a lunge at Mr Brougham, and glanced an eye at Mr Canning; *mystified* Mr Coleridge, and *stultified* Lord Liverpool in his place – in the Gallery. It was rare sport to see him, 'like an eagle in a dovecote, flutter the Volscians in Corioli.' He has found out the secret of attracting by repelling. Those whom he is likely to attack are curious to hear what he says of them. They go again, to show that they do not mind it. It is no less interesting to the bystanders, who like to witness this sort of *onslaught* – like a charge of cavalry, the shock, and the resistance. Mr Irving has, in fact, without leave asked or a licence granted, converted the Caledonian Chapel into a Westminster Forum or Debating Society, with the sanctity of religion added to it.

William Hazlitt, *The Spirit of the Age*[9]

George Borrow began with similar disapproval when he went, with some of his gypsy friends, to hear a sermon by a clergyman of the Church of England. His prejudice against anything that savoured of Nonconformity, outdone only by his immense bigotry against the Roman Catholic Church, was soon dispelled. He remembers his early years at East Dereham in Norfolk.

The clergyman now ascended the pulpit, arrayed in his black gown. The congregation composed themselves to attention, as did also my companions, who fixed their eyes upon the clergyman with a certain strange immovable stare, which I believe to be peculiar to their race. The clergyman gave out his text, and began to preach. He was a tall, gentlemanly man, seemingly between fifty and sixty, with greyish hair; his features were very handsome, but with a somewhat melancholy cast: the tones of his voice were rich and noble, but also with somewhat of melancholy in them. The text which he gave out was the following one, 'In what would a man be profited, provided he gained the whole world, and lost his own soul?'

And on this text the clergyman preached long and well: he did not read his sermon, but spoke it extempore; his doing so rather surprised and offended me at first; I was not used to such a style of preaching in a church devoted to the religion of my country. I compared it within my mind with the style of preaching used by the high-church rector in the old church of pretty D⟨ereham⟩, and I thought to myself it was very different, and being very different I did not like it, and I thought to myself how scandalised the people of D⟨ereham⟩ would have been had they heard it, and I figured to myself how indignant the high-church clerk would have been had any clergyman got up in the church of D⟨ereham⟩ and preached in such a manner. Did it not savour strongly of dissent, Methodism, and similar low stuff? Surely it did; why, the Methodist I had heard preach on the heath above the old city, preached in the same manner – at least he preached extempore; ay, and something like the present clergyman, for the Methodist spoke very zealously and with great feeling, and so did the present clergyman; so I, of course, felt rather offended with the clergyman for speaking with zeal and feeling. However, long before the sermon was over, I forgot the offence which I had taken, and listened to the sermon with much admiration, for the eloquence and powerful reasoning with which it abounded.

George Borrow, *Romany Rye*[10]

'Lewis Carroll' was the pseudonym of Charles Lutwidge Dodgson, who passed much of his life at Christ Church, Oxford, as a teacher of mathematics. His early biographer's account of his preaching shows a different side of the creator of Alice and the Snark.

On December 22, 1861, he was ordained deacon by the Bishop of Oxford.

He never proceeded to priest's orders, partly, I think, because he felt that if he were to do so it would be his duty to undertake regular parochial work, and partly on account of his stammering. He used, however, to preach not unfrequently, and his sermons were always delightful to listen to, his extreme earnestness being evident in every word.

'He knew exactly what he wished to say' (I am quoting from an article in *The Guardian*), 'and completely forgot his audience in his anxiety to explain his point clearly. He thought of the subject only, and the words came of themselves. Looking straight in front of him he saw, as it were, his argument mapped out in the form of a diagram, and he set to work to prove it point by point, under its separate heads, and then summed up the whole.'

One sermon which he preached in the University Church, on Eternal Punishment, is not likely to be soon forgotten by those who heard it. I, unfortunately, was not of that number, but I can well imagine how his clear-cut features would light up as he dwelt lovingly upon the mercy of that Being whose charity far exceeds 'the measure of man's mind.' It is hardly necessary to say that he himself did not believe in eternal punishment, or any other scholastic doctrine that contravenes the love of God.

He disliked being complimented on his sermons, but he liked to be told of any good effects that his words had had upon any member of the congregation. 'Thank you for telling me that fact about my sermon,' he wrote to one of his sisters, who told him of some such good fruit that one of his addresses had borne. 'I have once, or twice had such information volunteered; and it is a *great* comfort – and a kind of thing that is *really* good for one to know. It is *not* good to be told (and I never wish to be told), "Your sermon was so *beautiful.*" We shall not be concerned to know, in the Great Day, whether we have preached beautiful sermons, but whether they were preached with the one object, of serving God.'

He was always ready and willing to preach at the special service for College servants, which used to be held at Christ Church every Sunday evening; but best of all he loved to preach to children. Some of his last sermons were delivered at Christ Church, Eastbourne (the church he regularly attended during the Long Vacation), to a congregation of children. On those occasions he told them an allegory – *Victor and Arnion*, which he intended to publish in course of time – putting all his heart into the work, and speaking with such deep feeling that at times he was almost unable to control his emotion as he told them of the love and compassion of the Good Shepherd.

I have dwelt at some length on this side of his life, for it is, I am sure, almost ignored in the popular estimate of him. He was essentially a religious man in the best sense of the term, and without any of that morbid sentimentality which is too often associated with the word; and while his religion consecrated his talents, and raised him to a height which without it he could never have reached, the example of such a man as he was, so brilliant, so witty, so successful, and yet so full of faith, consecrates the very conception of religion, and makes it yet more beautiful.

S. D. Collingwood, *The Life and Letters of Lewis Carroll*[11]

John Henry Newman (1801–90) left many volumes of sermons, from both his Anglican and his Roman years, which are still good to read for their message and also for their style. His presence in the pulpit was impressive, as recalled by Matthew Arnold, himself a great Victorian writer. Arnold reverenced Newman for a time, then moved to a more sceptical position, but never forgot the early experience.

The name of Cardinal Newman is a great name to the imagination still; his genius and his style are still things of Power. But he is over eighty years old; he is in the Oratory at Birmingham; he has adopted, for the doubts and difficulties which beset men's minds to-day, a solution which, to speak frankly, is impossible. Forty years ago he was in the very prime of life; he was close at hand to us at Oxford; he was preaching in St Mary's pulpit every Sunday; he seemed about to transform and to renew what was for us the most national and natural institution in the world, the Church of England. Who could resist the charm of that spiritual apparition, gliding in the dim afternoon light through the aisles of St Mary's, rising into the pulpit, and then, in the most entrancing of voices, breaking the silence with words and thoughts which were a religious music – subtle, sweet, mournful? I seem to hear him still, say-ing, 'After the fever of life, after weariness and sicknesses, fightings and despondings, languor and fretfulness, struggling and succeeding; after all the changes and chances of this troubled, unhealthy state, at length comes death, at length the white throne of God, at length the beatific vision.' Or, if we followed him back to his seclusion at Littlemore, that dreary village by the London road, and to the house of retreat and the church which he built there – a mean house such as Paul might have lived in when he was tent-making at Ephesus, a church plain and thinly sown with worshippers – who could resist him there either, welcoming back to the severe joys of church-fellowship, and of daily worship and prayer, the firstlings of a generation which had well-nigh forgotten them? Again I seem to hear him: 'True faith does not covet comforts; they who realise that awful day, when they shall see Him face to face whose eyes are as a flame of fire, will as little bargain to pray pleasantly now as they will think of doing so then.'

Matthew Arnold, 'Emerson'[12]

The Baptist minister Charles Spurgeon (1834–92) was one of the most popular preachers of his day. The Metropolitan Tabernacle in South London, opened in 1861, was almost invariably full to capacity. The following description may be partisan and uncritical, but it gives some idea of the magnetism which he exercised.

Mr Spurgeon is not only popular; he represents the popularity of his time. He is as unlike the popular preacher of the past, as his Tabernacle, with its stage, pit, and galleries, is unlike Westminster Abbey. He is 'The Times' of modern evangelism. Many of his sermons would make good leading articles, and in the power, the profusion, and the rapidity with which they were poured forth, we are reminded of the steam press and the electric telegraph. And not the less is he emblematic of the times, that in his case the pulpit is stripped of all its common accessories. It is doubtful if the squat and somewhat round figure of the preacher would admit of improvement by gown and cassock. In an age, impatient of all kinds of pretence, he is anything but a clerical fop. There is no cant or whining about him; he is natural as the day; and were it not for time and place, few would suppose from look, tone, or style, that they listened to a sermon. It is difficult, indeed, at first, to account for Mr Spurgeon's popularity [...] It would be vain to fix on any one feature of the preacher in answer to this question. A combination of gifts as rare as startling, must account for his success in a career which, in the absence of any one of these gifts, might have proved a failure. There is the logical faculty appearing in the *lucidus ordo* [*clear order*] of his discourses, combined with a fancy which brings up images at will, and scatters around the plainest subject a copiousness of illustration with the dexterity of the juggler, who brings, out of an old hat, an endless shower of flowers, feathers, and all sorts of unexpected things. Then there is the marvellous memory of the man, which, like some nimble servitor, seems to be always ready to supply him with the stories of his reading as they are needed; the sonorous voice, ringing like a church bell; the terse Saxon English of his style, the volubility of his elocution, joined with that perfect self-control, which prevents it from degenerating into declamation, and imparts to it something like the measured tramp of military precision. The whole structure of his sermons is conversational, but then it is conversation through a speaking-trumpet. The speaker is on fire throughout, but it is not in occasional flashes of flame that the fire appears, but in the sustained white-heat of the furnace.

British and Foreign Evangelical Review, 1886[13]

Even livelier sermons might be heard from some independent preachers. Christmas Evans was one of the luminaries of the nineteenth-century Evangelical revival in Wales.

Many of his sermons were translations of our Lord's parables into Welsh; he cast away the Oriental dress, and darted an eye immediately into the spirit and meaning of the parable, and presented it in such a light that all hearing must see it too.

What, for instance, would you say if you saw the Prodigal Son quitting his father's house, in best beaver hat, blue coat and brass buttons, and top-boots – this at that time was the topmost height of finery in Wales – with a dangling spy-glass and a cigar? And when he preached this sermon near Llandiloes, and, directing his finger in the open air to a distant mountain, described the father as seeing him while yet a great way off, the heads of the thousands of the congregation were turned in the direction of the preacher's finger, expecting to see the father coming down from the hills too. Sometimes his parables entered more entirely into the pure region of fable; after a most eccentric fashion he described the faithful minister and the inconsistent office-bearers in a church, under the ideas of a dog and a tea-kettle – a kettle of water boiling on the

fire; the water must lift the lid, and a few drops fell upon a dog sleeping
on the hearth; he gave an angry growl, looked up, and soon went to sleep
again. A very little time elapsed before again the boiling spray fell upon
him, and this time more heavily than before; he uttered another growl,
but still slept on: but what could a kettle of water care for a growling dog?
– the fire burnt on – the water boiled on – it boiled furiously over; the
dog in agony started up to revenge himself on the kettle, and received the
full volume of boiling water for his pains. Thus Mr Evans chose to illus-
trate the relative position of a faithful ministry to unfaithful church-
members and officers.

E. P. Hood, *The Lamps of the Temple*[14]

*The anecdotal sermon can misfire, and Harriet Beecher Stowe certainly lost
patience with it. In her Introduction to one of her novels, she has a hit at
several types of clergy whom she dislikes.*

It is understood now that no paper is complete without its serial story,
and the spinning of these stories keeps thousands of wheels and spindles
in motion. It is now understood that whoever wishes to gain the public
ear, and to propound a new theory, must do it in a serial story. Hath any
one in our day, as in St Paul's, a psalm, a doctrine, a tongue, a revelation,
an interpretation – forthwith he wraps it up in a serial story, and presents
it to the public. We have prison discipline, free-trade, labour and capital,
woman's rights, the temperance question, in serial stories. We have
Romanism and Protestantism, High Church and Low Church and no
Church, contending with each other in serial stories, where each side
converts the other, according to the faith of the narrator.

We see that this thing is to go on. Soon it will be necessary that every
leading clergyman should embody in his theology a serial story, to be
delivered from the pulpit Sunday after Sunday. We look forward to
announcements in our city papers such as these: The Rev. Dr Ignatius, of
the Church of St. Mary the Virgin, will begin a serial romance, to be
entitled 'St Sebastian and the Arrows,' in which he will embody the
duties, the trials, and the temptations of the young Christians of our day.
The Rev. Dr Boanerges, of Plymouth Rock Church, will begin a serial
story, entitled 'Calvin's Daughter,' in which he will discuss the distinctive features of Protestant theology. The Rev. Dr Cool Shadow will go on

with his interesting romance of 'Christianity a Dissolving View,' – designed to show how everything is, in many respects, like everything else, and all things lead somewhere, and everything will finally end somehow, and that therefore it is important that everybody should encourage general sweetness, and have the very best time possible in this world.

H. B. Stowe, *My Wife and I*[15]

While British as well as American evangelists have often drawn large crowds to hear their preaching, the mass audience of the radio evangelist is an essentially American phenomenon. (Now, of course, it is television that makes the coverage even wider.) Aimée MacPherson was not strictly a member of the clergy, though she was called 'Sister', but she must have a place among the famous preachers. Discredited by scandals towards the end of her life, she had great success in the inter-war years. According to contemporary accounts, she was not physically attractive and yet exercised a fascination which some found almost sexual. Her strength was in her remarkable voice, developed through years of outdoor revivals and street meetings. It was deep, almost husky, and she used its full power and range to get her effects.

Father Charles E. Coughlin also gained a great following in the United States during the Depression. By writing, public speaking and broadcasting, he amassed a personal fortune and created a new political party which moved increasingly towards fascism and anti-Semitism. He was eventually discredited and disowned, but the years of his success leave a warning of how clerical influence can be misused. It is said that his radio appeals brought in as much as 20,000 dollars a week – an enormous sum for the 1930s. He used some of his profits to build a seven-storey headquarters with a huge crucified Christ across one side, and a new Church of the Little Flower (named after St Thérèse of Lisieux). He talked his way out of adverse criticism until at last his political opinions, as much as his monetary affairs, destroyed his reputation.

A very different kind of mass evangelist is the Baptist minister Billy Graham (born 1918), whose preaching in open meetings and through the media has attracted very large crowds. His campaign in Haringay Stadium, London, in 1954 had probably the largest attendance of any revival meeting ever held in that city. He invites people to 'come forward' at the end of his meetings and make a commitment of faith in consultation with a counsellor. He has been criticized for creating emotional responses which do not endure, but there is no doubt that he has brought many to a firm faith. Unlike some mass evangelists, he has never created his own sect but insists that converts and enquirers must be referred to local churches.

Most preachers have one or two multi-purpose sermons if something is required at short notice, but few are quite so adaptable as Canon Chasuble.

You would no doubt wish me to make some slight allusion to this tragic domestic affliction next Sunday. My sermon on the meaning of the manna in the Wilderness can be adapted to almost any occasion, joyful, or, as in the present case, distressing. I have preached it at Harvest celebrations, christenings, confirmations, on days of humiliation and festal days. The last time I delivered it was in the Cathedral, as a charity sermon on behalf of the Society for the Prevention of Discontent Among the Upper Classes. The Bishop, who was present, was much struck by some of the analogies I drew.

Oscar Wilde, The Importance of Being Earnest[16]

To conclude this chapter, here are two short warnings to all preachers.

> 'And now to God the Father,' he ends,
> And his voice thrills up to the topmost tiles:
> Each listener chokes as he bows and bends,
> And emotion pervades the crowded aisles.
> Then the preacher glides to the vestry-door,
> And shuts it, and thinks he is seen no more.
>
> The door swings softly ajar meanwhile,
> And a pupil of his in the Bible class,
> Who adores him as one without gloss or guile,
> Sees her idol stand with a satisfied smile
> And re-enact at the vestry-glass

Each pulpit gesture in deft dumb-show
That had moved the congregation so.

Thomas Hardy, *Collected Poems*[17]

He preached upon 'Breadth' till it argued him narrow –
The Broad are too broad to define
And of 'Truth' until it proclaimed him a Liar –
The Truth never flaunted a Sign.

Simplicity fled from his counterfeit presence
As Gold the Pyrites would shun –
What confusion would cover the innocent Jesus
To meet so enabled a Man!

Emily Dickinson, *Complete Poems*[18]

Chapter 6

Such Things as He Possesseth

The clergy have generally been among the lower-paid members of society, although until fairly recently there were great discrepancies in clerical incomes. The disciples of Jesus were enjoined to travel lightly and not to care for material wants, and the ideal of Holy Poverty continued through the centuries, especially in the rules of religious life. At the same time, the temporal power of the Church brought wealth, particularly in the accumulation of large estates, which the Reformation partly but not entirely transferred to secular possession. Writers have often contrasted the poverty of the many with the opulence of the few. Although many beneficed clergy were poorly off, the assistant curate (popularly known simply as 'the curate') has been the principal subject of their attention. While some served as support to the incumbent of a parish, for centuries both before and after the Reformation there were priests who lived on the income of their benefices while leaving the work to an ill-paid curate. It will be remembered that Chaucer's good Parson 'did not rent his benefice for hire'. An additional burden for the poor clergyman with a family was the need to keep up a standard of living appropriate to the professional classes on an income nearer to that of a manual worker. Things are better today, but it is certain that no one would seek holy orders for the sake of the money.

Two passages from the early seventeenth century give a glimpse of the extremes of fortune which a clergyman of the time might experience.

> He is the prelate of the parish here,
> And governs all the games, appoints the cheer.
> Writes down the bill of fare, pricks all the guests,
> Makes all the matches and the marriage feasts –
> Without the ward: draws all the parish wills,
> Designs the legacies, and strokes the gills

Of the chief mourners: and whoever lacks
Of all the kindred he hath first his blacks.
Thus holds he weddings up and burials
As the main thing: with the gossips' stalls
Their pews; he's top still at the public mess,
Comforts the widow and the fatherless
In funeral sad; sits 'bove the alderman;
For of the wardmote quest he better can
The mystery than the Levitic law:
That piece of clerkship doth his vestry awe.
He is, as he conceives himself, a fine
Well-furnished and apparelled divine.

Ben Jonson, *The Magnetic Lady*[1]

*A priest who could not get preferment to a parish incumbency might have to
be content with the post of tutor in a rich household. Joseph Hall (1574–
1636) was bishop successively of Exeter and Norwich.*

A gentle squire would gladly entertain
Into his house some trencher-chappelain,
Some willing man that might instruct his sons,
And that could stand to good conditions.
First, that he lie upon the truckle bed,
While his young master lieth overhead;
Second, that he do on no default
Ever presume to sit above the salt;
Third, that he never change his trencher twice;
Fourth, that he use all common courtesies,
Sit bare at meals, and one half rise and wait;
Last that he never his young master beat,
But he must ask his mother to define
How many jerks she would his breech should line;
All these observed, he would contented be,
To give five marks and winter livery.

Joseph Hall, *Virgidemiarum*[2]

The poor curate was not always a young man recently ordained. Many without influence remained in that position all their lives. This account of a mature family man with scholarly aspirations but no prospects was written by one who had himself served as a curate, but had better fortune.

Behold his dwelling! This poor hut he hires
Where he from view, though not from want, retires;
Where four fair daughters, and five sorrowing sons,
Partake his sufferings, and dismiss his duns
All join their efforts, and in patience learn
To want the comforts they aspire to earn;
For the sick mother something they'd obtain,
To soothe her grief and mitigate her pain;
For the sad father something they'd procure,
To ease the burden they themselves endure.
Virtues like these at once delight and press
On the fond father with a proud distress;
On all around he looks with care and love,
Grieved to behold, but happy to approve.

Then from his care, his love, his grief he steals,
And by himself an Author's pleasure feels:
Each line detains him; he omits not one,
And all the sorrows of his state are gone.
Alas! even then, in that delicious hour,
He feels his fortune, and laments its power.
Some Tradesman's bill his wandering eyes engage,
Some scrawl for payment thrust 'twixt page and page;
Some bold, loud rapping at his humble door,
Some surly message he has heard before,
Awake, alarm, and tell him he is poor.

An angry Dealer, vulgar, rich, and proud,
Thinks of his bill, and, passing, raps aloud;
The elder daughter meekly makes him way
'I want my money, and I cannot stay:
My mill is stopp'd; what, Miss, I cannot grind;
Go tell your father he must raise the wind.'

Still trembling, troubled, the dejected maid
Says, 'Sir! my father!' and then stops afraid
Even his hard heart is softened, and he hears
Her voice with pity; he respects her tears
His stubborn features half admit a smile,
And his tone softens – 'Well! I'll wait awhile.'

Pity! a man so good, so mild, so meek,
At such an age, should have his bread to seek;
And all those rude and fierce attacks to dread,
That are more harrowing than the want of bread;
Ah! who shall whisper to that misery peace!
And say that want and insolence shall cease?
'But why not publish?' – those who know too well,
Dealers in Greek, are fearful 'twill not sell;
Then he himself is timid, troubled, slow,
Nor likes his labours nor his griefs to show;
The hope of fame may in his heart have place,
But he has dread and horror of disgrace;
Nor has he that confiding, easy way,
That might his learning and himself display;
But to his work he from the world retreats,
And frets and glories o'er the favourite sheets.

George Crabbe (1754–1832), 'The Curate'[3]

Appeal to the absentee incumbent to raise the salary was not likely to succeed, according to the following dialogue. Dr Syntax is a clerical school-master who sets out on a vacation tour and meets many people and many misfortunes. He is at an inn when a fellow cleric is announced by the land-lady and warmly welcomed.

Syntax his brother Parson greeted
And begged him to be quickly seated;
'Come, take a pipe, and taste the liquor,
'Tis good enough for any vicar.'

CURATE

Alas! Sir, I'm no vicar; I,
Bound to an humble curacy,
With all my care can scarce contrive
To keep my family alive.
While the fat Rector can afford
To eat and drink like any lord;
But know, Sir, I'm a man of letters,
And ne'er speak evil of my betters.

SYNTAX

That's good; but when we suffer pain,
'Tis Nature's office to complain;
And when the strong oppress the weak,
Justice, though blind, will always speak.
Tell me, have you explained your case
With due humility and grace?
The great and wealthy must be flattered;
They love with praise to be bespattered:
Indeed, I cannot see the harm,
If thus you can their favour charm;
If by fine phrases you can bend
The pride of power to be your friend.

CURATE

I wrote, I'm sure, in humblest style
And prais'd his goodness all the while
I begg'd, as things had grown so dear,
He'd raise my pay ten pounds a year;
And, as I now had children five,
The finest little bairns alive,
While their poor, fond, and faithful mother
Would soon present me with another;
And, as the living brought him, clear,
At least a thousand pounds a year,
He'd grant the favour I implore,
Nor let me starve upon threescore.

SYNTAX
Now I should like without delay,
To hear what this rich man could say;
For I can well perceive, my friend,
That you did not obtain your end.

CURATE
The postman soon a letter brought,
Which cost me sixpence and a groat;
Nor can your friendly heart suggest
The rudeness which the page express'd.
'Such suits as yours may well miscarry,
For beggars should not dare to marry;
At least, for I will not deceive you;
I never, never will relieve you;
And if you trouble me, be sure
You shall be ousted from the cure.'
But I shall now, good sir, refrain,
Because I know 'twould give you pain,
From telling all that in his spite
The arch old scoundrel chose to write;
For know, Sir, I'm a man of letters,
And never will abuse my betters.

William Combe, *The Tour of Doctor Syntax*[4]

Sydney Smith had sympathy for the poor curate and was prepared to take up his cause against the episcopate. Herbert Marsh (1757–1839) became Bishop of Peterborough in 1819 and was known for his rigid adherence to the Establishment and his severity towards clergy of extreme Evangelical persuasion.

A Curate – there is something which excites compassion in the very name of a Curate!! How any man of Purple, Palaces, and Preferment, can let himself loose against this poor working man of God, we are at a loss to conceive – a learned man in an hovel, with sermons and saucepans, lexicons and bacon, Hebrew books and ragged children – good and patient – a comforter and a preacher – the first and purest pauper in the hamlet, and yet showing that, in the midst of his worldly misery, he has the heart of a gentleman, and the spirit of a Christian, and the kindness of a pastor; and this man, though he has exercised the duties of a clergyman for twenty years – though he has most ample testimonies of conduct from clergymen as respectable as any Bishop – though an Archbishop add his name to the list of witnesses, is not good enough for Bishop Marsh; but is pushed out in the street, with his wife and children, and his little furniture, to surrender his honour, his faith, his conscience, and his learning – or to starve! […] Men of very small incomes, be it known to his Lordship, have very often very acute feelings; and a Curate trod on feels a pang as great as when a Bishop is refuted.

The Wit and Wisdom of the Rev. Sydney Smith[5]

The lot of the curate a few decades later is described in a delightful nine-teenth-century book in which a young owl observes and reports on many Church affairs. In this instance, the curate is the bishop's appointment to replace an absent vicar. 'Involved' is a euphemism for 'bankrupt'.

The living is sequestered, and the vicar abroad, for he was so bad a manager of a small income that he got involved. So the bishop put a curate into the overgrown vicarage; and the curate has a stipend of eighty pounds a year. And on that the meek inoffensive man tries to live. He has furnished three rooms very poorly. And he lives very abstemiously, and his family are very shabbily clad. To Illford he came, with a very earnest desire not only to win souls, but to win hearts likewise. He will love the people if they will let him, and serve them faithfully. But he has the hardest of all problems to solve. How is a poor parson to win the respect of his purse-proud parishioners? As society is now constituted – covetousness and the love of money having eaten into the very heart's core of the people – mammon being as much, or rather tenfold more, the object of Englishmen's idolatry, than ever he was among those who first raised him into a deity, the poor clergyman is doubly obnoxious to the money-making portion of his flock; first, because he is poor; and secondly, because as being poor he is the more likely to come on them for aid towards the support of parochial institutions.

F. E. Paget, *The Owlet of Owlstone Edge*[6]

Another underpaid position was that of the 'perpetual curate', the incumbent of a parish appointed by a lay rector. He received a fixed stipend, usually very low, and had no benefit of tithes. Patrick Brontë (see p. 105) was the perpetual curate of Haworth. Trollope describes the distress of an educated man with a labourer's wage who was expected to take his place in a higher social class.

Mr Crawley only received one hundred and thirty pounds a year for performing the whole parochial duty of the parish of Hogglestock. And Hogglestock is a large parish. It includes two populous villages, abounding in brick-makers, a race of men very troublesome to a zealous parson who won't let men go rollicking to the devil without interference. Hogglestock has full work for two men; and yet all the funds therein applicable to parson's work is this miserable stipend of one hundred and thirty pounds a year. It is a stipend neither picturesque, nor time-honoured, nor feudal, for Hogglestock takes rank only as a perpetual curacy [...] There can be no doubt that Mr Crawley was a strict man, – a strict, stern, unpleasant man, and one who feared God and his own conscience. We must say a word or two of Mr Crawley and his concerns. He was now some forty years of age, but of these he had not been in possession even of his present benefice for more than four or five. The first ten years of his life as a clergyman had been passed in performing the duties and struggling through the life of a curate in a bleak, ugly, cold parish on the northern coast of Cornwall. It had been a weary life and a fearful struggle, made up of duties ill requited and not always satisfactorily performed, of love and poverty, of increasing cares, of sickness, debt, and death. For Mr Crawley had married almost as soon as he was ordained, and children had been born to him in that chill, comfortless Cornish cottage. He had married a lady well educated and softly nurtured, but not dowered with worldly wealth. They two had gone forth determined to fight bravely together; to disregard the world and the world's ways, looking only to God and to each other for their comfort. They would give up ideas of gentle living, of soft raiment, and delicate feeding. Others, – those that work with their hands, even the bettermost of such workers – could live in decency and health upon even such provision as he could earn as a clergyman. In such manner would they live so poorly and so decently, working out their work, not with their hands but with their hearts.

And so they had established themselves, beginning the world with one bare-footed little girl of fourteen to aid them in their small household matters; and for a while they had both kept heart, loving each other dearly, and prospering somewhat in their work. But a man who has once walked the world as a gentleman knows not what it is to change his position, and place himself lower down in the social rank. Much less can he know what it is so to put down the woman whom he loves. There are a thousand things, mean and trifling in themselves which a man despises when he thinks of them in his philosophy but to dispense with which puts his philosophy to so stern a proof.

Let any plainest man who reads this think of his usual mode of getting himself into his matutinal garments, and confess how much such a struggle would cost him. And then children had come. The wife of the labouring man does rear her children, and often rears them in health, without even so many appliances of comfort as found their way into Mrs Crawley's cottage; but the task to her was almost more than she could accomplish. Not that she ever fainted or gave way: she was made of the sterner metal of the two, and could last on while he was prostrate. And sometimes he was prostrate – prostrate in soul and spirit. Then would he complain with bitter voice, crying out that the world was too hard for him, that his back was broken with his burden, that his God had deserted him. For days and days, in such moods, he would stay within his cottage never darkening the door or seeing other faces than those of his own inmates. Those days were terrible both to him and her. He would sit there unwashed, with his unshorn face resting on his hand, with an old dressing-gown hanging loose about him, hardly tasting food, seldom speaking, striving to pray, but striving so frequently in vain. And then he would rise from his chair, and, with a burst of frenzy, call upon his Creator to remove him from this misery. In these moments she never deserted him. At one period they had had four children and though the whole weight of this young brood rested on her arms, on her muscles, on her strength of mind and body, she never ceased in her efforts to comfort him. Then at length falling utterly upon the ground, he would pour forth piteous prayers for mercy, and after a night of sleep would once more go forth to his work.

Anthony Trollope, *Framley Parsonage*[7]

By contrast, in the same diocese, Archdeacon Grantly has a well-paid living and spends accordingly. His breakfast leaves nothing to the imagination.

Let us observe the well-furnished breakfast-parlour at Plumstead Episcopi, and the comfortable air of all the belongings of the rectory. Comfortable they certainly were, but neither gorgeous, nor even grand; indeed, considering the money that had been spent there, the eye and taste might have been better served; there was an air of heaviness about the rooms which might have been avoided without any sacrifice of propriety; colours might have been better chosen and lights more perfectly diffused; but perhaps in doing so the thorough clerical aspect of the whole might have been somewhat marred; at any rate, it was not without ample consideration that those thick, dark, costly carpets were put down; those embossed, but sombre papers hung up; those heavy curtains draped so as to half exclude the light of the sun: nor were these old-fashioned chairs bought at a price far exceeding that now given for more modern goods, without a purpose. The breakfast-service on the table was equally costly and equally plain; the apparent object had been to spend money without obtaining brilliancy or splendour. The urn was of thick and solid silver, as were also the tea-pot, coffee-pot, cream-ewer, and sugar-bowl; the cups were old, dim dragon china, worth about a pound a piece, but very despicable in the eyes of the uninitiated. The silver forks were so heavy as to be disagreeable to the hand, and the bread-basket was of a weight really formidable to any but robust persons. The tea consumed was the very best, the coffee the very blackest, the cream the very thickest; there was dry toast and buttered toast, muffins and crumpets; hot bread and cold bread, white bread and brown bread, home-made bread and bakers' bread, wheaten bread and oaten bread; and if there be other breads than these, they were there; there were eggs in napkins, and crispy bits of bacon under silver covers; and there were little fishes in a little box, and devilled kidneys frizzling on a hot-water dish; which, by-the-by, were placed closely contiguous to the plate of the worthy archdeacon himself. Over and above this, on a snow-white napkin, spread upon the sideboard, was a huge ham and a huge sirloin; the latter having laden the dinner table on the previous evening. Such was the ordinary fare at Plumstead Episcopi.

Anthony Trollope, *The Warden*[8]

Ralph Waldo Emerson took a poor view of the mainstream churches. Bring-
ing the perspective of a country without an Established Church, he was
particularly critical of the wealth enjoyed by the bishops of the Church of
England. He did not think much of the system of appointment or of their
quality either.

When wealth accrues to a chaplaincy, a bishopric, or rectorship, it requires moneyed men for its stewards, who will give it another direction
than to the mystics of their day. Of course, money will do after its kind,
and will speedily work to unspiritualise and unchurch the people to
whom it was bequeathed. The class certain to be excluded from all
preferment are the religious – and driven to other churches – which is
nature's *vis medicatrix* [*healing power*].

The curates are ill-paid, and the prelates are overpaid. This abuse
draws into the church the children of the nobility, and other unfit
persons, who have a taste for expense. Thus a Bishop is only a surpliced
merchant. Through his lawn, I can see the bright buttons of the shop-
man's coat glitter. A wealth like that of Durham makes almost a
premium on felony. Brougham, in a speech in the House of Commons
on the Irish elective franchise, said, 'How will the reverend Bishops of
the other house be able to express their due abhorrence of the crime of
perjury, who solemnly declare in the presence of God, that when they are
called upon to accept a living, perhaps of £4000 a year, at that very
instant, they are moved by the Holy Ghost to accept the office and
administration thereof, and for no other reason whatever.' The modes of
initiation are more damaging than custom-house oaths. The Bishop is
elected by the Dean and Prebends of the cathedral. The Queen sends
these gentlemen a *congé d'élire*, or leave to elect; but also sends them the
name of the person whom they are to elect. They go into the cathedral,
chant and pray, and beseech the Holy Ghost to assist them in their
choice; and, after these invocations invariably find that the dictates of
the Holy Ghost agree with the recommendations of the Queen.

The church at this moment is much to be pitied. She has nothing left
but possession. If a Bishop meets an intelligent gentleman, and reads
fatal interrogations in his eyes, he has no resource but to take wine with
him. False position introduces cant, perjury, simony, and ever a lower
class of mind and character into the clergy: and, when the hierarchy is
afraid of science and education, afraid of piety, afraid of tradition, and

afraid of theology, there is nothing left but to quit a church which is no longer one.

Ralph Waldo Emerson, *English Traits*[9]

Dr Skinner could well be included among the clerical schoolmasters and headmasters, but his opulence and the self-important complacency that accompanies it must qualify him as one of the unpleasantly rich. His guest, Overton, is something of a self-portrait of the author.

The game had been a long one, and at half-past nine, when supper came in, we had each of us a few pieces remaining. 'What will you take for supper, Dr Skinner?' said Mrs Skinner in a silvery voice. He made no answer for some time, but at last in a tone of almost superhuman solemnity, he said, first, 'Nothing', and then 'Nothing whatever'.

By and by, however, I had a sense come over me as though I were nearer the consummation of all things than I had ever yet been. The room seemed to grow dark, as an expression came over Dr Skinner's face, which showed that he was about to speak. The expression gathered force, the room grew darker and darker. 'Stay', he at length added, and I felt that here at any rate was an end to a suspense which was rapidly becoming unbearable. 'Stay – I may presently take a glass of cold water – and a small piece of bread and butter'.

As he said the word 'butter' his voice sank to a hardly audible whisper; then there was a sigh as though of relief when the sentence was concluded, and the universe this time was safe.

Another ten minutes of solemn silence finished the game. The Doctor rose briskly from his seat and placed himself at the supper table. 'Mrs Skinner', he exclaimed jauntily, 'what are those mysterious-looking objects surrounded by potatoes?'

'Those are oysters, Dr Skinner.'

'Give me some, and give Overton some.'

And so on till he had eaten a good plate of oysters, a scallop shell of minced veal nicely browned, some apple tart, and a hunk of bread and cheese. This was the small piece of bread and butter.

The cloth was now removed and tumblers with teaspoons in them, a lemon or two and a jug of boiling water were placed upon the table. Then the great man unbent. His face beamed.

'And what shall it be to drink?' he exclaimed persuasively. 'Shall it be brandy and water? No. It shall be gin and water. Gin is the more wholesome liquor.'

So gin it was, hot and stiff too. Who can wonder at him or do anything but pity him? Was he not headmaster of Roughborough School? To whom had he owed money at any time? Whose ox had he taken, whose ass had he taken, or whom had he defrauded? What whisper had ever been breathed against his moral character? If he had become rich it was by the most honourable of all means – his literary attainments; over and above his great works of scholarship, his 'Meditations upon the Epistle and Character of St Jude' had placed him among the most popular of English theologians; it was so exhaustive that no one who bought it need ever meditate upon the subject again – indeed it exhausted all who had anything to do with it. He had made £5,000 by this work alone, and would very likely make another £5,000 before he died. A man who had done all this and wanted a piece of bread and butter had a right to announce the fact with some pomp and circumstance. Nor should his words be taken without searching for what he used to call a 'deeper and more hidden meaning.' Those who searched for this even in his lightest utterances would not be without their reward. They would find that 'bread and butter' was Skinnerese for oyster-patties and apple tart, and 'gin hot' the true translation of water.

Samuel Butler, *The Way of All Flesh*[10]

Cartwright, the Vicar of Wrexhill, has already appeared as a specimen of the bad clergyman (p. 37). He is a man of considerable wealth and rejoices in the prestige it gives him. He is arranging a nefarious scheme of inheritance with his nephew Stephen. The 'fancy fair' was the predecessor of the still-popular church bazaar. His calling it a 'Serious Fancy Fair' is a nice touch of pretended piety.

You know that on the twelfth of this month a Serious Fancy Fair is to be held in my grounds. Not only will all the rank and fashion of the county assemble on the occasion, but my park-gates will be open likewise to the people. At two o'clock a very splendid collation will be ready in five of my saloons; and it is after the company have risen and left the tables to resort once more to the booths in order to assist in the disposal of the remaining articles, that I shall permit every servant in my establishment to leave the mansion, and repair to witness the busy and impressive scenes in the booths. It will be a very impressive scene, cousin Stephen, for I shall myself pronounce a blessing upon the assembled crowd. From this I fear, my dear Stephen, that you must on this occasion absent yourself; but be assured; that as I speak those words of power, I will remember you.

Frances Trollope, *The Vicar of Wrexhill*[11]

By contrast, Patrick Brontë, father of three novelists, was the perpetual curate of Haworth in Yorkshire, an ill-paid position, as we have seen with Mr Crawley (p. 99). He was a man of strong Evangelical faith, and his social conscience sometimes got him into trouble, as Elizabeth Gaskell relates.

His strong, passionate Irish nature was, in general, compressed down with resolute stoicism; but it was there notwithstanding all his philosophic calm and dignity of demeanour; though he did not speak when he was annoyed or displeased. Mrs Brontë, whose sweet nature thought invariably of the bright side, would say, 'Ought I not to be thankful that he never gave me an angry Word?'

Mr Brontë was an active walker, stretching away over the moors for many miles, noting in his mind all natural signs of wind and weather, and keenly observing all the wild creatures that came and went in the loneliest sweeps of the hills. He has seen eagles stooping low in search of food for their young; no eagle is ever seen on those mountain slopes now.

He fearlessly took whatever side in local or national politics appeared to him right. In the days of the Luddites he had been for the peremptory interference of the law, at a time when no magistrate could be found to act, and all the property of the West Riding was in terrible danger. He became unpopular then among the mill-workers, and he esteemed his life unsafe if he took his long and lonely walks unarmed; so he kept the habit, which has continued to this day, of invariably carrying a loaded pistol about with him. It lay on his dressing-table with his watch; with his watch it was put on in the morning; with his watch it was taken off at night.

Many years later, during his residence at Haworth, there was a strike; the hands in the neighbourhood felt themselves aggrieved by the masters, and refused to work: Mr Brontë thought that they had been unjustly and unfairly treated, and he assisted them by all the means in his power to 'keep the wolf from their doors,' and avoid the incubus of debt. Several of the more influential inhabitants of Haworth and the neighbourhood were mill-owners; they remonstrated pretty sharply with him, but he believed that his conduct was right, and persevered in it.

His opinions might be often both wild and erroneous, his principles of action eccentric and strange, his views of life partial, and almost misanthropical; but not one opinion that he held could be stirred or modified by any worldly motive [...] He acted up to his principles of action; and, if any touch of misanthropy mingled with his view of mankind in general, his conduct to the individuals who came into personal contact with him did not agree with such view. It is true that he had strong and vehement prejudices, and was obstinate in maintaining them, and that he was not dramatic enough in his perceptions to see how miserable others might be in a life that to him was all-sufficient.

Elizabeth Gaskell, *The Life of Charlotte Brontë*[12]

Not all rich incumbents were guilty of self-indulgence and starving their curates. There were those who gave help to their poor parishioners, at a time when public welfare systems were little developed. They and their wives did not, however, fail to demand respect.

At the time when Laura arrived at Candleford Green a clergyman of the old type held the cure of souls of its inhabitants. He was an elderly man with what was then known as a fine presence, being tall and large rather than stout, with rosy cheeks, a lion-like mane of white hair, and an air of conscious authority. His wife was a dumpy little roly-poly of a woman who wore old, comfortable clothes about the village because, as she was once heard to say, 'Everybody here knows who I am, so why bother about dress?' For church and for afternoon calls upon her equals, she dressed in the silks and satins and ostrich feathers befitting her rank as the granddaughter of an earl and the wife of a vicar with large private means. She was said by the villagers to be 'a bit managing', but, on the whole, she was popular with them. When visiting the cottagers or mak-

ing purchases at the shops, she loved to hear and discuss the latest tit-
bit of gossip, which she was not above repeating – some said
with additions.

The church services were long, old-fashioned and dull, but all was
done decently and in order, and the music and singing were exception-
ally good for a village church at that date. Mr Coulsdon preached to his
poorer parishioners contentment with their divinely appointed lot in life
and submission to the established order of earthly things. To the rich,
the responsibilities of their position and their obligations in the way of
charity. Being rich and highly placed in the little community and
genuinely loving a country life, he himself naturally saw nothing wrong
in the social order, and, being of a generous nature, the duty of helping
the poor and afflicted was also a pleasure to him.

In cold, hard winters soup was made twice a week in the Vicarage
washing copper, and the cans of all comers were filled without question.
It was soup that even the very poor – connoisseurs from long and varied
experience of charity soups – could find no fault with – rich and thick
with pearl barley and lean beef gobbets and golden carrot rings and fat
little dumplings – so solidly good that it was said that a spoon would
stand in it upright. For the sick there were custard puddings, home-
made jellies and half-bottles of port, and it was an unwritten law in the
parish that, by sending a plate to the Vicarage at precisely 1.30 on any
Sunday, a convalescent could claim a dinner from the Vicarage joint.
There were blankets at Christmas, unbleached calico chemises for girls
on first going out in service, flannel petticoats for old women, and
flannel-lined waistcoats for old men.

Flora Thompson, *Candleford Green*[13]

*Clerical poverty was found in both town and country parishes, but the
nineteenth century saw an increase in the number of ill-paid clergy in urban
slum parishes. This one is not given a particular denomination: all the
churches took their share of the task.*

'Twas August, and the fierce sun overhead
Smote on the squalid streets of Bethnal Green,
And the pale weaver, through his windows seen,
In Spitalfields, look'd thrice dispirited.

I met a preacher there I knew, and said
'Ill and o'erwork'd, how fare you in this scene?'
'Bravely!' said he; 'for I of late have been
Much cheer'd with thoughts of Christ, the living bread'.

O human soul! as long as thou canst so
Set up a mark of everlasting light
Above the howling senses' ebb and flow,
To cheer thee, and to light thee if thou roam –
Not with lost toil thou labourest through the night
Thou mak'st the heaven thou hop'st indeed thy home.

Matthew Arnold, 'East London'[14]

*This clergyman belongs to the Established Church, but gains no temporal
advantage from it.*

A small blind street off East Commercial Road;
Window, door; window, door;
Every house like the one before;
Is where the curate, Mr Dowle, has found a pinched abode.
Spectacled, pale, moustache straw-coloured, and with a long thin face,
Day or dark his lodgings' narrow doorstep does he pace.

A bleached pianoforte, with its drawn silk plaitings faded,
Stands in his room, its keys much yellowed, cyphering, and abraded,
'Novello's Anthems' lie at hand, and also a few glees,
And 'Laws of Heaven for Earth' in a frame upon the wall one sees.

He goes through his neighbours' houses as his own, and none regards,
And opens their back-doors off-hand, to look for them in their yards:
A man is threatening his wife on the other side of the wall,
But the curate lets it pass as knowing the history of it all.

Freely within his hearing the children skip and laugh and say:
'There's Mister Dow-well! There's Mister Dow-well!' in their play;
And the long, pallid, devoted face notes not,
But stoops along abstractedly, for good, or in vain, God wot!

Thomas Hardy, 'An East-End Curate'[15]

The low incomes of such clergy made them more sympathetic to the poverty of those under their care. A Victorian novelist, writing of a period about a generation earlier, links clerical and lay poverty and reminds us how much the churches did in the way of poor relief and how desperately it was needed.

In a very populous district of London, somewhat north of Temple Bar, there stood, many years ago, a low, ancient church amidst other churches – for you know that London abounds in them. The doors of this church were partially open one dark evening in December, and a faint, glimmering light might be observed inside by the passers-by.

It was known well enough what was going on within, and why the light was there. The rector was giving away the weekly bread. Years ago a benevolent person had left a certain sum to be spent in twenty weekly loaves, to be given to twenty poor widows at the discretion of the minister. Certain curious provisos were attached to the bequest. One was that the bread should not be less than two days old, and should have been deposited in the church at least twenty-four hours before distribution. Another, that each recipient must attend in person. Failing personal attendance, no matter how unavoidable her absence, she lost the loaf: no friend might receive it for her, neither might it be sent to her. In that case, the minister was enjoined to bestow it upon 'any stranger widow who might present herself, even as should seem expedient to him': the word 'stranger' being, of course, used in contradistinction to the twenty poor widows who were on the books as the charity's recipients. Four times a year, one shilling to each widow was added to the loaf of bread.

A loaf of bread is not very much. To us, sheltered in our abundant homes, it seems as nothing. But, to many a one, toiling and starving in this same city of London, a loaf may be almost the turning-point between death and life. The poor existed in those days as they exist in these: as they always will exist: therefore it was no matter of surprise that a crowd of widow women, most of them aged, all in poverty, should gather round the church doors when the bread was being given out, each hoping that, of the twenty poor widows, some one might fail to appear, and the clerk would come to the door and call out her own particular name as the fortunate substitute. On the days when the shilling was added to the loaf, this waiting and hoping crowd would be increased four-fold.

Thursday was the afternoon for the distribution. And on the day we are now writing about, the rector entered the church at the usual hour: four o'clock. He had to make his way through an unusual number of outsiders; for this was one of the shilling days. He knew them all personally; was familiar with their names and homes; for the Rev. Francis Tait was a hard-working clergyman. And hard-working clergymen were more rare in those days than they are in these.

Of Scottish birth, but chiefly reared in England, he had taken orders at the usual age, and become curate in a London parish, where the work was heavy and the stipend small. Not that the duties attached to the church itself were onerous: but it was a parish filled with poor. Those familiar with such parishes know what this means, when the minister is sympathising and conscientious. For twenty years he remained a curate, toiling in patience, cheerfully hoping. Twenty years! It seems little to write; but it is a great deal; and Francis Tait, in spite of his hopefulness, sometimes found it so. Then promotion came. The living of this little church that you now see open was bestowed upon him. A poor living as compared with some others; and a poor parish, speaking of the social condition of its inhabitants. But the living seemed wealth compared with what he had earned as a curate; and as to his flock being chiefly composed of the poor, he had not been accustomed to anything else. Then the Rev. Francis Tait married; and another twenty years went by.

He stood in the church this evening; the loaves resting on the shelf overhead, against the door of the vestry, all near the entrance. A flaring tallow candle stood on the small table between him and the widows who clustered opposite. He was sixty-five years old now; a spare man of middle height, with a clear, pale skin, an intelligent countenance, and a thoughtful, fine grey eye. He had a pleasant word, a kind inquiry for all, as he put the shilling into their hands; the lame old clerk at the same time handing over the loaf of bread.

Mrs Henry Wood, *Mrs Halliburton's Troubles*[16]

Many Church of England clergy were poor; nearly all Nonconformist ministers were. This extract from a novel set in the last decade of the nineteenth century describes one in the Midlands, visiting a miner's wife who regards herself as 'superior' to her husband. It reveals a gentle, scholarly nature, combined with inability to relate effectively to some of his flock, a type of the quietly sacrificial life that often went unnoticed.

Mrs Morel had a visit every day from the Congregational clergyman. Mr Heaton was young, and very poor. His wife had died at the birth of his first baby, so he remained alone in the manse. He was a Bachelor of Arts of Cambridge, very shy and no preacher. Mrs Morel was fond of him, and he depended on her. For hours he talked to her, when she was well. He became the godparent of the child. Occasionally, the minister stayed to tea with Mrs Morel. Then she laid the cloth early, got out her best cups, with a little green rim, and hoped Morel would not come too soon; indeed, if he stayed for a pint, she would not mind this delay. She had always two dinners to cook, because she believed children should have their chief meal at midday, whereas Morel needed his at five o'clock. So Mr Heaton would hold the baby, whilst Mrs Morel beat up a batter-pudding or peeled the potatoes, and he, watching her all the time, would discuss his next sermon. His ideas were quaint and fantastic. She brought him judiciously to earth. It was a discussion of the wedding at Cana.

'When He changed the water into wine at Cana,' he said, 'that is a symbol that the ordinary life, even the blood, of the married husband and wife, which had before been uninspired, like water, became filled with the Spirit, and was as wine, because, when love enters, the whole spiritual constitution of a man changes, is filled with the Holy Ghost, and almost his form is altered.'

Mrs Morel thought to herself – 'Yes, poor fellow, his young wife is dead; that is why he makes his love into the Holy Ghost.'

They were halfway down their first cup of tea when they beard the sluther of pit-boots. 'Good gracious!' exclaimed Mrs Morel, in spite of herself. The minister looked rather scared. Morel entered. He was feeling rather savage. He nodded a 'How d'yer do' to the clergyman, who rose to shake hands with him.

'Nay,' said Morel, showing his hand, 'look thee at it! Tha niver wants ter shake hands wi' a hand like that, does ter? There's too much pick-haft and shovel-dirt on it.'

The minister flushed with confusion, and sat down again. Mrs Morel rose, carried out the steaming saucepan. Morel took off his coat, dragged his armchair to table and sat down, heavily.

'Are you tired?' asked the clergyman.

'Tired? I ham that,' replied Morel. 'You don't know what it is to be tired, as I'm tired.'

'No,' replied the clergyman.

'Why, look yer 'ere,' said the miner, showing the shoulders of his singlet. 'It's a bit dry now, but it's wet as a clout with sweat even yet. Feel it.'

'Goodness!' cried Mrs Morel. 'Mr Heaton doesn't want to feel your nasty singlet.'

The clergyman put out his hand gingerly.

'No, perhaps he doesn't,' said Morel; 'But it's all come out of *me* whether or not. An' iv'ry day all my singlet's wringin' wet. 'Aven't you got a drink, Missis, for a man when he comes home barkled up from the pit?'

'You know you drank all the beer,' said Mrs Morel, pouring out his tea.

'An' was there no more to be got?' Turning to the clergyman – 'A man gets that caked up wi' th' dust, you know – that clogged up down a coalmine, he *needs* a drink when he comes home.'

'I am sure he does,' said the clergyman.

'But it's ten to one if there's owt for him.'

'There's water – and there's tea,' said Mrs Morel.

'Water! it's not water as'll clear his throat.'

He poured out a saucerful of tea, blew it, and sucked it up through his great black moustache, sighing afterwards.

D. H. Lawrence, *Sons and Lovers*[17]

Dean Swift, with his typical biting irony, suggests that riches and poverty may be literally a matter of life and death.

That you, friend *Marcus*, like a stoick
Can wish to die, in strain heroick,
No real fortitude implies:
Yet, all must own, thy wish is wise.
Thy curate's place, thy fruitful wife,
Thy busy, drudging scene of life,
Thy insolent illiterate vicar,

Thy want of all-consoling liquor,
Thy thread-bare gown, thy cassock rent,
Thy credit sunk, thy money spent,
Thy week made up of fasting days,
Thy grate unconscious of a blaze,
And, to complete thy other curses,
The quarterly demands of nurses,
Are ills you wisely wish to leave,
And fly for refuge to the grave.
And, O what virtue you express
In wishing such afflictions less!

But, now should fortune shift the scene,
And make thy curate-ship a dean;
Or some rich benefice provide,
To pamper luxury and pride;
With labour small, and income great;
With chariot less for use than state;
With swelling scarf, and glossy gown,
And license to reside in town;
To shine, where all the gay resort,
At consort, coffee-house, or court;
And weekly persecute his grace
With visits, or to beg a place;
With underlings thy flock to teach,
With no desire to pray or preach;
With haughty spouse in vesture fine,
With plenteous meals and generous wine;
Would'st thou not wish, in so much ease,
Thy years as numerous as thy days?

Jonathan Swift, 'The Parson's Case'[18]

Chapter 7

Forsaking All Wordly and
Carnal Affections

From the earliest years of Christianity some have felt called to a dedicated life of obedience under a rule. The Rule of St Benedict, drawn up around the middle of the sixth century, was the foundation for the rules of the many orders of Western monasticism which developed. Poverty, chastity and obedience were the three basic vows of the rule. Religious communities were founded when Anglo-Saxon England became Christian, and flourished throughout the Middle Ages. The friars, notably the Franciscans, who appeared in England early in the thirteenth century, brought the reality of a community under rule but not limited to the physical confines of a monastery. The English abbeys and monasteries were suppressed at the time of the Reformation in the sixteenth century and their members dispersed. Dedication to the life under rule returned in the nineteenth century, with both Roman and Anglican orders of male and female religious. Like the parochial clergy, the religious have been both praised and condemned. The fat, jovial monk feasting and drinking is an image loved by some artists and is quaintly popular for Christmas cards. The reality contains some records of abuse and excess, far more of humility and devotion, serving God and his people through intercessory prayer and works of mercy. Not all the religious were, or are, ordained clergy but they deserve their place together.

About AD 660 the Saxon Queen Etheldreda left the court for the conventual life.

She had long requested the king, that he would permit her to lay aside worldly cares, and to serve only the true King, Christ, in a monastery; and having at length with difficulty prevailed, she went as a nun into the monastery of the Abbess Ebba, who was aunt to King Ecgfrid, at the place called the City Coludi, having taken the veil from the hands of the aforesaid Bishop Wilfrid; but a year after, she was herself made abbess in the country called Ely, where, having built a monastery, she began, by works and examples of a heavenly life, to be the virgin mother of very many virgins dedicated to God. It is reported of her, that from the time of her entering into the monastery, she never wore any linen but only woollen garments, and would rarely wash in any hot bath, unless just before any of the great festivals, as Easter, Whitsuntide, and the Epiphany, and then she did it last of all, after having, with the assistance of those about her, first washed the other servants of God there present; besides, she seldom did eat above once a day, excepting on the great solemnities, or some other urgent occasion, unless some considerable distemper obliged her. From the time of matins she continued in the church at prayer till it was day; some also say, that by the spirit of prophecy, she, in the presence of all, not only foretold the pestilence of which she was to die, but also the number of those that should be snatched away out of her monastery. She was taken to our Lord, in the midst of her flock, seven years after she had been made abbess.

Bede, *Ecclesiastical History of the English People*[1]

In the fourteenth century Chaucer's Prioress is a more lively, if less saintly, head of a convent.

There also was a Nun, a Prioress,
Who when she smiled was so demure and coy.
Her greatest oath was only, 'By Saint Loy!'
Her name indeed was Madam Eglantine.
Her singing of the services was fine,
Intoning through her nose in the right place.
When she spoke French it was with ease and grace,
Though in the style of Stratford down by Bow –
Parisian French, alas, she did not know.
At meals her manners were so very good
That she dropped from her lips no scrap of food.
Nor stuck her fingers in the sauce too far.
She could pick up a piece of food with care
So nothing ever fell upon her breast

She practised courtesy with a true zest.
He upper lip was always wiped so clean
That not the smallest spot of grease was seen
Inside her cup when drinking; then to eat
She reached out delicately for her meat.
Indeed she was good company to share,
Pleasant and friendly was her social air.
She tried to imitate the courtly style
With dignified behaviour all the while,
As one to whom folk reverence should render.
And in her sympathy she was so tender,
Her pity and compassion were so deep –
The mere sight of a mouse would make her weep
Caught in a trap, if it was dead or bleeding.
She had some little dogs, and kept them feeding
On roasted meat, or milk, or finest bread.
She would cry bitterly if one were dead,
Or by a sharp blow from a stick was hurt –
She was all sentiment and tender heart.
Her veil was gathered in the neatest wise,
Her nose was neat, and glassy-green her eyes.
Her mouth was small, and also soft and red,
And certainly she had a fair forehead –
The span of a whole hand across her eyes –
And certainly she was not small in size.
I noticed that her cloak was worn with grace.
She had some coral on her arm in place:
A set of beads, the large ones all in green
Holding a golden brooch of brightest sheen
On which was first inscribed a crownèd A
And after, Amor vincit omnia.

Geoffrey Chaucer, *The Canterbury Tales* [2]

Not all religious have been so gentle. In the Middle Ages the heads of the great houses wielded considerable power. The deeds of Abbot Samson of St Edmundsbury in the last decades of the twelfth century were recorded by a contemporary. In the nineteenth century Thomas Carlyle seized on the record as an example of the strong man in government which he believed his own time needed. He tells, in his inimitable style, an amusing story of one of Samson's victories.

By excommunication or persuasion, by impetuosity of driving or adroitness in leading, this Abbot, it is now becoming plain everywhere, is a man that generally remains master at last. He tempers his medicine to the malady, now hot, now cool; prudent though fiery, an eminently practical man. Nay sometimes in his adroit practice there are swift turns almost of a surprising nature! Once, for example, it chanced that Geoffrey Riddel, Bishop of Ely, a Prelate rather troublesome to our Abbot, made a request of him for timber from his woods towards certain edifices going on at Glemsford. The Abbot, a great builder himself, disliked the request; could not, however, give it a negative. While he lay, therefore, at his Manorhouse of Melford not long after, there comes to him one of the Lord Bishop's men or monks, with a message from his Lordship, That he now begged permission to cut down the requisite trees in Elmswell Wood, – so said the monk: Elms*well*, where there are no trees but scrubs and shrubs, instead of Elmset, our true *nemus* [*'grove', a wood with open spaces*] and high-towering oak-wood, here on Melford Manor. Elmswell? The Lord Abbot, in surprise, inquires privily of Richard his Forester; Richard answers that my Lord of Ely has already had his *carpentarii* in Elm*set*, and marked out for his own use all the best trees in the compass of it. Abbot Samson thereupon answers the monk. Elmswell? Yes surely, be it as my Lord Bishop wishes. The successful monk, on the morrow morning, hastens home to Ely; but, on the morrow morning, directly after mass, Abbot Samson too was busy. The successful monk, arriving at Ely, is rated for a goose and an owl; is ordered back to say that Elmset was the place meant. Alas, on arriving at Elmset, he finds the Bishop's trees, they and a hundred more, all felled and piled, and the stamp of St Edmund's Monastery burnt into them, 'for roofing of the great tower we are building there. Your importunate Bishop must seek wood for Glemsford edifices in some other *nemus* than this.' A practical Abbot!

Thomas Carlyle, *Past and Present*[3]

Members of religious orders in many countries have suffered from suppression and annexation. The dissolution of the English monasteries was carried out with cruelty to those whose consciences resisted it. Abbot Whiting of Glastonbury was one of the victims.

He was ready to do everything consistent with his duty as a subject: he received the visitors always with friendly hospitality, but now they had come to try him upon the rights of his monastery, he became at once a changed man; from being tottering and feeble, he grew strong at the indignity, and neither bribes, promises, nor threats, could induce him to yield to the extortionate demands of the visitors. They, upon his refusal, arrested him on the spot, carried him back to the abbey, and, in their own language, 'proceeded that night to search his study for letters and books.' They declared they found, secreted in his study, a book of arguments against the king's divorce, with bulls, pardons, and a 'Life of Becket', but *'we could not find any letter that was material.'* They then examined the abbot once more, and took down his answers, which they compelled him to sign. After this he was taken to the Tower and confined, *'being but a very weak man and sickly'* [...] A charge of high treason was got up against the abbot, and he was tried at Wells the fourteenth of November, and condemned with two of the monks [...] The trial must have been illegal, since the Abbot was allowed no time to seek advice or prepare his defence.

The next day, the fifteenth November, he was taken with the two monks from Wells to Glastonbury. Here, as a last indignity, he was drawn through the town upon a hurdle to the Tor Hill, where he was to be executed. He then asked pardon of God, and submitted to his fate patiently. He was hanged, and after he had been cut down, his head was struck off; his body divided into quarters, the head being placed over the gate of his abbey, and a quarter sent to each of the four towns, Wells, Bath, Ilchester, and Bridgwater. The two monks suffered with him, and the memory of that deed is not extinct amongst the peasantry to this day, the Tor being still pointed out as the spot where 'poor Abbot Whiting *was murdered*'.

O. T. Hill, *English Monasticism*[4]

In the Middle Ages the friars, travelling and preaching in different places, were generally popular among the people, though less so with the parish clergy. They were also satirized as sometimes failing in their vows, particularly that of chastity. After the Reformation, their legend continued, and they could be presented on the stage to an audience who had never seen one in the flesh. The tale of Friar Bacon who made a magical brazen head was the subject of one play. He speaks about his occult powers to two visitors from the University of Oxford.

Seeing you come as friends unto the friar,
Resolve you, doctors, Bacon can by books,
Make storming Boreas thunder from his cave,
And dim fair Luna to a dark eclipse.
The great arch-ruler, potentate of hell,
Trembles when Bacon bids him, or his fiends,
Bow to the force of his Pentageron.
What art can work, the frolic friar knows,
And therefore will I turn my magic books,
And strain out necromancy to the deep.
I have contrived and framed a head of brass,
(I made Belcephon hammer out the stuff)
And that by art shall read philosophy;
And I will strengthen England by my skill,
That if ten Caesars lived and reigned in Rome,
With all the legions Europe doth contain,
They should not touch a grass of English ground.
The work that Ninus reared at Babylon,
The brazen walls framed by Semiramis,
Carved out like to the portal of the sun,
Shall not be such as rings the English strond,
From Dover to the market place of Rye.

Robert Greene, *Friar Bacon and Friar Bungay*[5]

Shakespeare presents a friar whose skill is medical rather than occult. We find Friar Lawrence, before his well-meant but disastrous plan to help the young lovers Romeo and Juliet, gathering herbs at daybreak.

The grey-ey'd morn smiles on the frowning night,
Checkering the Eastern clouds with streaks of light;
And flecked darkness like a drunkard reels
From forth day's path and Titan's fiery wheels.
Now, ere the sun advance his burning eye
The day to cheer and night's dank dew to dry,
I must upfill this osier cage of ours
With baleful weeds and precious-juiced flowers.
The earth that's nature's mother is her tomb.
What is her burying grave, that is her womb;
And from her womb children of divers kind
We sucking on her natural bosom find;
Many for many virtues excellent,
None but for some, and yet all different.
O, mickle is the powerful grace that lies
In plants, herbs, stones, and their true qualities;
For naught so vile that on the earth doth live
But to the earth some special good doth give;
Nor aught so good but, strained from that fair use,
Revolts from true birth, stumbling on abuse.
Virtue itself turns vice, being misapplied,
And vice sometimes by action dignified.
Within the infant rind of this small flower
Poison hath residence, and medicine power;
For this, being smelt, with that part cheers each part;
Being tasted, slays all senses with the heart.
Two such opposed kings encamp them still
In man as well as herbs – grace and rude will;
And where the worser is predominant,
Full soon the canker death eats up that plant.

William Shakespeare, *Romeo and Juliet*[6]

Nicholas Ferrar (1592–1637) founded a small mixed community at Little Gidding in Huntingdonshire. They followed a rule of austere life and regular prayer in the Anglican tradition, a discipline which was not observed again until the nineteenth century. The community continued after the death of Ferrar until it was destroyed by a Parliamentarian force in 1646, at the beginning of the English Civil War. Ferrar did not proceed beyond the order of deacon, which explains why the local vicar celebrated the Sunday Communion.

Holy Communion was regularly celebrated on the first Sunday of every month, and on the great Festivals of the Church, the vicar of Steeple Gidding acting as celebrant, and Nicholas Ferrar assisting as deacon. Those of the servants who received the Communion dined on that day with Mrs Ferrar and the rest of the family. The Saturday afternoon preceding was employed by the careful master of the house in explaining that sacred mystery to the younger, and in exhorting the elder and in preparing them all for that best and noblest entertainment of such holy souls. Of the weekday routine we have the following account.

They rose at four; at five went to the oratory to prayers; at six said the psalms of the hour (for every hour had its appointed psalms), with some portion of the Gospel, till Mr Ferrar had finished his Concordance, when a chapter of that work was substituted in place of the portion of the Gospel. Then they sang a short hymn, repeated some passages of Scripture, and at half-past six went to church to matins. At seven said the psalms of the hour, sang the short hymn, and the children went to breakfast. Then the young people repaired to their respective places of instruction. The old gentlewoman [*Nicholas Ferrar's mother*] took her chair, inspecting her daughters and grandchildren as they sat at their books or other good employments in great silence, or at least avoiding all vain talking and jesting that was not convenient. No hour but had its business. Eight, nine, ten o'clock come, those hours had their several companies, that came and did as at former hours: psalms said and a head of the Concordance, the organs playing, the hymn sung at each hour, as the clock struck, that gave notice to all of the time passing. At ten, to the church to Litany every day of the week, as their bishop had given them leave. At eleven to dinner (after saying the hourly office). At which seasons were regular readings in rotation, from the Scripture, from the Book of Martyrs, and from short histories drawn up by Mr Ferrar, and adapted to the purpose of moral instruction. Recreation was permitted till one; then the bell tolled for the boys to school, and those that had their turns came up into the great chamber again, to say their psalms and head of Concordance, sing a hymn and play on the organ whilst they sung. There old Mrs Ferrar commonly sat till four o'clock, and, as before, each hour had its performance. Church at four for Evensong; supper at five, or sometimes six. Diversions till eight. Then prayers in the oratory, where a hymn was sung, the organs playing, and afterwards all retired to their respective apartments.

H. P. K. Skipton, The Life and Times of Nicolas Ferrar⁷

At a time when interest in the story of Little Gidding was being revived, it was introduced into a popular novel. The eponymous hero of the book, seeking spiritual fulfilment, comes on a visit.

He asked to see Mr Ferrar, and was shown by a manservant into a fair spacious parlour, where Mr Ferrar presently came to him. Inglesant was disappointed at his appearance, which was plain and not striking in any way, but his speech was able and attractive. Johnny apologized for his bold visit, telling him how much taken he had been by his book, and by what he had heard of him and his family; and that what he had heard did not interest him merely out of curiosity, as he feared it might have done many, but out of sincere desire to learn something of the holy life which doubtless that family led.

To this Mr Ferrar replied that he was thankful to see any one who came in such a spirit, and that several, not only of his own friends, as Mr Crashaw the poet, but many young students from the University at Cambridge came to see him in a like spirit, to the benefit, he hoped, of both themselves and of him. He said with great humility, that although on the one hand very much evil had been spoken of him which was not true, he had no doubt that, on the other, many things had been said about their holiness and the good that they did which went far beyond the truth. For his own part, he said he had adopted that manner of life through having long seen enough of the manners and vanities of the world; and holding them in low esteem, was resolved to spend the rest of his life in mortifications and devotion, in charity, and in constant preparation for death. That his mother, his elder brother, his sisters, his nephews and nieces, being content to lead this mortified life, they spent their time in acts of devotion and by doing such good works as were within their power, such as keeping a school for the children of the next parishes, for teaching of whom he provided three masters who lived constantly in the house. That for ten years they had lived this harmless life, under the care of his mother, who had trained her daughters and granddaughters to every good work; but two years ago they had lost her by death, and as his health was very feeble he did not expect long to be separated from her, but looked forward to his departure with joy, being afraid of the evil times he saw approaching.

J. H. Shorthouse, *John Inglesant*[8]

Men and women have taken religious vows for many reasons, and left many types of secular life behind them. This nun speaks movingly for some who have found peace but not forgetfulness in the conventual life.

I loved him; yes, where was the sin?
   I loved him with my heart and soul;
   But I pressed forward to no goal,
There was no prize I strove to win.
Show me my sin that I may see:
Throw the first stone, thou Pharisee.

I loved him, but I never sought
   That he should know that I was fair.
   I prayed for him; was my sin prayer?
I sacrificed, he never bought;
He nothing gave, he nothing took;
We never bartered look for look.

My voice rose in the sacred choir,
   The choir of nuns: do you condemn
   Even if when kneeling among them
Faith, zeal, and love, kindled a fire,
And I prayed for his happiness
Who knew not; was my error this?

I only prayed that in the end
   His trust and hope may not be vain;
   I prayed not we may meet again:
I would not let our names ascend,
No not to Heaven, in the same breath
Nor will I join the two in death.

Oh sweet is death, for I am weak
   And weary, and it giveth rest.
   The crucifix lies on my breast,
And all night long it seems to speak
Of rest; I hear it through my sleep,
And the great comfort makes me weep.

Oh sweet is death that bindeth up
   The broken and the bleeding heart.
   The draught chilled, but a cordial part
Lurked at the bottom of the cup;
And for my patience will my Lord
Give an exceeding great reward.

Yea the reward is almost won,
   A crown of glory and a palm.
   Soon I shall sing the unknown psalm;
Soon gaze on light, not on the sun;
And soon with surer faith shall pray
For him, and cease not night nor day.

My life is breaking like a cloud –
   God judgeth not as man doth judge –
   Nay, bear with me: you need not grudge
This peace; the vows that I have vowed
Have all been kept: Eternal Strength
Holds me, though mine own fails at length.

Bury me in the Convent-ground
   Among the flowers that are so sweet;
   And lay a green turf at my feet,
Where thick trees cast a gloom around;
At my head let a cross be, white
Through the long blackness of the night.

Now kneel and pray beside my bed
   That I may sleep being free from pain
   And pray that I may wake again
After His likeness who hath said
(Faithful is He who promiseth)
We shall be satisfied therewith.

Christina Rossetti, 'Three Nuns'[9]

An Irish monk reveals the same tension between obedience and desire.

I go with silent feet and slow
As all my black-robed brothers go;
I dig a while and read and pray,
So portion out my quiet day
Until the evening time, and then
Work at my book with cunning pen.
If she would turn to me a while,
If she would turn to me and smile,
My book would be no more to me
Than some forgotten phantasy,
And God no more unto my mind
Than a dead leaf upon the wind.

Seamas O'Sullivan, 'The Monk'[10]

The calm acceptance of a religious vocation is perfectly expressed in these few lines of a nun about to take her vows.

I have desired to go
Where springs not fail,
To fields where flies no sharp and sided hail
And a few lilies blow.

And I have asked to be
Where no storms come,
Where the green swell is in the havens dumb,
And out of the swing of the sea.

G. M. Hopkins, 'Heaven-Haven'[11]

The creation of Anglican sisterhoods which followed the Oxford Movement met with much opposition and suspicion. William Walsh, a vehement denouncer of all 'Puseyite' doings, was particularly angry about the convents. He quotes from a book by Margaret Goodman published in 1863. Her frequent italics are retained here as in his extracts.

There is certainly in this 'Rule of Holy Poverty' something which looks very much like what City men term 'sharp practice'. It is a grand scheme for relieving English ladies of their money. 'A lady' writes the Rev. W. G. Cookesley, 'who joined Dr Pusey's establishment, as a Sister, carried into the common stock a capital producing, I believe, so large a sum as £1200 *per annum*; when she subsequently left the Society, which she did to join the Church of Rome, she did not possess a penny!' Here we are face to face with another very serious evil, which sadly needs a remedy at the hands of Parliament. A Sisterhood which retains the property of a Sister who desires to leave its walls, ought to be compelled by law to return her fortune, after deducting a reasonable amount for her support while in the Convent. This 'Rule of Holy Poverty' is manifestly unjust on the face of it. A provision should be made, in every case, which shall secure the pecuniary rights of each Sister, and not leave her dependent – should she decide upon leaving the Sisterhood – on the doubtful charity of the authorities. But even if such a provision were made, something more should be done to remove the difficulties which surround a Sister desirous of leaving a Sisterhood. Miss Goodman, writing from the stand point of one who had practical experience, informs us that:

'The fact that these Conventual establishments are closed against all unwelcome visitation, and that any of the inmates may be secluded from all intercourse and communication with their family and friends, at the will of the Superior, is, if not a breach of the law of England, *at least an alarming and dangerous innovation, and in direct opposition to the spirit of civil and religious liberty in this country. Since it is possible for a young girl to be kept secretly*, in strict seclusion, in a Convent professedly connected with the Church of England, not only *against her own inclinations, but against the wishes of her parents and friends*, and even in despite of their efforts to remove or communicate with her, it is superfluous to add that this fact is one of grave importance, *and demands the consideration of the Legislature.* The unfortunate inmates of lunatic asylums, private as well as public, are shielded by the law from ill usage and unjustifiable restraint; surely the inmates of Religious Houses, who devote themselves to the good offices of nursing and comforting the sick and afflicted, teaching ignorant adults and training children – or even if solely engaged in prayer and worship – ought not to he left entirely to the tender mercies of high-handed and uncontrolled power, exercised by irresponsible Superiors, whose authority is absolute.'

If what Miss Goodman here states be true – and I have discovered no reason for doubting it – it follows that Ritualistic Convents are, in some instances, nothing better than jails for innocent young ladies, and consequently that, like jails, they ought to be under Government Inspection. Nominally, in most if not all of these Convents, the Sisters may be free to leave when they please; but even here *moral* bolts and bars are used which more effectually prevent their escape than any material ones could.

'A Sister', writes Miss Goodman, 'under some circumstances would find it very difficult to leave. Those who enter Sisterhoods abandon family ties; they acquire peculiar habits; are ignorant of the state of things without their Nunnery gates [...] I have known several Sisters who have spent every penny of their capital; and Dr Pusey also knows them much better than I do. Without money; without friends; without clothes (Sisters who persist in leaving Miss Sellon's are sent forth in Sisters' garb, and they are instructed to send everything back as soon as they can clothe themselves); without an idea which way to look for occupation; what is a Sister to do who leaves a Nunnery?'

William Walsh, *The Secret History of the Oxford Movement*[12]

Until well into the nineteenth century, the hospital nurse was seldom a woman of high professional quality: Dickens' Mrs Gamp was found more often than Florence Nightingale. The improvement in standards coincided with the growth of sisterhoods and some women found that they had a vocation both to nursing and to the religious life. Such a one was Dorothy Pattison (1832–78). Her feminist biographer believed that she 'made what many must think was the greatest mistake of her life [when she] join-ed a High Church Sisterhood'. Nevertheless, she is warm in her praise of 'Sister Dora'.

She had a very strong personal influence for good over the poor rough people, both men and women, for whom she worked. Her religion was one more of deeds than of words, and they saw that both in word and deed it was genuine. Many a one has dated a new start in life from the time he came under her care. Sometimes patients, waking in the night, would find her praying by their bedsides, and it touched them deeply to see how sincerely and truly she cared for them. Although she had the hearty sense of fun already alluded to, no man could over venture on a coarse word or jest in her presence, and she inspired a good 'tone' in the wards even when they were occupied by the roughest and poorest. As time went on there was hardly a slum or court in the lowest part of Walsall where she was not known, and hardly a creature in the town that did not feel he owed something to her. Although most of her time was given to healing bodily troubles, all her patients felt that she cared for something higher in them than their bodies. She joined heartily in several missions that were started with the object of reaching the lowest and most outcast; she would go quite fearlessly at midnight into the haunts of the most degraded men and women of the town, and induce them, for a while at least, to pause and consider what their lives had been given to them for.

Mrs Henry Fawcett, 'Sister Dora'[13]

We have already met the 'Owlet' (p. 98). He gives a pessimistic (and very politically incorrect) idea of what a future Mother Superior might be like – unless male authority should prevail.

Sisterhoods will be formed: the fashion will spread. It is high time that the energies of our English women should be used, which for generations have been running to waste. People see and feel this more strongly day by day: and a movement in favour of sisterhoods will be the result. You can no more stop it than Mrs Partington with her mop could check the tide of the Atlantic, or than Sir George Noodle can extinguish Convocation, or Sheriff Doodle in Scotland can obliterate Episcopacy. Sisterhoods will come. But how? Are they, one after another to be a succession of failures, harassed by persecution from without, and split asunder by dissensions from within? Are they to be looked upon by good men with suspicion, and are they to give a handle to bad men for profaneness? Is the Dissenter to exult over them as Romanizing? Is the Romanist to point to them as evidence that no associated work of love undertaken by the Church of England can flourish and endure? Do we wish to see such a state of things?

We can bring it about easily if we do. Look out a clever, enthusiastic woman, with a strong will of her own, and no stronger will from without to control it. Make her the Head of the Sisterhood, without any man to come with the weight of years, authority, and holiness, to say to her, 'This must not be.' 'That would be very silly, or very unreasonable, or very improper, or very cruel, or very injudicious, and therefore I positively forbid it.' Do this, and you will do the devil's work, in frustrating a means of good as effectually as he could wish. You will get sisterhoods in all the slavish misery of nuns, and with none of the protection of convents – a pack of unhappy women, forbidden to exercise common sense, and rendered morbid, oversensitive, and indevout by the system which the uncontrolled Superior exercises over them. And not rarely you will have that good lady herself lose her personal influence, and utterly check her own spiritual progress, through the unlimited indulgence of her talent for government.

F. E. Paget, *The Owlet of Owlstone Edge*[14]

The ideal of monastic discipline was sometimes adopted without entering a regular community. The Anglo-Catholic priest C. F. Lowder had a long and fruitful ministry in East London. He was the founder of the Society of the Holy Cross. The celibate clergy who lived an active life while keeping a daily rule showed that the two vocations were not incompatible.

The first bell for rising was rung at 6.30; we said Prime in the oratory at 7; Matins was said at St Peter's and St Saviour's at 7.30; the celebration of the Holy Eucharist followed. After breakfast, followed by Terce, the clergy and teachers went to their respective work – some in school, some in the study or district. Sext was said at 12.45, immediately before dinner, when the household were again assembled; on Fridays and fast days some book, such as the 'Lives of the Saints' or Ecclesiastical History, was read at table. After dinner, rest, letters, visiting, or school work, as the case might be, and then tea at 5.30 p.m. After tea, choir practice, classes, reading, or visiting again until Evensong at 8 p.m. After service the clergy were often engaged in classes, hearing confessions, or attending to special cases. Supper at 9.15, followed by Compline, when those who had finished their work retired to their rooms. It was desired that all should be in bed at 11 p.m., when the gas was put out; but, of course, in the case of the clergy, much of whose work was late in the evening with those who could not come to them at any other time, it was impossible absolutely to observe this rule. In an active community the rules of the house must yield to the necessities of spiritual duties.

M. Trench, *Charles Lowder: a Biography*[15]

Inspired by the revival of the religious life in the nineteenth century, Joseph Lyne (1837–1908), known as Father Ignatius, wished to revive the Benedictine order for Anglicans. He inaugurated a monastery at Capel-y-ffin near Llanthony in Wales. He was also famous as a mission preacher. As this description by another clergyman shows, he was not free from personal eccentricity, but he gained much devotion from his small circle of followers.

At 10.45 started across the fields to walk to Capel y Ffin. I came in sight of the little Capel y Ffin squatting like a stout grey owl among its seven great black yews. I hastened on, and in front of the Capel House farm there was the sunny haired girl washing at a tub as usual by the brook side, the girl with the blue eyes, not the blue of the sky, but the blue of the sea. 'Is Father Ignatius here?' I asked. 'Yes, at least he was here this morning.' I asked a mason at work upon the building if Father Ignatius was there. 'Here he is with his brother,' said the mason. A black robed and cowled monk was walking fast along the bottom of the field towards a barn with Clavering Lyne. Clavering came up to me, but the monk walked quickly on without looking round. Clavering took me to his father and mother, who were sitting on a garden seat under a tree in a pretty little dingle. They had just arrived unexpectedly from Pontrilas having driven up the valley as I came down. It was curious, our meeting thus as it were by chance.

Mr and Mrs Lyne came up out of their dingle and Mrs Lyne brought up Father Ignatius and introduced us. He struck me as being a man of gentle simple kind manners, excitable, and entirely possessed by the one idea. He always spoke to his father and mother as 'Papa' and 'Mamma' and called me 'Father'. I could not persuade him that my name was not

Venables. His head and brow are very fine, the forehead beautifully rounded and highly imaginative. The face is a very saintly one and the eyes extremely beautiful, earnest and expressive, a dark soft brown. When excited they seem absolutely to flame. He wears the Greek or early British tonsure all round the temples, leaving the hair of the crown untouched. His manner gives you the impression of great earnestness and singlemindedness. The voice and manner are very like Clavering's and it was with difficulty that I could tell which of the two was speaking if I did not see them. Father Ignatius wore the black Benedictine habit with the two loose wings or pieces falling in front and behind, two violet tassels behind, the knotted scourge girdle, a silver cross on the breast, and a brazen or golden cross hanging from the rosary of black beads under the left arm.

We walked round the place and then climbed the steep bank above and looked down upon the building. Mrs Lyne gathered some whin-berries and gave them to us to eat. They were very nice. They grew along the ground on tiny bushes among a very small delicately twisted pink heath. We saw the monks and novices below issuing from a barn where they had engaged for an hour or so in an 'examination of conscience'. One of the monks was gazing at us. He had conceived an irrepress-ible desire to see Mrs Lyne again. He did not wish to intrude upon her approach or address her. He simply wanted to see her at a respectful distance and admire her afar off. Mr Lyne said the monk was a man of few and simple wants, content with a little and thankful for small mercies. Because the monk had said that if he could see Mrs Lyne he would be perfectly happy.

Mrs Lyne not having much faith in the larder or resources of the monastery, especially on a Friday, had wisely taken the precaution of bringing with her an honest leg of mutton and two bottles of wine. The monasterial garden provided potatoes and French beans, very good, and we had luncheon under the tree in the dingle, waited on by the novices also cowled and robed in black like the monks. They addressed Father Ignatius as 'dear Father' whenever they spoke to him and bent the knee whenever they approached or passed him.

The Diary of Francis Kilvert, 2 September 1870[16]

The revival of the religious life brought back many of the traditional orders. In this extract, several friends, one of whom feels drawn to this vocation, are visiting a Carthusian monastery. The novelist who is the narrator, himself a Roman Catholic priest, offers an impression of a twentieth-century monk.

The door suddenly opened, and a little man in white came in, closing it behind him.

Now I wish to describe this man carefully, because he made a very singular and wholly indefinable impression on me. As he shook hands, first with Chris, and was then introduced to each of us, making us sit down, and listening to explanations, I was observing him violently.

He was small, not above five feet four; he was dressed in a greyish white of some woolly-looking material; his scapular was linked, front to back, at the height of his knees, by a broad band. His hands were hidden, as he sat, beneath his scapular that, like the tunic beneath, fell into stiff, ungraceful folds. His whole head and face were shaven to a bluish-black colour, and the rest of his complexion was almost colourless. His mouth was small and compressed, his nose was slightly hooked, and his ears projected a little. His voice was almost toneless, it said things without a touch of emotion; and he seemed rather tired. But he was not at all pathetic or picturesque. He wore ordinary black boots.

To analyse in words a psychological impression is always difficult, but with this man it appears impossible; for there seemed to be no atmosphere about him at all. Yet there was one sensation that I remember distinctly, of a negative character. It was that, as I looked at the others in his presence, the three seemed strangely shrunken and mean. It was as if we were all plebeians in the presence of a prince – coarse ill-bred, empty-headed bourgeois. Yet there was not in his air anything remarkable. It was we who were remarkably small and rather coarse, not he that was remarkably great or ethereal. He seemed the normal man, we the abnormal. He did not bring with him a spiritual aroma such as I had expected; he did not say searching or suggestive or oracular sentences. He told us some facts as to the number of monks at present in the house – there were about a hundred fathers, I think he said; he told us about the room we were sitting in, and the date of the foundation of the house – all in that same rather insignificant but perfectly steady voice. Looking back on him now, I think I should say that he was a man simply and entirely uninterested in the things that interest the world; and perfectly secretive about things that interested him. Things other than his own business had no personal relation to him at all. It was nothing to him that this parlour resembled a fifth-rate morning-room, nor that four strangers from the world sat there eyeing and listening to him. I could see that, if he had permitted himself to be so, he would have been bored. As it was, he took it all in the day's work; yet, so far as he had any inclination at all, it was for a return to his cell as soon as might be.

R. H. Benson, *The Conventionalists*[17]

Thomas Merton joined the silent Trappist order. His writings have helped the spirituality of many people and continue to be popular. Prayer and meditation fill much of the monastic life, but nearly all Rules since that of St Benedict have also enjoined manual labour. The holiness of work as part of the total commitment is described here.

How sweet it is out in the fields, at the end of the long summer afternoons! The sun is no longer raging at you, and the woods are beginning to throw long blue shadows over the stubble fields where the golden shocks are standing. The sky is cool, and you can see the pale half-moon smiling over the monastery in the distance. Perhaps a clean smell of pine comes down to you, out of the woods, on the breeze, and mingles with the richness of the fields and of the harvest. And when the undermaster claps his hands for the end of work, and you drop your arms and take off your hat to wipe the sweat out of your eyes, in the stillness you realize how the whole valley is alive with the singing of crickets, a constant universal treble going up to God out of the fields, rising like the incense of an evening prayer to the pure sky: *laus perennis*! [*meaning perpetual praise*]

And you take your rosary out of your pocket, and get in your place in the long file, and start swinging homeward along the road with your boots ringing on the asphalt and deep, deep peace in your heart! And on your lips, silently, over and over again, the name of the Queen of Heaven, the Queen also of this valley: 'Hail Mary, full of grace, the Lord is with Thee ...! And the Name of her Son, for Whom all this was made in the first place, for Whom all this was planned and intended, for Whom the whole of creation was framed, to be His Kingdom. 'Blessed is the fruit of Thy womb, Jesus!'

'Full of grace!' The very thought, over and over, fills our own hearts with more grace: and who knows what grace overflows into the world from that valley, from those rosaries, in the evenings when the monks are swinging home from work!

Thomas Merton, *Seven Storey Mountain*[18]

Chapter 8

An Honourable Estate

The question of clerical celibacy has been a cause of considerable controversy. It is clear that some at least of the Apostles were married, and St Paul seems to have been rather resentful that St Peter and others were accompanied by their wives on their missionary travels (1 Corinthians 9:5). The rule for the professed religious required celibacy, but it was only gradually enforced on the secular clergy, and not made definitive in the Western Church until the twelfth century (the rules in the East are different). The sixteenth-century Reformation brought permission to marry for all but Roman Catholic clergy, and with it there came a new dimension in clerical life. The wife and children of the priest or minister were expected to have the same high standards of character and conduct, and were liable to be judged harshly for any lapses. Many wives were a great strength to their husbands, others a hindrance or a burden. Some lived unremarked under the shadow of his work, others made their presence forcefully felt. The children might feel isolated from their contemporaries in the parish and sometimes suffered – and still suffer – from teasing or bullying. The record, both factual and fictional, tells of the delights and the trials of the clerical family – perhaps not much different from the lot of laypeople, but sometimes complicated by the expectations laid on the clergy and the need to keep up appearances in poverty. Today it may be the husband who is the lay partner in a clerical household – but that is another story, which has not yet found a place in literature.

It took some time for the idea of married clergy to meet approval in all quarters. Queen Elizabeth I took a poor view of it: her farewell to Archbishop Parker's wife has already been recorded (p. 48). Unable to reverse the new freedom, she did her best to restrict it.

Of the Injunctions which Elizabeth published, for the guidance of her clergy and laity in religious matters, in the first year of her reign, the twenty-ninth runs thus: 'Item, although there be no prohibition by the word of God, nor any example of the Primitive Church, but that the Priests and Ministers of the Church may lawfully, for the avoiding of fornication, have an honest and sober wife, and that for the same purpose the same was by Act of Parliament in the time of our dear brother King Edward the Sixth made lawful: whereupon a great number of the clergy of this Realm were then married, and so continue, yet because there hath grown offence, and some slander to the Church by lack of discreet and sober behaviour in many ministers of the Church, both in choosing of their wives and indiscreet living with them, the remedy whereof is necessary to be sought, it is thought therefore very necessary, that no manner of priest or deacon shall hereafter take to his wife any manner of woman without the advice and allowance first had upon good examination by the bishop of the same diocese, and two justices of the peace of the same shire, dwelling next to the place where the same woman hath most made her abode before her marriage, nor without the good will of the parents of the said woman, if she have any living, or two of the next of her kinsfolks, or, for lack of knowledge of such, of her master or mistress where she serveth. And before she shall be contracted in any place, she shall make a good and certain proof thereof to the minister, or to the congregation assembled for that purpose, which shall be upon some holyday where divers may be present. And if any shall do otherwise, that then they shall not be permitted to minister either the word or the sacraments of the Church, nor shall be capable of any ecclesiastical benefice, and for the manner of marriages of any bishops, the same shall be allowed and approved by the metropolitan of the province, and also by such commissioners as the Queen's Majesty thereunto shall appoint.'

[*The injunction was not always totally successful.*]

The Elizabethan complainants against the Dean and Chapter of Worcester charged the clerical ladies of the Cathedral Close with arrogance, insolence, idleness, and inordinate love of dress; and the splendour of their attire was all the more offensive to many of their censors because the gentlewomen of the Church were indebted for much of it to the despoliation of the Cathedral vestiaries, from which store-rooms large quantities of silk gowns, embroidered vestments, fine linen robes, and other paraphernalia of Catholic Ritualism had been

taken in the course of the ordinary operations of ecclesiastical purifi-
cation, and had been converted into millinery for canons' wives and
daughters.

J. C. Jeafferson, *A Book about the Clergy*[1]

*According to his early biographer, one of the Elizabethan clergy who might
have wished that celibacy was still enforced was the saintly Richard Hooker
(p. 4). Some modern scholars question the accuracy of Waltons' story, but it
is related with circumstantial detail. Hooker was befriended in illness by a
woman in London, whom he trusted to find him a suitable wife.*

Now, the wife provided for him was her daughter Joan, who brought
neither beauty nor portion: and for her conditions, they were too like
that wife's, which is by Solomon compared to a dripping house: so that
the good man had no reason to 'rejoice in the wife of his youth;' but too
just cause to say with the holy Prophet, 'Woe is me, that I am constrained
to have my habitation in the tents of Kedar!'

This choice of Mr Hooker's – if it were his choice – may be wondered
at [...] And by this marriage the good man was drawn from the tran-
quillity of his College; from that garden of piety, of pleasure, of peace,
and a sweet conversation, into the thorny wilderness of a busy world;
into those corroding cares that attend a married Priest, and a country
Parsonage; which was Drayton-Beauchamp in Buckinghamshire, not far
from Aylesbury, and in the Diocese of Lincoln; to which he was presented by John Cheney, Esq – then Patron of it – the 9th of December, 1584,
where he behaved himself so as to give no occasion of evil, but as St Paul
adviseth a minister of God – 'in much patience, in afflictions, in
anguishes, in necessities, in poverty and no doubt in long-suffering,' yet
troubling no man with his discontents and wants.

And in this condition he continued about a year; in which time his
two pupils, Edwin Sandys and George Cranmer, took a journey to see
their tutor; where they found him with a book in his hand – it was the
Odes of Horace – he being then like humble and innocent Abel, tending
his small allotment of sheep in a common field; which he told his pupils
he was forced to do then, for that his servant was gone home to dine, and
assist his wife to do some necessary household business. But when his

servant returned and released him, then his two pupils attended him to his house, where their best entertainment was his quiet company, which was presently denied them; for Richard was called to rock the cradle; and the rest of their welcome was so like this, that they stayed but till morning, which was time enough to discover and pity their tutor's condition; and they having in that time rejoiced in the remembrance, and then paraphrased many of the innocent recreations of their younger days, and other like diversions, and thereby given him as much present comfort as they were able, they were forced to leave him to the company of his wife Joan, and seek themselves a quieter lodging for next night. But at their parting from him, Mr Cranmer said, 'Good tutor, I am sorry your lot is fallen in no better ground, as to your parsonage; and more sorry that your wife proves not a more comfortable companion, after you have wearied yourself in your restless studies.' To whom the good man replied, 'My dear George, if Saints have usually a double share in the miseries of this life, I, that am none, ought not to repine at what my wise Creator hath appointed for me; but labour – as indeed I do daily – to submit mine to his will, and possess my soul in patience and peace.'

Isaac Walton, The Life of Richard Hooker[2]

George Herbert was a priest of exemplary piety and kindness (p. 5). His own precepts for the life of a clergy family may seem severe and almost oppressive to the modern reader, but it would have been idyllic in comparison with many contemporary realities.

The Parson is very exact in the governing of his House, making it a copy and model for his Parish. He knows the temper and pulse of every person in his house, and accordingly either meets with their vices, or advanceth their virtues. His wife is either religious, or night and day he is winning her to it. Instead of the qualities of the world, he requires only *three* of her. *First,* a training up of her children and maids in the fear of God, with prayers, and catechizing and all religious duties. *Secondly,* a curing and healing of all wounds and sores with her own hands; which skill either she brought with her, or he takes care she shall learn it of some religious neighbour. Thirdly, a providing for her family in such sort, as that neither they want a competent sustentation, nor her husband be brought in debt. His children he first makes Christians, and then Commonwealth's men; the one he owes to his heavenly Country, the other to his earthly, having no title to either, except he do good to both. Therefore having seasoned them with all piety, not only of words in praying, and reading; but in actions, in visiting other sick children, and tending their wounds, and sending his charity by them to the poor, and sometimes giving them a little money to do it of themselves, that they get a delight in it, and enter favour with God, who weighs even children's actions (1 Kings 14:12–13). He afterwards turns his care to fit all their dispositions with some calling, not sparing the eldest, but giving him the prerogative of his father's profession, which happily for his other children he is not able to do. Yet in binding them Apprentices (in case he think fit to do so) he takes care not to put them into vain trades, and unbefitting the reverence of their Father's calling, such as are Taverns for men, and Lace-making for women; because those trades, for the most part, serve but the vices and vanities of the world, which he is to deny and not augment.

George Herbert, *A Priest to the Temple*[3]

Being the wife and children of a saintly man has not always guaranteed a comfortable life. We have seen something of the Little Gidding community (p. 121). If George Herbert expected much of a parson's family, Nicolas Ferrar demanded more.

As the children grew older Ferrar used to undertake their religious instruction himself, giving up several hours daily for that purpose. He placed great stress upon the learning by heart of passages of Scripture, and especially of the whole Book of Psalms, upon which he used to comment at length and clearly. But above all things he was anxiously attentive to daily catechetical lectures, according to the doctrine of the Church of England. Undenominational education was evidently far from his thoughts. As the four elder nieces, the daughters of Mrs Collett, grew up, they were required to take the housekeeping in turn for a month at a time, and their accounts were regularly kept and audited. There was an infirmary for sick members of the household, and a sort of out-patients' room was provided, where surgical and other help was given to such of their neighbours as required it, and here Ferrar's own medical knowledge stood him in excellent stead. The surgeon's chest and the provision of medicines was regulated with the same exactness as everything else in the household, and the young ladies were required to dress the wounds of those who were hurt, in order to give them readiness and skill in this employment, and to habituate them to the virtues of humility and tenderness of heart. The dispensary was under Ferrar's own care. Thus says the chronicler, 'did Mr Ferrar form his nieces to be wise and useful, virtuous and valuable women.'

H. P. K. Skipton, *The Life and Times of Nicolas Ferrar*[4]

Family life brought much joy and comfort to the clergy, but it sometimes also brought problems. Goldsmith's worthy though somewhat self-righteous parish priest Dr Primrose loses his private capital and has to live on his meagre stipend, but his wife and daughters do not accept the reality of their social decline.

When Sunday came, it was indeed a day of finery, which all my sumptuary edicts could not restrain. Howellsoever I fancied my lectures against pride had conquered the vanity of my daughters, yet I still found them secretly attached to all their former finery; they still loved laces, ribands, bugles, and catgut; my wife herself retained a passion for her crimson paduasoy, because I formerly happened to say it became her.

The first Sunday, in particular, their behaviour served to mortify me. I had desired my girls the preceding night to be dressed early the next day; for I always loved to be at church a good while before the rest of the congregation. They punctually obeyed my directions; but when we were assembled in the morning at breakfast, down came my wife and daughters, dressed out in all their former splendour; their hair plastered up with pomatum, their faces patched to taste, their trains bundled up into a heap behind, and rustling at every motion. I could not help smiling at their vanity, particularly that of my wife, from whom I expected more discretion. In this exigence, therefore, my only resource was to order my son, with an important air, to call our coach. The girls were amazed at the command; but I repeated it with more solemnity than before. 'Surely, my dear, you jest,' cried my wife; 'we can walk it perfectly well: we want no coach to carry us now.' 'You mistake, child', returned I, 'we do want a coach; for if we walk to church in this trim, the very children in the parish will hoot after us.' 'Indeed,' replied my wife,

'I always imagined that my Charles was fond of seeing his children neat and handsome about him.' 'You may be as neat as you please', interrupted I, 'and I shall love you the better for it; but all this is not neatness, but frippery. These rufflings, and pinkings, and patchings, will only make us hated by all the wives of our neighbours. No, my children', continued I, more gravely, 'those gowns may be altered into something of a plainer cut; for finery is very unbecoming in us, who want the means of decency. I do not know whether such flouncing and shredding is becoming even in the rich, if we consider, upon a moderate calculation, that the nakedness of the indigent world may be clothed from the trimmings of the vain.'

This remonstrance had the proper effect: they went with great composure, that very instant, to change their dress; and the next day I had the satisfaction of finding my daughters, at their own request, employed in cutting up their trains into Sunday waistcoats for Dick and Bill, the two little ones; and what was still more satisfactory, the gowns seemed improved by this curtailing.

Oliver Goldsmith, *The Vicar of Wakefield*[5]

With his usual eye for a rural idyll, Wordsworth portrays a more harmonious clerical family. The 'Wanderer' enjoys his visit to a country parsonage: but perhaps he is not very tactful in making so much of the wife's faded appearance.

But lo! Where from the rocky garden-mount
Crowned by its antique summer-house, descends
Light as the silver fawn, a radiant Girl;
For she hath recognised her honoured friend,
The Wanderer ever welcome! A prompt kiss
The gladsome child bestows at his request
And, up the flowery lawn as we advance,
Hangs on the old Man with a happy look,
And with a pretty restless hand of love.
We enter – by the Lady of the Place
Cordially greeted. Graceful was her port;
A lofty stature undepresed by time,
Whose visitation had not wholly spared

The finer lineaments of form and face,
To that complexion brought which prudence trusts in
And wisdom loves. But when a stately ship
Sails in smooth weather by the placid coast
On homeward voyage – what if wind and wave
And hardship undergone in various climes,
Have caused her to abate the virgin pride,
And that full trim of inexperienced hope
With which she left her haven – not for this
Should the sun strike her, and the impartial breeze
Play on her streamers, fails she to assume
Brightness and touching beauty own,
That charm all eyes. So bright, so fair, appeared
This goodly Matron, shining in the beams
Of unexpected pleasure. Soon the board
Was spread, and we partook a plain repast.

William Wordsworth, *The Excursion*[6]

When parish livings were in the hands of a particular family, there could be tensions with blood relations as well as domestic difficulties. Nor was a younger son of the family always blessed with a true vocation to holy orders. Bute Crawley and his wife are not on the best of terms with his brother, the local squire and landlord.

The Reverend Bute Crawley was a tall, stately, jolly, shovel-hatted man, far more popular in his county than the Baronet his brother. At college he pulled stroke-oar in the Christchurch boat, and had thrashed all the best bruisers of the 'town'. He carried his taste for boxing and athletic exercises into private life; there was not a fight within twenty miles at which he was not present, nor a race, nor a coursing match, nor a regatta, nor a ball, nor an election, nor a visitation dinner, nor indeed a good dinner in the whole county, but he found means to attend it. You might see his bay-mare and gig-lamps a score of miles away from his Rectory House, whenever there was any dinner-party at Fuddleston, or at Roxby, or at Wapshot Hall, or at the great lords of the county, with all of whom he was intimate. He had a fine voice; sang 'A southerly wind and a cloudy sky'; and gave the 'whoop' in chorus with general applause.

He rode to hounds in a pepper-and-salt frock, and was one of the best fishermen in the county.

Mrs Crawley, the rector's wife, was a smart little body, who wrote this worthy divine's sermons. Being of a domestic turn, and keeping the house a great deal with her daughters, she ruled absolutely within the rectory, wisely giving her husband full liberty without. He was welcome to come and go, and dine abroad as many days as his fancy dictated, for Mrs Crawley was a saving woman and knew the price of port wine. Ever since Mrs Bute carried off the young Rector of Queen's Crawley (she was of a good family, daughter of the late Lieutenant-Colonel Hector MacTavish, and she and her mother played for Bute and won him at Harrowgate), she had been a prudent and thrifty wife to him. In spite of her care, however, he was always in debt. It took him at least ten years to pay off his college bills contracted during his father's lifetime. In the year 179–, when he was just clear of these incumbrances, he gave the odds of 100 to 1 (in twenties) against Kangaroo, who won the Derby. The Rector was obliged to take up the money at a ruinous interest, and had been struggling ever since. His sister helped him with a hundred now and then, but of course his great hope was in her death – when 'hang it' (as he would say), 'Matilda *must* leave me half her money'.

So that the Baronet and his brother had every reason which two brothers possibly can have for being by the ears. Sir Pitt had had the better of Bute in innumerable family transactions. Young Pitt not only did not hunt, but set up a meeting-house under his uncle's very nose. Rawdon, it was known, was to come in for the bulk of Miss Crawley's property. These money transactions – these speculations in life and death – these silent battles – for reversionary spoil – make brothers very loving towards each other in Vanity Fair. I, for my part, have known a five-pound note to interpose and knock up a half century's attachment between two brethren; and can't but admire, as I think what a fine and durable thing Love is among worldly people.

W. M. Thackeray, *Vanity Fair*[7]

The popular image of the oppressive Victorian family is countered by this charming picture of the home life of Charles Kingsley. A vigorous controversialist and champion of many causes, he seems to have been a model of love and gentleness as a family man. Here we see the author of The Water

Babies *rather than the man whose attack provoked Newman to write his* Apologia Pro Vita Sua.

To see him at his best and highest was to see him in his home – to see 'the tender, adoring husband, so gentle and so strong' – the father who treated his daughters like princesses, his sons as trusted companions, his servants as friends, those faithful servants who thought no labour heavy to give him ease and comfort, and who, when they followed their be-loved master to the grave, had lived half a life-time in his service. It was truly said of him, that in 'that inner circle all men knew that he was to his children and servants a yet "finer gentleman", to use the grand old English word he loved to use, than he was in the finest circles'. 'Pitiful and courteous' – he carried out this apostolic precept in his home; and however difficult life might be to himself, his daily care was to make it easy to those around him. Like a brave man as he was, he kept his feelings of depression, and those dark hours of wrestling with doubt and dis-appointment and anxiety, which must come to every thinking, feeling human being, within the sanctuary of his own heart, unveiled only to one on earth, and to his Father in Heaven. And when he came out of his study in the morning, and met his children and guests at breakfast, he would greet them with bright courtesy and that cheerful disengaged temper acquired by strict self-discipline, which enabled him to enter into all their interests, and the joy and playfulness of the moment. The family gatherings were the brightest hours in the day, lit up as they were with his marvellous humour. Bright – not only because of the joy his great heart took in his nearest and dearest – but bright on the Bible principle – that 'a merry heart is a continual feast', and sunshine neces-sary to the development and actual health and growth of all things, especially the young. 'I wonder', he would say, 'if there is so much laugh-ing in any other home in England as in ours.' He became a light-hearted boy once more in the presence of his children, and still more remarkably so in that of his aged mother, when he saw her face clouded with depres-sion during her later years, which were spent under his roof. He brought sunshine into her room whenever he entered it, as well as the strong spiritual consolation which she needed, and received in his daily minis-trations by her bedside morning and evening.

Charles Kingsley: His Letters and Memories of his Life[8]

The wives of difficult clergy – perhaps like the wives of difficult husbands in other professions – sometimes took the easy way of acquiescence and lived with their own thoughts. The wife of the Revd Theobald Pontifex, a veritable tyrant in his own household, is one such.

Yet I imagine that Christina was on the whole happier than her husband. She had not to go and visit sick parishioners, and the management of her house and the keeping of her accounts afforded as much occupation as she desired. Her principal duty was, as she well said, to her husband – to love him, honour him, and keep him in a good temper. To do her justice she fulfilled this duty to the uttermost of her power. It would have been better perhaps if she had not so frequently assured her husband that he was the best and wisest of mankind, for no one in his little world ever dreamed of telling him anything else, and it was not long before he ceased to have any doubt upon the matter. As for his temper, which had become very violent at times, she took care to humour it on the slightest sign of an approaching outbreak. She had early found that this was much the easiest plan. The thunder was seldom for herself. Long before her marriage even she had studied his little ways, and knew how to add fuel to the fire as long as the fire seemed to want it, and then to damp it judiciously down, making as little smoke as possible. In money matters she was scrupulousness itself.

Samuel Butler, *The Way of All Flesh*[9]

Mrs Proudie, wife of the Bishop of Barchester, is probably the most famous clerical wife in literature, a byword for the domineering and interfering type. Trollope describes her with his usual ironical reserve.

It is not my intention to breathe a word against the character of Mrs Proudie, but still I cannot think that with all her virtues she adds much to her husband's happiness. The truth is that in matters domestic she rules supreme over her titular lord, and rules with a rod of iron. Nor is this all. Things domestic Dr Proudie might have abandoned to her, if not voluntarily, yet willingly. But Mrs Proudie is not satisfied with such home dominion, and stretches her power over all his movements, and will not even abstain from things spiritual. In fact, the bishop is henpecked ...

This lady is habitually authoritative to all, but to her poor husband she is despotic. Successful as has been his career in the eyes of the world, it would seem that in the eyes of his wife he is never right. All hope of defending himself has long passed from him; indeed he rarely even attempts self-justification; and is aware that submission produces the nearest approach to peace which his own house can ever attain.

Mrs Proudie has not been able to sit at the boards and committees to which her husband has been called by the state; nor, as he often reflects, can she make her voice heard in the House of Lords. It may be that she will refuse to him permission to attend to this branch of a bishop's duties; it may be that she will insist on his close attendance to his own closet. He has never whispered a word on the subject to living ears, but he has already made his fixed resolve. Should such an attempt be made he will rebel. Dogs have turned against their masters, and even Neapolitans against their rulers, when oppression has been too severe. And Dr Proudie feels within himself that if the cord be drawn too tight, he also can muster courage and resist.

[But to supplement this description, we must see Mrs Proudie in action. At her reception, Mr Slope has fallen for the charm of the disabled daughter of one of the canons. Joseph Grimaldi (1779–1837) was the most famous clown of his day.]

When she reached the room above, she found it absolutely deserted, except by the guilty pair. The signora was sitting very comfortably up to her supper, and Mr Slope was leaning over her and administering to her wants. They had been discussing the merits of Sabbath-day schools, and the lady had suggested that as she could not possibly go to the children, she might be indulged in the wish of her heart by having the children brought to her.

'And when shall it be, Mr Slope?' said she.

Mr Slope was saved the necessity of committing himself to a promise by the entry of Mrs Proudie. She swept close up to the sofa so as to confront the guilty pair, stared full at them for a moment, and then said as she passed on to the next room, 'Mr Slope, his lordship is especially desirous of your attendance below; you will greatly oblige me if you will join him.' And so she stalked on.

Mr Slope muttered something in reply, and prepared to go downstairs. As for the bishop's wanting him, he knew his lady patroness well enough to take that assertion at what it was worth; but he did not wish to make himself the hero of a scene, or to become conspicuous for more gallantry than the occasion required.

'Is she always like this?' said the signora.

'Yes – always – madam,' said Mrs Proudie, returning; 'always the same – always equally adverse to impropriety of conduct of every description;' and she stalked back through the room again, following Mr Slope out of the door.

The signora couldn't follow her, or she certainly would have done so. But she laughed loud, and sent the sound of it ringing through the lobby and down the stairs after Mrs Proudie's feet. Had she been as active as Grimaldi she could probably have taken no better revenge.

'Mr Slope,' said Mrs Proudie, catching the delinquent at the door, 'I am surprised that you should leave my company to attend on such a painted Jezebel as that.'

'But – she's lame, Mrs Proudie, and cannot move. Somebody must have waited upon her.'

'Lame,' said Mrs Proudie; 'I'd lame her if she belonged to me. What business had she here at all? – such impertinence – such affectation.'

In the hall and adjacent rooms all manner of cloaking and shawling was going on, and the Barchester folk were getting themselves gone. Mrs Proudie did her best to smirk at each and every one, as they made their adieux, but she was hardly successful. Her temper had been tried fearfully.

Anthony Trollope, *Barchester Towers*[10]

Not all clergy wives were, or are, like Mrs Proudie. Mrs Walton has lost her own child and is kind to a little girl visiting the parsonage. Perhaps both characters are a little too good to be credible, but the description is sympathetic.

For a moment a slight pang of envy crossed Amy's mind, as her cousins' grandeur was contrasted with her own insignificance; but it was soon forgotten when she found herself seated, as usual, on a low stool by the side of Mrs Walton, who, with one hand placed upon hers, and the other fondly smoothing her dark hair, heard with real pleasure her description of all she had been doing since her last visit and, as Amy became more and more animated, the old rector himself was attracted to the window, and for a few moments, while watching the bright eyes and sweet smile of his young favourite, could almost have imagined he was again listening to the voice of his own child. Mrs Walton was several years younger than her husband, but rheumatic attacks of a very painful kind had rendered her nearly helpless, so that the difference between them appeared much less than it really was. Age and infirmity had subdued her naturally quick, eager disposition, into a calm and almost heavenly peace, without in the least diminishing her interest in everything that was passing around her. Her mind, like her dress, seemed to be totally different from that of the everyday world; the dress was fashioned according to the custom of years gone by; the mind, of those which were to come; and few could converse with her without feelings of respect, almost amounting to awe, for her goodness, her patience, her meekness, her charity, her abstraction from all earthly cares. Amy could not as yet fully appreciate all her excellence, though she could understand it in some degree. She had never heard Mrs Walton spoken of but with reverence; and, perhaps, half the pleasure she felt in talking so freely to her arose from the consciousness of being petted and loved by one to whom persons so much older than herself agreed in looking up. There was an additional reason for Amy's enjoyment on this evening; she had, willingly – and unknown to her mother – resolved to give up her favourite volume of fairy tales, that she might go on with the frock for Susan Reynolds and even before the tea-things were brought in, she produced her basket, and began working industriously; and from having thus denied her own inclination in one instance, everything else appeared doubly delightful.

Elizabeth Sewell, *Amy Herbert*[11]

Accounts of clergy wives have mostly been written by men, with emphasis on the husband's position. Here is a different view, from one of the most perceptive women novelists. Dorothea, carried away by idealism and hero-worship, has married Casaubon, a middle-aged priest, dry and lacking in emotion, who can afford to leave most of his work to a curate and concentrate on his research. He is trying to write a 'Key to All Mythologies' and once admits that 'I live too much with the dead'. On her honeymoon in Rome, Dorothea is alone while Casaubon is out pursuing his own interests.

There is a reference to Richard Hooker whose marital problems are described above (p. 137).

How was it that in the weeks since her marriage, Dorothea had not distinctly observed but felt with a stifling depression, that the large vistas and wide fresh air which she had dreamed of finding in her husband's mind were replaced by ante-rooms and winding passages which seemed to lead nowhither? I suppose it was that in courtship everything is regarded as provisional and preliminary, and the smallest sample of virtue or accomplishment is taken to guarantee delightful stores which the broad leisure of marriage will reveal. But the door-sill of marriage once crossed, expectation is concentrated on the present. Having once embarked on your marital voyage, it is impossible not to be aware that you make no way and that the sea is not within sight – that, in fact, you are exploring an enclosed basin.

In their conversation before marriage, Mr Casaubon had often dwelt on some explanation or questionable detail of which Dorothea did not see the bearing; but such imperfect coherence seemed due to the brokenness of their intercourse, and, supported by her faith in their future, she had listened with fervid patience to a recitation of possible arguments to be brought against Mr Casaubon's entirely new view of the Philistine god Dagon and other fish-deities, thinking that hereafter she should see this subject which touched him so nearly from the same high ground whence doubtless it had become so important to him. Again, the matter-of-course statement and tone of dismissal with which he treated what to her were the most stirring thoughts, was easily accounted for as belonging to the sense of haste and preoccupation in which she herself shared during their engagement. But now, since they had been in Rome, with all the depths of her emotion roused to tumultuous activity, and with life made a new problem by new elements, she had been becoming more and more aware, with a certain terror, that her mind was continually sliding into inward fits of anger or repulsion, or else into forlorn weariness. How far the judicious Hooker or any other hero of erudition would have been the same at Mr Casaubon's time of life, she had no means of knowing, so that he could not have the advantage of comparison; but her husband's way of commenting on the strangely impressive objects around them had begun to affect her with a sort of mental shiver: he had perhaps the best intention of acquitting himself worthily, but only of acquitting himself. What was fresh to her mind was worn out to his; and such capacity of thought and feeling as had ever been stimulated in him by the general life of mankind had long shrunk to a sort of dried preparation, a lifeless embalmment of knowledge.

George Eliot, *Middlemarch*[12]

Mrs Proudie might terrorize a diocese, but there were also wives who effectively took over the running of their husband's parish. Edward Underwood was the senior curate in a parish where he had been happy until circumstances changed.

In the first pleasure of a strong, active, and enterprising man, at finding his plans unopposed by authority, Mr Underwood had been delighted with his rector's ready consent to whatever he undertook, and was the last person to perceive that Mr Bevan, though objecting to nothing, let all the rough and tough work lapse upon his curates, and took nothing but the graceful representative part. Even then, Mr Underwood had something to say in his defence. Mr Bevan was valetudinarian in his habits and besides – he was in the midst of a courtship – after his marriage he would give his mind to his parish. For Mr Bevan, hitherto a confirmed and rather precise and luxurious bachelor, to the general surprise, married a certain Lady Price, the young widow of an old admiral, and with her began a new *régime*.

My Lady, as every one called her, since she retained her title and name, was by no means desirous of altering the ornamental arrangements in church, which she regarded with pride; but she was doubly anxious to guard her husband's health, and she also had the sharpest eye to the main chance. Hitherto, whatever had been the disappointments and shortcomings at the Rectory, there had been free-handed expenditure, and no stint either in charity or the expenses connected with the service; but Lady Price had no notion of taking on her uncalled-for outlay. The parish must do its part, and it was called on to do so in modes that did not add to the Rector's popularity. Moreover, the arrangements were on the principle of getting as much as possible out of everybody, and no official failed to feel the pinch. The Rector was as bland, gentle, and obliging as ever; but he seldom transacted any affairs that he could help; and in the six years that had elapsed since the marriage, every person connected with the church had changed, except Mr Underwood.

Yet, perhaps, as senior curate, he had felt the alteration most heavily. He had to be, or to refuse to be, my Lady's instrument in her various appeals; he came in for her indignation at wastefulness, and at the un-authorised demands on the Rector; he had to feel what it was to have no longer unlimited resources of broth and wine to fall back upon at the Rectory; he had to supply the shortcomings of the new staff brought in on lower terms – and all this, moreover, when his own health and vigour were beginning to fail.

Lady Price did not like him or his family. They were poor, and she distrusted the poor; and what was worse, she knew they were better born and better bred than herself and had higher aims. Gentle Mrs Under-wood, absorbed in household cares, no more thought of rivalry with her than with the Queen; but the soft movement, the low voice, the quiet sweep of the worn garments, were a constant vexation to my Lady, who having once pronounced the curate's wife affected, held to her opinion. With Mr Underwood she had had a fight or two, and had not conquered, and now they were on terms of perfect respect and civility on his side, and of distance and politeness on hers. She might talk of him half con-temptuously, but she never durst show herself otherwise than civil, though she was always longing to bring in some more deferential person in his place; and, whenever illness interfered with his duties, she spoke largely to her friends of the impropriety of a man's undertaking what he could not perform.

Charlotte M. Yonge, *The Pillars of the House*[13]

This highly idealized view of the clerical family in the nineteenth century may bring an ironical laugh from present-day parish clergy and their wives. The modern 'rustic hoydens' would probably react with language that would have deeply shocked the author.

Of the influence of the prosperous clerical home on the rural parish in which it is situated it would be difficult to speak with excessive praise. Much is often said of the good effects wrought by the personal character and exertions of the country rector who, in the customary absence of the territorial magnates of his district, discharges the functions of a benevolent squire, no less than the duties of a spiritual adviser, to the peasantry of his parish; but though I cordially concur in the praise universally bestowed by intelligent laymen on the zeal, efficiency, and beneficial labours of our country clergy, I am disposed to regard the influence of the average clerical household as scarcely less conducive to our national health than the influence of the average pastor. In the purely agricultural parish, in which there are no resident gentry outside the rectory garden, the clerical home is often the one social power which softens the manners, elevates the minds, and mitigates the distresses, of a rude and indigent community. From its kitchen, timely aid flows to the sick villagers who would, but for its Christian care, be left altogether to the harsh and unfeeling ministrations of the poor law. Its inmates are the comforters of the aged, and the voluntary instructors of the infantile population. Of incalculable value also is the clerical home as a school of manners to the offspring of petty farmers and small tradesmen, of ignorant artisans and boorish labourers. The pleasant arts, the graceful courtesies, the dress and refined ways of the ladies of the parsonage are imitated – always awkwardly, sometimes with touches of grotesque exaggeration – by the women of the lowly households that look to their 'betters' for guidance on matters of decorum and taste, no less than on matters of opinion and duty. Sometimes the young ladies of a rectory in a wild and primitive district are heard to speak disapprovingly, and even with irritation, of the quickness with which their new fashions of toilet and diversion are parodied rather than copied by their humble imitators in the village street, and the kitchens of adjacent farmsteads. But instead of wishing to repress this imitative habit, they should regard its results as gratifying proofs and significant demonstrations of their influence upon their humble neighbours. The rustic hoydens and serving-girls who copy their parson's young ladies in such matters as crinolines and bonnets, ribbons and hair-stuffers, strive also to imitate their gentle voices and winning modes of address, their reverential demeanour in church and good humour to the world.

J. C. Jeafferson, *A Book about the Clergy*[14]

Barbara Pym, a novelist who combined humorous observation with sympathetic insight into the lives of the clergy, describes what must be one of the most stressful events for an incumbent's wife: a visit from his predecessor, especially one who seems to have gone on to higher things. Jane Cleveland, an intelligent but not very well-organized vicar's wife, has been unexpectedly entertaining the previous couple. After some difficult conversation, they take their leave.

There was a pause and the Canon stood up. 'Well, my dear,' he turned to his wife. 'I think we shall have to be on our way.'

'We are to have luncheon with the Bishop,' Mrs Pritchard explained. 'We left the motor outside.'

Going out to luncheon and in a motor, thought Jane, seeing a high Edwardian electric brougham and Mrs Pritchard in a dust-coat and veiled motoring cap. But well-bred people talked like this even to-day, Jane believed. She hoped they would get a good meal at the Palace, but was prudent enough not to make any enquiries.

In the hall Canon Pritchard paused and held out his hands with a vague gesture. Jane thought for one wild moment that he was attempting to give her some kind of a blessing, but it appeared that he wanted to wash.

'Yes, of course,' said Jane, showing him into the little cloak-room. 'I wonder if there is a clean towel?' she added, knowing that there could not possibly be one.

'Yes, thank you, there is,' Canon Pritchard called out. Jane supposed that Mrs Glaze must have put one there when she heard them arrive, and she now realised that had they been able to stay to lunch an adequate meal would have been provided. Mrs Pritchard would have been able to say, 'We drove over to the Clevelands in the motor and stayed to luncheon.'

Mrs Pritchard did not appear to want to wash. No doubt the Palace offered better amenities, Jane decided, as they stood rather uncertainly in the hall.

'You must come over to luncheon one day,' Mrs Pritchard observed, 'and bring your husband.'

'Thank you. We should like to very much,' Jane said.

Canon Pritchard came out of the cloakroom and the three of them went out to the motor, which was not of an Edwardian type, rather to Jane's disappointment.

Barbara Pym, Jane and Prudence[15]

The clerical family is usually imagined as a clergyman in the company of his wife and children. But it may be the parental generation which gives domestic support. The Revd Septimus Crisparkle, an amiable Canon of the imaginary Cloisterham Cathedral (based on Rochester in Kent), lives happily with his mother. She still regards him as in need of motherly care and tries to look after his mental and physical health. When he seems troubled, she offers him a glass of wine and a biscuit from her splendid store-cupboard – but she has another cupboard too, which Dickens describes with his customary exuberant detail.

The Reverend Septimus yielded himself up quite as willing a victim to a nauseous medicinal herb-closet [...] To what amazing infusions of gentian, peppermint, gilliflower, sage, parsley, thyme, rue, rosemary, and dandelion, did his courageous stomach submit itself! In what wonderful wrappers, enclosing layers of dried leaves, would he swathe his rosy and contented face, if his mother suspected him of a toothache! What botanical blotches would he cheerfully stick upon his cheek, or forehead, if the dear old lady convicted him of an imperceptible pimple there! Into this herbaceous penitentiary, situated on an upper staircase landing: a low and narrow whitewashed cell, where bunches of dried leaves hung from rusty hooks in the ceiling, and were spread out upon shelves, in company with portentous bottles: would the Reverend Septimus submissively be led, like the highly popular lamb who has so long and unresistingly been led to the slaughter, and there would he, unlike that lamb, bore nobody but himself. Not even doing that much, so that the old lady were busy and pleased, he would quietly swallow what was given him, merely taking a corrective dip of hands and face into the great bowl of dried rose-leaves, and into the other great bowl of dried lavender, and then would go out, as confident in the sweetening powers of Cloisterham Weir and a wholesome mind, as Lady Macbeth was hopeless of those of all the seas that roll.

In the present instance the good Minor Canon took his glass of Constantia with an excellent grace, and, so supported to his mother's satisfaction, applied himself to the remaining duties of the day. In their orderly and punctual progress they brought round Vesper service and twilight.

Charles Dickens, *The Mystery of Edwin Drood*[16]

Chapter 9

Factious, Peevish and Perverse

The Victorian age is generally regarded, with some truth, as a period of piety and faith. Despite the growth of agnosticism, arising from various causes, it was certainly one in which Christianity was a firm background to much of the thought and writing. But faith was marred by internal controversies between the churches and within them. Although Roman Catholics were freed from civil disabilities in 1829, the restoration of the English hierarchy in 1850 brought a new wave of hostility. The Oxford Movement, reaffirming the catholic continuity of the Church of England, roused suspicions of concealed Romanism. In the next generation, the successors of the Movement introduced advanced ceremonial into Anglican services and revived the practice of private confession: the result was, in extreme cases, legal persecution and judicial punishment. All these and other matters were given an outlet by the growth of book production and particularly the novel. Books were written to attack or to defend every imaginable religious position: the 'church novel' became a recognized sub-genre, attracting many minor writers as well as a few leading ones like Anthony Trollope and Charlotte M. Yonge. Passages in other chapters show that there was often love and harmony as well, but some of the more acerbic disputes have their own fascination today. We may give thanks that the present time, with all its traumas and troubles, has discovered the importance of ecumenical co-operation and mutual respect.

Even before Queen Victoria came to the throne, some people thought that the Church was not as it had been, and regretted the greater learning, earnestness and attention to ecclesiastical detail of the new clergy. Mary Russell Mitford set her objections in the fictional town of 'Belford Regis', based on Reading, in Berkshire. Parson Adams is the amiable and innocent clergyman in Henry Fielding's novel Joseph Andrews *whom we have already met (p. 74).*

Of late years, there has been a prodigious change in the body clerical. The activity of the dissenters, the spread of education, and the immense increase of population, to say nothing of that 'word of power', Reform, have combined to produce a stirring spirit of emulation amongst the younger clergy, which has quite changed the aspect of the profession. Heretofore, the 'church militant' was the quietest and easiest of all vocations; and the most slender and ladylike young gentleman, the 'mamma's darling' of a great family, whose lungs were too tender for the bar, and whose frame was too delicate for the army, might be sent with perfect comfort to the snug curacy of a neighbouring parish, to read Horace, cultivate auriculas, christen, marry, and bury, about twice a quarter, and do duty once every Sunday. Now times are altered; prayers must be read and sermons preached twice a day at least, not forgetting lectures in Lent, and homilies at tide times; workhouses are to be visited; schools attended, boys and girls taught in the morning, and grown-up bumpkins in the evening; children are to be catechized; masters and mistresses looked after; hymn-books distributed; bibles given away; tract societies fostered amongst the zealous, and psalmody cultivated amongst the musical. In short, a curate, nowadays, even a country curate, much more if his parish lie in a great town, has need of the lungs of a barrister in good practice, and the strength and activity of an officer of dragoons.

Now this is just as it ought to be. Nevertheless, I cannot help entertaining certain relentings in favour of the well-endowed churchman of the old school, round, indolent and rubicund, at peace with himself and with all around him, who lives in quiet and plenty in his ample parsonage-house, dispensing with a liberal hand the superfluities of his hospitable table, regular and exact in his conduct, but not so precise as to refuse a Saturday night's rubber in his own person, or to condemn his parishioners for their game of cricket on Sunday afternoons; charitable in word and deed, tolerant, indulgent, to the widest extent of that widest word; but, except in such wisdom (and it is of the best), no wiser than that eminent member of the church, Parson Adams.

M. R. Mitford, *Belford Regis*[1]

*Roman Catholics gained freedom from civil disabilities in 1829, but sus-
picion and hostility against them remained strong for many years, aggra-
vated for some by the restoration of the hierarchy in 1850. Charles Kingsley,
for all his admirable qualities, was excessively bigoted in this respect.
He gives a brief picture of a suave and ingratiating priest, probably based on
Newman, who had entered the Roman Catholic Church in 1845. Lancelot
has come to him seeking news of his cousin Luke who has taken the same
step. Despite the outward courtesy of exchange, Kingsley's quotation marks
around 'conversion' and 'Father' are revealing authorial comment.*

At last, in despair of obtaining tidings of his cousin by any other method,
Lancelot made up his mind to apply to a certain remarkable man, whose
'conversion' had preceded Luke's by about a year, and had, indeed,
mainly caused it.

He went, and was not disappointed. With the most winning courtesy
and sweetness, his story and his request were patiently listened to.

'The outcome of your speech, then, my dear sir, as I apprehend it, is a
request to me to send back the fugitive lamb into the jaws of the well-
meaning, but still lupine wolf?'

This was spoken with so sweet and arch a smile, that it was impossible
to be angry.

'On my honour, I have no wish to convert him. All I want is to have
human speech of him – to hear from his own lips that he is content.
Whither should I covert him? Not to my own platform – for I am
nowhere. Not to that which he has left, for if he could have found standing ground there, he would not have gone elsewhere for rest.'

'Therefore they went out from you, because they were not of you,' said
the 'Father', half aside.

'Most true, sir. I have felt long that argument was useless with those
whose root-ideas of Deity, man, earth and heaven, were as utterly different from my own, as if we had been created by two different beings.'

'Do you include in that catalogue those ideas of truth, love, and
justice, which are Deity itself? Have you no common ground in them?'

'You are an older and a better man than I. It would be insolent in me
to answer that question, except in one way … and –'

'In that you cannot answer it. Be it so. You shall see your cousin. You
may make what efforts you will for his re-conversion. The Catholic
Church,' continued he, with one of his arch, deep-meaning smiles, 'is

not like Popular Protestantism, driven into shrieking terror at the
approach of a foe. She has too much faith in herself, and in Him who
gives to her the power of truth, to expect every gay meadow to allure
away her lambs from the fold' …

[*Afterwards Lancelot thinks, with a rather odd anatomical metaphor:*]
'What a man! Or rather, the wreck of what a man! Oh for such a heart,
with the thews and sinews of a truly English brain!'

Charles Kingsley, Yeast[2]

*The writings of Dickens are full of pious sentiments, but also rich in
criticisms of institutional religion. He was particularly hard on the many
dissenting groups of his time, though, not wishing to offend the reading
public, he seldom specified any one of them. Here, after a satirical view of a
dry, formal service in an Anglican church, he turns to an even more savage
attack on a Nonconformist chapel.*

Enter a less orthodox place of religious worship and observe the contrast. A small close chapel with a whitewashed wall, and plain deal pews
and pulpit, contains a close-packed congregation, as different in dress as
they are opposed in manner, to that we have just quitted. The hymn is
sung – not by paid singers, but by the whole assembly at the loudest pitch
of their voices, unaccompanied by any musical instrument, the words
being given out, two lines at a time, by the clerk. There is something in
the sonorous quavering of the harsh voices, in the lank and hollow faces
of the men, and the sour solemnity of the women, which bespeaks this a
stronghold of intolerant zeal and ignorant enthusiasm. The preacher
enters the pulpit. He is a coarse, hard-faced man of forbidding aspect,
clad in rusty black, and bearing in his hand a small plain Bible from
which he selects some passage for his text, while the hymn is concluding.
The congregation fall upon their knees, and are hushed into profound
stillness as he delivers an extempore prayer, in which he calls upon the
Sacred Founder of the Christian faith to bless his ministry, in terms of
disgusting and impious familiarity not to be described. He begins his
oration in a drawling tone, and his hearers listen with silent attention.
He grows warmer as he proceeds with his subject, and his gesticulation
becomes proportionately violent. He clenches his fists, beats the book

upon the desk before him, and swings his arms wildly about his head. The congregation murmur their acquiescence in his doctrines: and a short groan occasionally bears testimony to the moving nature of his eloquence. Encouraged by these symptoms of approval, and working himself up to a pitch of enthusiasm amounting almost to frenzy, he denounces sabbath-breakers with the direst vengeance of offended Heaven. He stretches his body half out of the pulpit, thrusts forth his arms with frantic gestures, and blasphemously calls upon the Deity to visit with eternal torments those who turn aside from the word, as interpreted and preached by – himself. A low moaning is heard, the women rock their bodies to and fro, and wring their hands; the preacher's fervour increases, the perspiration starts upon his brow, his face is flushed, and he clenches his hands convulsively, as he draws a hideous and appalling picture of the horrors preparing for the wicked in a future state. A great excitement is visible among his hearers, a scream is heard, and some young girl falls senseless on the floor. There is a momentary rustle, but it is only for a moment – all eyes are turned towards the preacher. He pauses, passes his handkerchief across his face, and looks complacently round. His voice resumes its natural tone, as with mock humility he offers up a thanksgiving for having been successful in his efforts, and having been permitted to rescue one sinner from the path of evil. He sinks back into his seat, exhausted with the violence of his ravings; the girl is removed, a hymn is sung, a petition for some measure for securing the better observance of the Sabbath, which has been prepared by the good man, is read; and his worshipping admirers struggle who shall be the first to sign it.

Charles Dickens, *Reprinted Pieces*[3]

The first years of the Oxford Movement were followed by a growth of more Catholic belief and practice in the Church of England. The 'Puseyites', named after E. B. Pusey who succeeded Newman as head of the movement, were disliked by Anglicans of a lower persuasion. A satirical portrait of an advanced Puseyite priest picks out several of the features which most annoyed their opponents, in their conduct of worship, language and sartorial appearance. The MB coat and waistcoat were the long, buttoned garments favoured by them. It stood for 'Mark of the Beast', said to be derived from the notes of a sardonic clerical tailor. We have read how Mr Slope abhorred 'a full-breasted black silk waistcoat' (p. 32).

Who does not recognise, when he meets them in the railway or the street, the clipped shirt-collar, the stiff and tie-less neckcloth, the M.B. coat and cassock waistcoat, the cropped hair and unwhiskered cheek? Who does not know that the wearer of this costume will talk of 'the Holy Altar', and 'the Blessed Virgin,' 'Saint Ignatius Loyola,' and 'Saint Alphonso de Liguori'? And that he will date his letters on 'the eve of St Chad,' or 'the Morrow of St Martin?' Who has not seen the youthful Presbyter bowing to the altar, and turning his back on the people? Who has not heard him intoning the prayers, and preaching in his surplice on the 'holy obedience,' due from laity to priesthood? Who is ignorant that he reads the offertory after his sermon, and sends round little bags at the end of long poles, which are thrust in the faces of the worshippers to extort their contributions? Who has not noticed the gaudy furniture of his church, the tippeted altar, the candles blazing at noon-day, the wreaths of flowers changing their colour with feast or fast, the medieval emblems embroidered on the altar-cloth?

W. J. Conybeare, 'Church Parties'[4]

A novelist who had little time for any of the churches aims his deadly satire against a Puseyite priest. Ernest Pontifex is the son of strict Evangelical parents (we met his mother on p. 145), newly ordained to a London parish. The title 'Senior Curate' is not often heard today when curates are few, but it was important in the Victorian church hierarchy.

His rector was a moderate High Churchman of no very pronounced views – an elderly man who had had too many curates not to have long since found out that the connection between rector and curate, like that between employer and employed in every other walk of life, was a mere matter of business. He had now two curates, of whom Ernest was the junior; the senior curate was named Pryer, and when this gentleman made advances, as he presently did, Ernest in his forlorn state was delighted to meet them.

Pryer was about twenty-eight years old. He had been at Eton and at Oxford. He was tall, and passed generally for good-looking; I only saw him once for about five minutes, and then thought him odious both in manners and appearance. Perhaps it was because he caught me up in a way I did not like. I had quoted Shakespeare for lack of something better to fill up a sentence – and had said that one touch of nature made the whole world kin. 'Ah,' said Pryer, in a bold, brazen way which displeases me, 'but one touch of the unnatural makes it more kindred still,' and he gave me a look as though he thought me an old bore and did not care two straws whether I was shocked or not. Naturally enough, after this I did not like him.

This, however, is anticipating, for it was not till Ernest had been three or four months in London that I happened to meet his fellow-curate, and I must deal here rather with the effect he produced upon my godson than upon myself. Besides being what was generally considered good-looking, he was faultless in his get-up, and altogether the kind of man whom Ernest was sure to be afraid of and be taken in by. The style of his dress was very High Church, and his acquaintances were exclusively of the extreme High Church party, but he kept his views a good deal in the background in his rector's presence, and that gentleman, though he looked askance on some of Pryer's friends, had no such ground of complaint against him as to make him sever the connection. Pryer, too, was popular in the pulpit, and, take him all round, it was probable that many worse curates would he found for one better. When Pryer called on my hero, as soon as the two were alone together, he eyed him all over with a quick penetrating glance and seemed not dissatisfied with the result – for I must say here that Ernest had improved in personal appearance under the more genial treatment he had received at Cambridge. Pryer, in fact, approved of him sufficiently to treat him civilly, and Ernest was immediately won by anyone who did this. It was not long before he discovered that the High Church party, and even Rome itself, had more to say for themselves than he had thought.

[*Ernest soon gets into trouble with Pryer by suggesting that they might follow the example of the evangelists who preached at street meetings. Pryer's response shows Victorian sectarianism at its worst.*]

Ernest broached this to Pryer, who treated it as something too outrageous to be even thought of. Nothing, he said, could more tend to lower the dignity of the clergy and bring the Church into contempt. His manner was brusque, and even rude.

Ernest ventured a little mild dissent; he admitted it was not usual, but something at any rate must be done, and that quickly. This was how Wesley and Whitfield had begun that great movement which had kindled religious life in the minds of hundreds of thousands. This was no time to be standing on dignity. It was just because Wesley and Whitfield had done what the Church would not that they had won men to follow them whom the Church had now lost.

Pryer eyed Ernest searchingly, and after a pause said, 'I don't know what to make of you, Pontifex; you are at once so very right and so very wrong. I agree with you heartily that something should be done, but it must not be done in a way which experience has shown leads to nothing but fanaticism and dissent. Do you approve of these Wesleyans? Do you hold your ordination vows so cheaply as to think that it does not matter whether the services of the Church are performed in her churches and with all due ceremony or not? If you do – then, frankly, you had no business to be ordained; if you do not, then remember that one of the first duties of a young deacon is obedience to authority. Neither the Catholic Church, nor yet the Church of England, allows her clergy to preach in the streets of cities where there is no lack of churches.'

Samuel Butler, *The Way of All Flesh*[5]

The country parson and diarist Francis Kilvert, visiting his old university, Oxford, in May 1876, went to a service at St Barnabas', an advanced Anglo-Catholic church of imposing Byzantine design – the 'ceremonial church of St Silas' in Hardy's Jude the Obscure. *Despite the presence of the good Father Stanton (p. 11), Kilvert's reaction was – in every sense of the word – low.*

The service at St Barnabas was at 8 o'clock, and the evening light was setting behind the lofty Campanile as we entered. The large Church was almost full, the great congregation singing like one man. The clergy and choir entered with a procession, incense bearers and a great gilt cross, the thurifers and acolytes being in short white surplices over scarlet cassocks and the last priest in the procession wearing a biretta and a chasuble stiff with gold. The Magnificat seemed to be the central point in the service and at the words 'For behold from henceforth all generations shall call me blessed' the black biretta and golden chasuble (named Shuttleworth) advanced, was 'censed' by the thurifer, then took the censer from him and censed the cross, the banners, the lights and the altar, till the Church was all in a fume. At least so Mayhew said. I myself could not see exactly what was done though I knew some ceremony was going on. It appeared to me to be pure Mariolatry. Father Stanton took for his text 'He is altogether lovely,' *Canticles* ii. The matter was not original or interesting, and the manner was theatrical and overdone. I should think every eye in that great congregation was quite dry. The text was repeated constantly in a very low die-away tone. The sermon came after the Third Collect. I was disappointed in it and so I think were many more. After the service there was an offertory and a processional hymn, and then round came the procession down the South aisle and up the nave in the following order. First the thurifer in short white surplice and scarlet cassock swinging a chained censer high in the air and bringing it back with a sudden check and violent jerk which brought the incense out in a stifling cloud. Next an acolyte in a similar dress bearing aloft a great gilt cross. Then three banners waving and moving above the heads of the people in a weird strange ghostly march, as the banner-bearers steered them clear of the gaslights. After them came two wand-bearers preceding the clergy, Father Stanton walking in the midst and looking exhausted, the rear of the procession being brought up by the hideous figure of the emaciated ghost in the black biretta and golden chasuble.

As we came out of Church Mayhew said to me, '*Well*, did you ever see such a function as that?' No, I never did and I don't care if I never do again. This was the grand function of the Ascension at St Barnabas, Oxford. The poor humble Roman Church hard by is quite plain, simple and Low Church in its ritual compared with St Barnabas in its festal dress on high days and holidays.

Diary of Francis Kilvert[6]

Samuel Reynolds Hole (1819–1904), Dean of Rochester, was in favour of the principles of the Oxford Movement, but disliked the practices of some of its later followers. His problem with an unfamiliar service-book may find a sympathetic response from clergy today who have met the unexpected when visiting a strange church.

Of course there were in all this, as in all great revivals, notably the Wesleyan, men who have a zeal not according to knowledge, and who insist on transgressing the boundaries marked out by their leader. There are men who rejoice in walking on the rims of rocks, standing on the tip ends of precipices, skating on thin ice, going where they are forbidden to go.

There were, moreover, extravagances of ritual which not only enraged opponents and bewildered simple folks, but estranged the sympathies of many who desired a reverent and beautiful service, but were pained and offended by 'the last new dodge from Rome'.

I went to a high celebration in a London church, and, arriving after the service had commenced, was never able to distinguish one word of it, and only knew by close observation what part of the office we had reached. On another occasion I went to celebrate at the altar of an absent priest, and was actually unable to find the service in a book which was there, full of hieroglyphics and illustrations to me unintelligible. I was wondering whether I could repeat from memory the more important portions, when I saw in the hand of the little server behind me a small twopenny Prayer Book, and this supplied all my need. In my own church, a stranger, officiating in my absence, remained so long bending over the altar that my worthy churchwarden feared that he had some paralytic or apoplectic seizure, and went to his relief.

S. R. Hole, *Memories*[7]

Another admirer of the Tractarians who was annoyed by the later Puseyites was J. H. Shorthouse, a former Quaker who defends the old 'High Church' against the innovators in the person of a fictional priest who influences the narrator's boyhood.

The old-fashioned High Church notions of Mr de Foi led him to the observance of many practices since supposed to be modern innovations, a generation at least before Ritualists, so-called, were heard of. He observed the eastward position at the Holy Communion, he invariably bowed to the altar, and he read morning prayers on Wednesdays, Fridays, and Saints' days in the little church in the chase. The bell was rung to call to these services, but no one was ever known to attend, until one morning, when I was about eight years of age, happening by chance to be in the neighbourhood with my nurse, I insisted upon going in, and, conceiving an intense liking to the ceremony, we never, or rarely, failed to form the entire congregation. After service Mr de Foi generally accompanied us towards the house, and in this way the friendship between the man and the child – the kindly interest on the one hand, and the intense devotion on the other – grew up. It was in these walks, through the beds of fern and bracken, that I began to love him, and even as a child to apprehend the lofty teaching of his Christian Idealism.

J. H. Shorthouse, *Sir Percival*[8]

The Anglo-Catholic influence soon spread to the United States, there to meet both enthusiastic reception and hostile rejection as it had in England. Mrs Potiphar, an American Episcopalian, writes to her friend about the new priest. Her husband is notably less impressed.

I've so many things to tell you that I hardly know where to begin […] I was uncertain for a long time how to have my prayer-book bound. Finally, after thinking about it a great deal, I concluded to have it done in pale blue velvet, with gold clasps, and a gold cross upon the side. To be sure, it's nothing very new. But what is new nowadays? Sally Shrimp has had hers done in emerald, and I know Mrs Croesus will have crimson for hers, and those people who sit next us in church (I wonder who they are; it's very unpleasant to sit next to people you don't know; and, positively, that girl, the dark-haired one with large eyes, carries the same muff she did last year; it's big enough for a family) have a kind of brown morocco binding. I must tell you one reason why I fixed upon the pale blue. You know that aristocratic-looking young man in white cravat and black pantaloons and waistcoat, whom we saw at Saratoga a year ago, and who always had such a beautiful sanctimonious look, and such small white hands; well, he is a minister, as we supposed, 'an unworthy candidate, an unprofitable husband', as he calls himself in that delicious voice of his. He has been quite taken up among us. He has been asked a good deal to dinner, and there was hope of his being settled as colleague to the Doctor, only Mr Potiphar (who can be stubborn, you know) insisted that the Rev. Cream Cheese, though a very good young man, he didn't doubt, was addicted to candlesticks. I suppose that's something awful. But could you believe anything awful of him? I asked Mr Potiphar what he meant by saying such things.

'I mean,' said he, that lie, 'that he's a Puseyite, and I've no idea of being tied to the apron-strings of the Scarlet Woman'.

Dear Caroline, who *is* the Scarlet Woman? Dearest, tell me upon your honour, if you have over heard any scandal of Mr Potiphar.

'What is it about candlesticks?' said I to Mr Potiphar. 'Perhaps Mr Cheese finds gas too bright for his eyes; and that's his misfortune, not his fault.'

'Polly', said Mr Potiphar – who will call me Polly, although it sounds so very vulgar – 'please not to meddle with things you don't understand. You may have Cream Cheese to dinner as much as you choose, but I will not have him in the pulpit of my church.'

The same day, Mr Cheese happened in about lunch-time, and I asked him if his eyes were really weak.

'Not at all,' said he. 'Why do you ask?'

Then I told him that I had heard that he was so fond of candlesticks.

Ah! Caroline, you should have seen him then. He stopped in the midst of pouring out a glass of Mr P.'s best old port, and, holding the decanter in one hand and the glass in the other, he looked so beautifully sad, and said in that sweet low voice:

'Dear Mrs Potiphar, the blood of the martyrs is the seed of the church.' Then he filled up his glass and drank the wine off with such a mournful, resigned air, and wiped his lips so gently with his cambric handkerchief (I saw that it was a hemstitch), that I had no voice to ask him to take a bit of the cold chicken, which he did, however, without my asking him. But when he said in the same low voice, 'A little more breast, dear Mrs Potiphar,' I was obliged to run into the drawing-room for a moment to recover myself.

Well, after he had lunched, I told him that I wished to take his advice upon something connected with the church (for a prayer-book is, you know, dear), and he looked so sweetly at me, that, would you believe it, I almost wished to be a Catholic, and to confess three or four times a week, and to have him for my confessor. But it's very wicked to wish to be a Catholic, and it wasn't real much, you know: but somehow I thought so. When I asked him in what velvet he would advise me to have my prayer-book bound, he talked beautifully for about twenty minutes. I wish you could have heard him. I'm not sure that I understood much of what he said – how should I? – but it was very beautiful. Don't laugh, Carrie, but there was one thing I did understand, and which, as it came pretty often, quite helped me through: it was, 'Dear Mrs Potiphar'; you can't tell how nicely he says it. He began by telling me that it was very important to consider all the details and little things about the church. He said they were all timbales or cymbals – or something of that kind; and then he talked very prettily about that stole, and the violet and scarlet capes of the cardinals and purple chasubles, and the lace edge of the Pope's little short gown.

George William Curtis, 'Rev. Cream Cheese and the New Livery'[9]

While some fulminated against what seemed to be 'Romish' practices in the Church of England, others were acerbic about extremely 'Low' churchmanship. George Russell looks back without pleasure from his later Anglo-Catholic position at the clergy of the parish church when he was young. Benjamin Jowett (1817–93), Master of Balliol College, Oxford, was distrusted in some quarters for his article in Essays and Reviews, *the controversial volume of liberal theology published in 1860.*

Our clerical staff consisted of the incumbent (who became a 'Vicar' by Act of Parliament in 1868) and a curate. Our list of services was as follows: Sunday – 11 a.m., Morning Prayer, Litany, Table-prayers, and Sermon; 6 p.m., Evening Prayer, and Sermon. There was Evening Prayer with a sermon on Thursdays, and a prayer-meeting in the schoolroom on Tuesday evenings. There were no extra services in Lent or Advent, nor on any Holy Days except Good Friday and Ascension Day. The Holy Communion was administered after Morning Service on the first Sunday of the month, and on Christmas and Easter Days; and after Evening Service on the third Sunday. The black gown was, of course, worn in the pulpit, and I remember a mild sensation caused by the disuse of bands. The prayers were preached; the Psalms were read; and the hymn-book in use was 'The Church and Home Metrical Psalter and Hymnal' – a quaint compilation which I have never seen elsewhere. It would not be easy to describe the dreariness of the services; and the preaching corresponded to them. This is curious, for Evangelical preaching generally was rousing and effective. I remember that we heard preaching of that type from strangers who occasionally 'took duty' or 'pleaded for Societies'; but our own pastors always expatiated on justification by Faith only. I cannot recall any other subject; and, even in enforcing this, 'Pulpit-eloquence', topical allusions, and illustrations whether from nature or from books, were rigidly eschewed. 'As dull as a sermon' is a proverbial saying which for me in early boyhood had an awful truth.

It has been stated in an earlier chapter that I discovered the Sacramental System of the Church by the simple method of studying the Prayer Book. Certainly I got no help in that direction from my spiritual pastors. The incumbent was, I should think, the Lowest Churchman who ever lived. He was a Cambridge man; a thorough gentleman; well-read; wholly devoted to his sacred calling; and fearless in his assertion of what he believed to be right. (He once refused to let Jowett preach in our pulpit, though the noble patron made the request.) He was entirely insensible to poetry, beauty, romance, and enthusiasm; but his mind was essentially logical, and he followed his creed to its extremest consequences. Baptismal grace, of course, he absolutely denied. He prepared me for Confirmation, and he began his preparation by assailing my faith in the Presence and the Succession. He defined Confirmation as 'a coming of age in the things of the soul'. I perfectly remember a sermon preached on 'Sacrament Sunday', which ended with some such words as these, 'I go to yonder table today; not expecting to meet the Lord, because I know He will not be there'. I have seldom heard the doctrine of the Real Absence stated with equal frankness.

G. W. E. Russell, *Fifteen Chapters of Autobiography*[10]

W. H. Mallock, a writer of Anglo-Catholic sympathies, was an undergraduate at Balliol College when Jowett, mentioned by Russell above, was Master. He brings him as the Broad Churchman 'Dr Jenkinson' into an imaginary house-party at which a number of eminent Victorians are present under disguised names. Dr Jenkinson's version of Mattins may be found uncomfortably close to the eclecticism of some present-day liberalism.

Presently a sound was heard. A door opened, and Dr Jenkinson, in his ordinary dress, entered the stalls. He looked deliberately round him for a moment, as though he were taking stock of those present; then, selecting the central stall as a kind of *prie-dieu*, he knelt down facing his congregation, and after a moment's pause began to read the service in a simple, earnest voice. Lady Ambrose, however, though she knew her prayer-book as well as most women, could not for the life of her find the place. The reason was not far to seek. The Doctor was opening the proceedings with the following passage from the Koran, which he had once designed to use in Westminster Abbey as the text of a missionary sermon.

'Be constant in prayer', he began, in a voice tremulous with emotion, 'and give alms: and what good ye have sent before for your souls, ye shall find it with God. Surely God seeth that which ye do. They say, Verily none shall see Paradise except they be Jews or Christians. This is their wish. Say ye, Produce your proof of this if ye speak truth. Nay, but he who resigneth himself to God, and doeth that which is right, he shall have his reward with his Lord; there shall come no fear on them, neither shall they be grieved.'

Dr Jenkinson then went on to the Confession, the Absolution, and a number of other selections from the English morning service, omitting, however, the creed, and concluded the whole with a short prayer of St Francis Xavier's.

W. H. Mallock, *The New Republic*[11]

Some of the smaller Nonconformist churches were powerful in bringing faith and worship to the neglected poor in the industrial towns. The sad aspect was that they could become narrowly exclusive and dependent on the prejudices of the minister. A novelist who knew that world from childhood shows this side of the picture.

The prayer over, Mr Broad rose and said that he was there that night to discharge a most painful duty – one which, if he had taken counsel with flesh and blood, he would most gladly have avoided. But he was a humble servant of their common Lord and Master. It behoved him to cease not to warn every one night and day; to remember that the Holy Ghost had made him an overseer to feed the church of God which He had purchased with His precious blood. He had done nothing in this matter without constant recurrence to the footstool of grace, and he had also consulted with some of his dear brethren in Christ whom he saw near him. They would have observed that Brother Allen and his family had for some time absented themselves from the means of grace. He should have said nothing upon this point if they had joined any other

Christian community. If even they had attended the Established Church, he would have been silent, for he was free to confess that in other religious bodies besides their own God had faithful servants who held fast to the fundamental doctrines of His Book. But it was notorious, alas! that his dear brother had gone NOWHERE! In the face of the apostolic command not to forsake the assembling of themselves together, what could they do but suspect that his dear brother's belief had been undermined – sapped, he would say? But to that point he would return presently. Then again, they were all familiar with the circumstances attending the late political contest in the county. He knew that many of his dear brethren differed one from another concerning matters relating to this world, although they were all, blessed be God, one in Christ, members of His Body. He himself had thought it better to follow, as far as he could, the example of his Lord and Master, to render unto Caesar the things that are Caesar's, and to lead a quiet and peaceable life in all godliness and honesty. He would not for a moment, however, condemn any who differed from him in carnal policy. But his dear Brother Allen and his son had overstepped the line; and, considering this was a mixed church, he was of opinion that they should have acted – what should he say – with more Christian consideration. More than this, Mr George Allen was known to have abetted an unruly mob, a position highly unbecoming, he might say, to one occupying the position of member at Tanner's Lane. But he might, perhaps, be permitted to dwell for a moment on another point. His dear Brother Allen and his son had – there was no doubt of it – consorted with infidels, one of whom had been convicted by the laws of his country – a *convict* – and it was through their instrumentality that his brethren had been led to wander from the fold. This was the secret of the calamity which had overtaken the church. Wolves, he would say – yes, wolves, grievous wolves – had entered in, not sparing the flock.

Mark Rutherford (W. H. White), *The Revolution in Tanner's Lane*[12]

There were more extreme sects in the nineteenth century. We have met Edward Irving as a preacher (p. 81). Newman gave a fictional and unsympathetic portrayal of an Irvingite in a novel which is by no means wholly autobiographical but which draws on his own experience in moving to Rome. Charles Reding, a young Oxford graduate who is taking the same path, is visited by a number of people who try to dissuade him, including the Revd Alexander Highfly. In the Iliad *Glaucus gives his golden armour in exchange for the bronze armour of Diomede, and Highfly claims to be offering a similar exchange of value.*

Mr Highfly was a man of gentlemanlike appearance and manner; his language was refined, and his conduct was delicate; so much so that Charles at once changed his tone in speaking to him. He came to Mr Reding, he said, from a sense of duty; and there was nothing in his conversation to clash with that profession. He explained that he had heard of Mr Reding's being unsettled in his religious views, and he would not lose the opportunity of attempting so valuable an accession to the cause to which he had dedicated himself.

'I see', said Charles, smiling, 'I am in the market.'

'It is the bargain of Glaucus with Diomede', answered Mr Highfly, 'for which I am asking your co-operation. I am giving you the fellowship of Apostles.'

'It is, I recollect, one of the characteristics of your body,' said Charles, 'to have an order of Apostles, in addition to Bishops, Priests, and Deacons.'

'Rather', said his visitor, 'it is the special characteristic; for we acknowledge the orders of the Church of England. We are but completing the Church system by restoring the Apostolic College.'

'What I should complain of,' said Charles, 'were I at all inclined to listen to your claims, would be the very different views which different members of your body put forward.'

'You must recollect, sir,' answered Mr Highfly, 'that we are under Divine teaching, and that truth is but gradually communicated to the Church. We do not pledge ourselves what we shall believe to-morrow by anything we say to-day.'

'Certainly,' answered Reding, 'things have been said to me by your teachers which I must suppose were only private opinions, though they seemed to be more.'

'But I was saying,' said Mr Highfly, 'that at present we are restoring the Gentile Apostolate. The Church of England has Bishops, Priests, and Deacons, but a Scriptural Church has more; it is plain it ought to have Apostles. In Scripture Apostles had the supreme authority, and the three Anglican orders were but subordinate to them.'

'I am disposed to agree with you there,' said Charles. Mr Highfly looked surprised and pleased.

'We are restoring,' he said, 'the Church to a more Scriptural state; perhaps, then, we may reckon on your co-operation in doing so? We do not ask you to secede from the Establishment, but to acknowledge the Apostolic authority to which all ought to submit.'

J. H. Newman, *Loss and Gain*[13]

Edward Irving was the most prominent, and for a time the most successful, proponent of a new sect. There were many others who gathered a smaller following but were a challenge to the other denominations. No clergy appear in person in this conversation, but it reveals the tension between parochial and house churches. The enthusiast Barbara Neville has come to live near the orthodox Lady Olivia. The conversation, with its abundance of descriptive authorial comments, somehow catches the tone of the period.

'Barbara!' said Lady Olivia, on her first Sunday after being settled at the cottage, 'we shall be in very good time for church by setting out, in half an hour, when the bells begin to ring; it is only a ten minutes walk.'

'I do not propose attending church *at all* while I am settled here', replied Miss Neville, with a self-satisfied look.

'No!' exclaimed Lady Olivia, in an accent of the most unfeigned astonishment.

'No!' answered Miss Neville, in an oracular tone. 'I consider that Mr Arnold does not preach as he ought to do.'

'My dear Barbara! I trust you are not serious,' replied Lady Olivia, in a tone of earnest remonstrance. 'Pray consider what you are about! Mr Arnold is the clergyman of this parish deservedly beloved and respected by all his congregation, to whom he acts the part of a faithful and diligent pastor.'

'That is your opinion!' said Miss Neville, dryly.

'And that of all who know his worth and excellence, as I do,' added Lady Olivia. 'He has long known each individual amongst his congregation personally, and, far from confining his ministrations to the pulpit, he teaches, exhorts, and prays with them in their own houses, and watches as one who knows he must give an account. Mr Arnold may not be exactly according to your taste as a preacher, but he gives us a good, plain wholesome diet, and is himself a most sincere and exemplary Christian.'

'There is always a strong tinge of Arminianism in what he calls the practical exhortation at the end of his sermons,' replied Miss Neville, shaking her head, 'and that will never do for me.'

'But, Barbara, we have no other church within reach,' said Lady Olivia, in a persuasive tone. 'It must surely require much stronger objections to justify your forsaking the assembling of ourselves together.'

'Let me tell you,' replied Miss Neville, in a confidential voice, and with a very significant look, 'Mr Arnold is still *quite* in the dark!'

'Do you really mean, then, always to remain at home on Sundays?' inquired Lady Olivia, in a tone of unaffected regret.

'Not exactly,' answered Miss Neville. 'Some of my friends who live in this neighbourhood are to meet on alternate weeks at each other's houses for conference and prayer, when Mr Harvey has agreed to preside.'

'Mr Harvey, the friend of Sir Francis!' exclaimed Lady Olivia, with astonishment, almost amounting to incredulity.

'Yes,' said Miss Neville, decidedly. 'Mr Harvey, who *was once* a friend of Sir Francis, and of many others whom he now abjures. He is, as Miss Rachel Stodart says, "a splendid Christian".'

'You cannot surely be in earnest, Barbara,' replied Lady Olivia. 'Why! it is but a short year since he began to consider these subjects at all! What can he teach you that will not be still better enforced within the house of God, by one who has been a pious and conscientious clergyman of our church for thirty years? Oh, Barbara! beware of false teachers and false prophets; let us be diffident of our own judgement, and careful to ascertain that we have the sanction of God's own word for all we do, and His glory as our first object. One thing more you must pardon me for hinting, with the most sincere regret if it should at all hurt your feelings. Viewing this subject as I do, it is my earnest wish that no meeting, such as you describe, may ever be held in this house.'

Jane Sinclair, *Modern Accomplishments*[14]

Social class could be as divisive as levels of churchmanship. The light satire of Trollope does not conceal the painful snobbishness from which many clergy must have suffered.

Mr Samuel Prong was a little man, over thirty, with scanty, light-brown hair, with a small, rather upturned nose, with eyes by no means deficient in light and expression, but with a mean mouth. His forehead was good, and had it not been for his mouth his face would have been expressive of intellect and of some firmness. But there was about his lips an assumption of character and dignity which his countenance and body generally failed to maintain; and there was a something in the carriage of his head and in the occasional projection of his chin, which was intended to add to his dignity, but which did, I think, only make the failure more palpable. He was a devout, good man; not self-indulgent; perhaps not more self-ambitious than it becomes a man to be; sincere, hardworking, sufficiently intelligent, true in most things to the instincts of his calling, but deficient in one vital qualification for a clergyman of the Church of England; he was not a gentleman. May I not call it a necessary qualification for a clergyman of any church? He was not a gentleman. I do not mean to say that he was a thief or a liar; nor do I mean hereby to complain that he picked his teeth with his fork and misplaced his 'h's'. I am by no means prepared to define what I do mean – thinking, however, that most men and most women will understand me. Nor do I speak of this deficiency in his clerical aptitudes as being injurious to him simply – or even chiefly – among folk who are themselves gentle; but that his efficiency for clerical purposes was marred altogether, among high and low, by his misfortune in this respect. It is not the owner of a good coat that sees and admires its beauty. It is not even they who have good coats themselves who recognise the article on the back of another. They who have not good coats themselves have the keenest eyes for the coats of their better-clad neighbours. As it is with coats, so it is with that which we call gentility. It is caught at a word, it is seen at a glance, it is appreciated unconsciously at a touch by those who have none of it themselves. It is the greatest of all aids to the doctor, the lawyer, the member of Parliament – though in that position a man may perhaps prosper without it – and to the statesman; but to the clergyman it is a vital necessity. Now Mr Prong was not a gentleman.

Anthony Trollope, *Rachel Ray*[15]

Hostility and suspicion lingered into the twentieth century. The accusation that Anglo-Catholics were secretly plotting to bring the whole country to the Roman obedience was still being made. In a discourse intended to be serious but so exaggerated as to read like a parody, an Anglican priest – 'a little man with a taste for plottings and stratagems' – declares himself to a woman who has come to make enquiries on behalf of the Roman Catholic establishment. He belongs to the 'Sacred Society of Nicodemus'.

His sallow cheeks flared for a moment and his eyes shone. 'I am content to suffer,' he cried earnestly; 'I do not ask for applause, for notoriety, for the fame of a moment. I work for eternity, and I work slowly. You say I have introduced reforms into this parish, but you complain that they come slowly; yet, do you consider, that while these reforms come so slowly and yet so certainly, my vicar has never guessed for a moment that I am even a ritualist, and the richest members of the congregation actually, believe that I am opposed to advanced Churchmanship? Father Severn – with all his brilliant gifts – is suspected. He could not enter this parish. The Evangelicals name him, quote him, denounce him. He is openly on the side of Ritualism, and therefore he is checked at every turn by the very boldness of his tactics. But I, madam, I can go into the stoniest places of Protestantism and plant there, in the name and under the shadow of that wicked pervert, Martin Luther, the blessed seed of Holy Church. What says Frà Di Bruno? "Nicodemus was a disciple of Jesus Christ in secret." Newman, Ward, Manning – what did they do but fling themselves off the ship and save themselves; but we, madam, labour rather to save the ship and bring her into the harbour of God's almighty safety than seek the selfish security of our own peace of mind. The Society of Nicodemus is a society of martyrs, a society of patriots; for the sake of our country's salvation we remain among members of a schismatic Church whose Thirty-nine Articles – forty stripes save one – odious as they are, we are willing to bear upon our backs for the greater glory of the true Church's ultimate triumph.'

Harold Begbie, *The Priest*[16]

Let us end this rather unhappy chapter with a pleasant gathering that would cause no surprise today but was not so very long ago the stuff of fiction. The vision was there, and the reality would follow in the next century. Squire Fordham has arranged a Christmas party to welcome back his son who has been abroad for some years.

Then all that afternoon might be seen a most wonderful sight, more especially when the company came into the drawing-room before dinner. The fine young lawyers and officers talking amicably with the wife and daughter of the Methodist minister, and the Squire's lady, who was grand-daughter of an Earl, turning over engravings with his son. And, still more wonderful, the Rev. Augustine Bernard and his cousin the Rector of Woodcote engaged in friendly talk with the Methodist minister himself. The Rev. Augustine Bernard! who had an embroidered altar cloth and wax candles in his church, and services on all Saints' days and holy days, who had all the old pews taken down and replaced with open seats, and who had erected, with the help of his brother, a screen and font of the most 'severe taste'! And these clergymen (who were such 'high Anglicans' that the ministers of the little dissenting chapels in their villages did little else but preach against them as followers of the 'beast and the scarlet woman') not only talked amicably with the dissenter, but found that on many subjects they thought wonderfully alike; and the Methodist minister found, to his astonishment, that the high churchmen knew quite as much about the poor of their parishes as he did of his. And all these wonderful things happened because Richard Fordham came home from abroad; or rather, let us say, because of that blessed Christmas spirit in which all men equally put their trust, and whose influence makes the whole world own its kinship, the rich and the poor, the wise and the simple, the highly and the lowly born.

J. H. Shorthouse, 'The Fordhams of Severnstoke'[17]

Chapter 10

Joyful in the Lord

The ability to laugh is an important part of a full life in faith. The Bible shows little sense of laughter as we understand it: when people laugh, or indeed when God is said to laugh, it is usually in scorn and triumph over enemies. But Jesus often used irony, exaggerated images and verbal puns, and the Jewish tradition is rich in humour. The best jokes, whether their target is religious or secular, are usually told by insiders who can appreciate the element of humour in what they value. It has been said that a miserable Christian is a powerful work of the Devil. Occasional exasperation with the clergy and what they represent can be dispelled by a good story against them. If this is added to an innate British delight in eccentricity, it is not surprising that there is a rich store of clerical humour over the centuries. There have been clergy who were wilfully eccentric, others who were in- voluntarily so, and many who have shown a good sense of the comic and even ridiculous aspects of their calling. Not all stories which purport to be true need be taken as literally so. Anecdotes soon gather around a person with a reputation for wit or for oddity, and the line between fact and fiction is perhaps more blurred in this chapter than in others.

John Skelton (c. 1460–1529) was a poet who gained royal favour in spite of his satirical and sometimes scurrilous verse. He was tutor to Henry VIII as Prince of Wales and became Vicar of Diss in Norfolk, England, where his conduct sometimes fell short of what might be expected of a priest. However, he finds a place among the eccentric rather than the 'bad'. As well as allegorical and satirical poems, he wrote the morality play Magnyfycence. *It has been suggested that the poem 'Who Killed Cock Robin?' was derived from Skelton's poem 'Phyllp Sparrow', a mock elegy on the pet bird of a nun called Jane Scrope in which he parodied the church Burial Service.*

Anecdotes about him were circulating not many years after his death.

When he learned that he had been reported to the bishop for fathering a child, he freely admitted it, held up the baby in the pulpit, and asked the congregation whether it was not 'as fair as the best of yours'. Nevertheless, he decided to try to appease the bishop with the gift of a brace of pheasants but, on arrival at the episcopal palace, was denied entrance. He decided to cross the palace moat by means of a plank, from which he fell into the water. He appeared dripping wet before the bishop, who berated him as a fool. 'You will accept my pheasants if you know their names', said Skelton. When the bishop enquired further, he replied, 'This one is called Alpha, the first, and this one Omega, the last; in other words, if it pleases your lordship to accept them, be sure that it's the first present I've ever given you, but also, by God, the last.'

John Donne (1572–1631) was one of the most remarkable men of his time. A great writer of both poetry and prose, he was brought up a Roman Catholic, went over to the Church of England, in which he was ordained, and eventually became Dean of St Paul's Cathedral, London. It was decided that a monument to him should be set up at St Paul's during his lifetime and that he should arrange the details. His response was somewhat unusual.

A monument being resolved upon, Dr Donne sent for a carver to make for him in wood the figure of an Urn, giving him directions for the compass and height of it; and to bring with it a board, of the just height of his body. These being got, then without delay a choice Painter was got to be in readiness to draw his picture, which was taken as followeth. Several charcoal fires being first made in his large study, he brought with him into that place his winding-sheet in his hand, and having put off all his clothes, had this sheet put on him, and so tied with knots at his head and feet, and his hands so placed as dead bodies are usually fitted, to be shrouded and put into their coffin, or grave. Upon this Urn he thus stood, with his eyes shut, and with so much of the sheet turned aside as might shew his lean, pale, and death-like face, which was purposely turned towards the East, from whence he expected the second coming of his and our Saviour Jesus. In this posture he was drawn at his just height; and when the picture was fully finished, he caused it to be set by his bedside, where it continued and became his hourly object till his death, and was then given to his dearest friend and executor Dr Henry King, then chief Residentiary of St Paul's, who caused him to be thus carved in one entire piece of white marble, as it now stands in that Church.

Isaac Walton, *The Life of Dr John Donne*[1]

Rowland Hill (1744–1833) was a deacon in the Church of England but did not take priest's orders, as the bishops to whom he applied objected to his practice of preaching outside the regular jurisdiction of the Church. He became an independent preacher, with his own chapels in Gloucestershire and later in London, where he exercised his ready and sometimes caustic humour.

One day when the attendance was scantier than usual, a sudden shower of rain came on and the building at once rapidly filled. The preacher did not allow this to pass unnoted, saying: 'I have often heard of religion being used as a cloak, but never before as an umbrella.' Then too, when preaching at Wapping he is reported to have said: 'There are among you some great sinners, some large sinners – and I may say some Whopping sinners.'

When he was preaching once on behalf of a public charity, a note was handed up to him asking if it would be right for a bankrupt to contribute in response to his appeal. Hill referred to this in the course of his sermon, and said decidedly that such a person could not do so in Christian honesty. 'But, my friends', he added, 'I would advise you who are not insolvent not to pass the plate this evening, as if you do the people will be sure to say: "There goes the bankrupt"!' [...]

A member of his congregation said, 'Oh, Mr Hill, how is it that you say such out-of-the-way things in your sermons?' to receive the reply, 'Why, some of you are such out-of-the-way sinners.'

One of his 'out-of-the-way things' was when announcing from the pulpit the amount of a liberal collection he said: 'You have behaved so well on this occasion that we mean to have another collection next Sunday. I have heard it said of a good cow, that the more you milk her the more she will give.'

A member of his congregation wrote a letter of remonstrance to Rowland Hill – who was then over eighty – about his journeying to chapel in his brougham, asking triumphantly: 'Is this the way our Lord used to attend Divine Worship?' The preacher read out this letter from the pulpit on the following Sunday, admitting with an air of ingenuous penitence that Our Saviour had not been in the habit of using a brougham. 'But, to atone for my indiscretion', he added, 'if the writer of this letter will come into the vestry after service next Sunday, bringing along with him a saddle and bridle, I will ride *him* home!'

Walter Jerrold, *A Book of Famous Wits*[2]

The clerical father of the poet Samuel Taylor Coleridge (1772–1834) was a loved pastor and a good preacher, but he was sometimes a trial to his family and friends.

On another occasion he dined with the bishop, who had great pleasure and delight in his society, when the following ludicrous scene took place. The bishop had a maiden daughter, past the meridian of life, who was always glad to see and converse with the 'dear good old man' (his usual appellation), and who was also kind enough to remind him of his little *Forgets* in society, and rouse him from his absent moods. It not being the fashion in his day for gentlemen to wear braces, his small-clothes, receding from his waistcoat, left a space in his black dress, through which often appeared a portion of his linen. On these occasions, the good lady would draw his attention to this appearance, by saying in an undertone, 'A little to this side, Mr Coleridge', or to that as the adjustment might require. This hint was as instantly attended to as his embarrassed manner, produced by a sense of the kindness, would permit. On the day above alluded to, his kind friend sat next to him, dressed, as was then the fashion, in a smart party-going muslin apron. Whilst in earnest conversation with his opposite neighbour, on the side next the lady appeared the folds of his shirt, through the hiatus before described, so conspicuously as instantly to attract her notice. The hint was immediately given: 'Mr Coleridge, a little on the side next me'; and was as instantly acknowledged by the usual reply, 'Thank you, ma'am, thank you', and the hand set to work to replace the shirt; but unfortunately, in his nervous eagerness, he seized on the lady's apron, and appropriated the greater part of it. The appeal of 'Dear Mr Coleridge, do stop!' only increased his embarrassment, and also his exertions to dispose, as he thought, of his shirt; till the lady, to put a stop to the titter of the visitors, and relieve her own confusion, untied the strings, and thus disengaging herself, left the room, and her friend in possession of her apron […]

I have heard Coleridge relate the following anecdote of his father. The old gentleman had to take a short journey on some professional business, which would detain him from home for three or four days: his good wife, in her care and watchfulness, had packed a few things in a small trunk, and gave them in charge to her husband, with strong injunctions that he was to put on a clean shirt every day. On his return home, his wife went to search for his linen, when, to her dismay, it was not in the trunk. A closer search, however, discovered that the vicar had strictly obeyed her injunctions, and had put on daily a clean shirt, but had forgotten to remove the one underneath. This might have been the pleasantest and most portable mode of carrying half a dozen shirts in winter, but not so in the dog-days.

James Gillman, *The Life of Samuel Taylor Coleridge*[3]

The Church has never lacked a number of belligerent clergy. Nearly contemporary with the gentle Coleridge, though a fictional creation, is this parson who is returning home from a convivial evening.

The Reverend Doctor Folliott took his departure about ten o'clock, to walk home to his vicarage. There was no moon, but the night was bright and clear, and afforded him as much light as he needed. He paused a moment by the Roman camp, to listen to the nightingale; repeated to himself a passage of Sophocles; proceeded through the park gate, and entered the narrow lane that led to the village. He walked on in a very pleasant mood of the state called reverie; in which fish and wine, Greek and political economy, the Sleeping Venus he had left behind, and poor dear Mrs Folliott, to whose fond arms he was returning, passed as in a camera obscura, over the tablets of his imagination. Presently the image of Mr Eavesdrop, with a printed sketch of the Reverend Doctor F, presented itself before him, and he began mechanically to flourish his bamboo. The movement was prompted by his good genius, for the uplifted bamboo received the blow of a ponderous cudgel, which was intended for his head. The reverend gentleman recoiled two or three paces, and saw before him a couple of ruffians, who were preparing to renew the attack, but whom, with two swings of his bamboo, he laid with cracked sconces on the earth, where he proceeded to deal with them like corn beneath the flail of the thresher. One of them drew a pistol, which went off in the very act of being struck aside by the bamboo, and lodged a bullet in the brain of the other. There was then only one enemy, who vainly struggled to rise, every effort being attended with a new and more signal prostration. The fellow roared for mercy. 'Mercy, rascal!' cried the divine; 'what mercy were you going to show me, villain? What! I warrant me, you thought it would be an easy matter, and no sin, to rob and murder a parson on his way home from dinner. You said to yourself, doubtless, "We'll waylay the fat parson (you irreverent knave) as he waddles home (you disparaging ruffian) half-seas-over" (you calumnious vagabond).' And with every dyslogistic term, which he supposed had been applied to himself, he inflicted a new bruise on his rolling and roaring antagonist. 'Ah, rogue!' he proceeded, 'you can roar now, marauder; you were silent enough when you devoted my brains to dispersion under your cudgel. But seeing that I cannot bind you, and that I intend you not to escape, and that it would be dangerous to let you rise, I will disable you in all your members, I will contund [*pound*] you as Thestylis did strong-smelling herbs, in the quality whereof you do most gravely partake, as my nose beareth testimony, ill weed that you are. I will beat you to a jelly, and I will then roll you into the ditch, to lie till the constable comes for you, thief.'

'Hold! hold, reverend sir!' exclaimed the penitent culprit. 'I am disabled already in every finger, and in every joint. I will roll myself into the ditch, reverend sir.'

'Stir not, rascal,' returned the divine, 'stir not so much as the quietest leaf above you, or my bamboo rebounds on your body, as hail in a thunderstorm. Confess, speedily, villain; are you simple thief, or would you have manufactured me into a subject for the benefit of science? Ay, miscreant caitiff, you would have made me a subject for science, would you? You are a schoolmaster abroad, are you? You are marching with a detachment of the march of mind, are you? You are a member of the Steam Intellect Society, are you? You swear by the learned friend, do you?'

'Oh no, reverend sir,' answered the criminal, 'I am innocent of all these offences, whatever they are, reverend sir. The only friend I had in the world is lying dead beside me, reverend sir.'

The reverend gentleman paused a moment, and leaned on his bamboo. The culprit, bruised as he was, sprang on his legs, and went off in double quick time. The Doctor gave him chase, and had nearly brought him within arm's length, when the fellow turned at right angles, and sprang clean over a deep dry ditch. The divine, following with equal ardour, and less dexterity, went down over head and ears into a thicket of nettles. Emerging with much discomposure, he proceeded to the village, and roused the constable; but the constable found, on reaching the scene of action, that the dead man was gone, as well as his living accomplice.

Thomas Love Peacock, *Crotchet Castle*[4]

R. S. Hawker (1804–75) must occupy an eminent place in the ranks of eccentric clergy. He was Vicar of Morwenstow in Cornwall, loved for his benevolence and hospitality, and credited with initiating the Harvest Festival service. His ways were unpredictable and his choice of clerical dress was unusual.

Mr Hawker [...] was rather peculiar in his dress. At first, soon after his induction to Morwenstow, he wore his cassock; but in time abandoned this inconvenient garb, in which he found it impossible to scramble about his cliffs. He then adopted a claret-coloured coat, with long tails. He had the greatest aversion to anything black: the only black things he would wear were his boots. These claret-coloured coats would button over the breast, but were generally worn open, displaying beneath a knitted blue fisherman's jersey. At his side, just where the Lord's side was pierced, a little red cross was woven in the jersey. He wore fishing-boots reaching above his knee. The claret-coloured cassock coats, when worn out, were given to his servant-maids, who wore them as morning dresses when going about their dirty work.

'See there! the parson is washing potatoes!' or, 'See there! the parson is feeding the pigs!' would be exclaimed by the villagers, as they saw his servant girls engaged on their work, in their master's house.

At first he went about in a college cap; but after speedily made way for a pink or plum-coloured beaver hat without a brim, the colour of which rapidly faded to a tint of pink, the blue having disappeared. When he put on coat, jersey or hat he wore it till it was worn out; he had no best suit.

Once he had to go to Hartland, to the funeral of a relative. On the way he had an accident – his carriage upset, and he was thrown out. When he arrived at Hartland, his relations condoled with him on his upset.

'Do, Hawker, let me find you a new hat: in your fall you have knocked the brim off yours,' said one.

'My dear –' he answered, 'priests of the Holy Eastern Church wear no brims to their hats; and I wear none, to testify the connection of the Cornish Church with the East, before ever Augustine set foot in Kent.' And he attended the funeral in his brimless hat. He wore one of these peculiar coloured hats, bleached almost white, at the funeral of his first wife, in 1863, and could hardly be persuaded to allow the narrowest possible band of black crape to be pinned round it. The pink hats were, however, abandoned, partly because they would not keep their colour; and a priest's wide-awake, claret-coloured like the coat, was adopted in its place.

'My coat,' said he, when asked by a lady why he wore one of such a cut and colour, 'my coat is that of an Armenian archimandrite.' But this he said only from his love of hoaxing persons who asked him impertinent questions.

S. Baring-Gould, *The Vicar of Morwenstow*[5]

There were parish priests not quite so eccentric as Hawker who nevertheless followed their calling in an idiosyncratic way. An affectionate fictional portrait of one of them pays tribute to his benevolence, even if other aspects left something to be desired.

You already suspect that the Vicar did not shine in the more spiritual functions of his office; and indeed, the utmost I can say for him in this respect is, that he performed those functions with undeviating attention to brevity and despatch. He had a large heap of short sermons, rather yellow and worn at the edges, from which he took two every Sunday, securing perfect impartiality in the selection by taking them as they came, without reference to topics; and having preached one of these sermons at Shepperton in the morning, he mounted his horse and rode hastily with the other in his pocket to Knebley, where he officiated in a wonderful little church, with a checkered pavement which had once rung to the iron tread of military monks, with coats of arms in clusters on the lofty roof, marble warriors and their wives without noses occupying a large proportion of the area, and the twelve apostles, with their heads very much on one side, holding didactic ribbons, painted in fresco on the walls. Here, in an absence of mind to which he was prone, Mr Gilfil would sometimes forget to take off his spurs before putting on his surplice, and only become aware of the omission by feeling something mysteriously tugging at the skirts of that garment as he stepped into the reading-desk. But the Knebley farmers would as soon have thought of criticising the moon as their pastor. He belonged to the course of nature, like markets and toll-gates and dirty bank-notes; and being a vicar, his claim on their veneration had never been counteracted by an exasperating claim on their pockets.

George Eliot, 'Mr Gilfil's Love Story'[6]

Sydney Smith's opinions on several matters have already been quoted, and he may be allowed also to present himself as he looks back over his busy and idiosyncratic clerical life. He is annoyed by the proposals of the Ecclesiastical Commission of 1833 to reduce the privileges of cathedral chapters.

You tell me I shall be laughed at as a rich and over-grown Churchman. Be it so. I have been laughed at a hundred times in my life, and care little or nothing about it. If I am well provided for now – I have had my full share of the blanks in the lottery as well as the prizes. Till thirty years of age I never received a farthing from the Church; then £50 per annum for two years – then nothing for ten years – then £500 per annum, increased for two or three years to £800, till in my grand climacteric, I was made Canon of St Paul's; and before that period, I had built a Parsonage-house with farm offices for a large farm, which cost me £4000, and had reclaimed another from ruins at the expense of £2000. A lawyer, or a physician in good practice, would smile at this picture of great ecclesiastical wealth; and yet I am considered as a perfect monster of ecclesiastical prosperity.

I should be very sorry to give offence to the dignified ecclesiastics who are in the Commission: I hope they will allow for the provocation, if I have been a little too warm in the defence of St Paul's which I have taken a solemn oath to defend. I was at school and college with the Archbishop of Canterbury: fifty-three years ago he knocked me down with the chessboard for checkmating him – and now he is attempting to take away my patronage. I believe these are the only two acts of violence he ever committed in his life; the interval has been one of gentleness, kindness, and the most amiable and high-principled courtesy to his Clergy.

The Wit and Wisdom of the Rev. Sydney Smith[7]

A number of clergy from the Anglican Church in Ireland moved to England in search of a milieu more congenial than the Roman Catholic majority of their native country. Patrick Brontë (p. 105) was one of them. They were usually of a particularly strong Evangelical inclination and this, together with the incurable English weakness for finding the Irish amusing, created some fictional characters, or rather caricatures. Charles Kingsley was not only prejudiced against Roman Catholics (p. 157); this Protestant clergy-man could be included in the Victorian section, but he is endearing enough to be with the eccentrics.

As Lancelot walked up to the Priory that morning, the Reverend Panurgus O'Blareaway dashed out of a cottage by the roadside, and seized him unceremoniously by the shoulders. He was a specimen of humanity which Lancelot could not help at once liking and despising; a quaint mixture of conceit and earnestness, uniting the shrewdness of a stockbroker with the frolic of a schoolboy broke loose. He was rector of a place in the west of Ireland, containing some ten Protestants and some thousand Papists. Being, unfortunately for himself, a red-hot Orangeman, he had thought fit to quarrel with the priest, in consequence of which he found himself deprived both of tithes and congregation; and after receiving three or four Rockite letters, and a charge of slugs through his hat (of which he always talked as if being shot at was the most pleasant and amusing feature of Irish life), he repaired to England, and there, after trying to set up as a popular preacher in London, declaiming at Exeter Hall, and writing for all the third-rate magazines, found himself incumbent of Lower Whitford. He worked there, as he said himself, 'like a horse'; spent his mornings in the schools, his afternoons in the cottages; preached four or five extempore sermons every week to overflowing congregations; took the lead, by virtue of the 'gift of the gab' at all 'religious' meetings for ten miles round; and really did a great deal of good in his way. He had an unblushing candour about his own worldly ambition, with a tremendous brogue; and prided himself on exaggerating deliberately both of these excellences.

'The top of the morning to ye, Mr Smith. Ye haven't such a thing as a cegar about ye? I've been preaching to school-children till me throat's as dry as the slave [*sleeve*] of a lime-burner's coat.'

Charles Kingsley, Yeast[8]

The Victorian – and later – habit of finding the Irish amusing is not one for the English to be proud of, but perhaps an Irish writer may be allowed some latitude. Charles Lever (1806–72) practised as a doctor in Ireland and wrote novels of Irish life. The narrator, a guardsman, gets a lift from a local priest, whose brogue is broad, but not impenetrable.

I am by no means certain that the prejudices of my English education were sufficiently overcome to prevent my feeling a kind of tingling of shame as I took my place beside Father Tom Loftus in his gig. Early as it was, there were still some people about; and I cast a hurried glance around, to see if our equipage was not as much a matter of amusement to them as of affliction to me.

When Father Tom first spoke of his 'dennet' I innocently pictured to myself something resembling the indigenous productions of Loughrea. 'A little heavy or so,' thought I; 'strong for country roads – mayhap somewhat clumsy in the springs, and not over-refined about the shafts.' Heaven help my ignorance! I never fancied a vehicle whose component parts were two stout poles, surmounting a pair of low wheels, high, above which was suspended, on two lofty C springs, the body of an ancient buggy; the lining of a bright scarlet, a little faded and dimmed by time, bordered by a lace of the most gaudy pattern; a flaming coat of arms with splendid blazonry and magnificent quarterings, ornamented each panel of this strange-looking tub, into which, for default of steps, you mounted by a ladder.

'Eh, Father,' said I, 'what have we here? this is surely not the –'

'Ay, captain,' said the good priest, as a smile of proud satisfaction curled his lip, 'that's "the convaniency"; and a pleasanter and an easier never did man sit in – a little heavy, to be sure; but then one can always walk up the hills, and if they're very stiff ones entirely, why it's only throwing out the ballast.'

'The ballast! – what do you mean?'

'Just them,' said he, pointing with his whip to some three, or four huge pieces of lime-stone rock that lay in the bottom of the gig; 'there's seven – maybe eight stone weight; every pound of it.'

'And for heaven's sake', said I, 'why do you carry that mass of rubbish along with you?'

'I'll just tell you then. The road has holes in it you could bury your father in, and when the convaniency gets into one of them, she has a way of springing up into the air, that if you're not watching, is sure to pitch you out – maybe into the bog at the side – maybe on the beast's back: I was once actually thrown into a public-house window, where there was a great deal of fun going on, and the bishop came by before I extricated myself. I assure you I had hard work to explain it to his satisfaction.'

There was a lurking drollery in his eye, as he said these last few words, that left me to the full as much puzzled about the accident as his worthy diocesan. 'But look at the springs,' he continued, 'there's a metal for you! and do you mind the shape of the body? it's for all the world like the ancient *curriculus*. And look at Bathershin himself – the ould varmint! sure he's classical too – hasn't he a Roman nose? and ain't I a Roman myself? So get up, captain – *ascendite ad currum* – get into the shay. And now for the *doch an dhurrus* – the stirrup-cup, Mrs Doolan: that's the darlin'. Ah, there's nothing like it! *Sit mihi lagena ad summum plena.* [*May the flask be filled to the brim for me.*] Here captain, take a pull – beautiful milk punch!'

Draining the goblet to the bottom, which I confess was no unpleasant task, I pledged my kind hostess, who, curtseying deeply, refilled the vessel for Father Tom.

'That's it, Mary; froth it up, acushla. Hand it here, my darling – my blessing on you.'

As he spoke, the worthy Father deposited the reins at his feet, and lifted the cup with both hands to his mouth; when suddenly the little window over the inn-door was burst open, and a loud tally-ho was shouted out, in accents the wildest I ever listened to. I had barely time to catch the merry features of poor Tipperary Joe, when the priest's horse, more accustomed to the hunting field than the high-road, caught up the welcome sound, gave a wild toss of his head, cocked up his tail, and, with a hearty bang of both hind legs against the front of the chariot, set off down the street as if the devil were after him. Feeling himself at liberty, as well as favoured by the ground, which was all down hill, the pace was really terrific. It was some time before I could gather up the reins, as Father Tom, jug and all, had been thrown at the first shock on his knees to the bottom of the 'convaniency', where, half-suffocated by fright and the milk punch that went wrong with him, he bellowed and coughed with all his might.

'Hold him tight – ugh, ugh, ugh! not too hard – don't check him for the love of – ugh, ugh, ugh! the reins is rotten and the traces no better – ugh, ugh, ugh! Bad luck to the villains, why didn't they catch his head? – and the *stultus execrabilis*! – the damned fool! how he yelled!'

Almost fainting with laughter, I pulled my best at the old horse, not, however, neglecting the priest's caution about the frailty of the harness. This, however, was not the only difficulty I had to contend with, for the 'curriculus', participating in the galloping action of the horse, swung upwards and downwards, backwards and forwards, and from one side to the other – all at once too – in a manner so perfectly addling, that it was not before we reached the first turnpike that I succeeded in arresting our progress. Here a short halt was necessary for the priest to recover himself, and examine whether either his bones or any portion of the harness had given way: both had happily been found proof against mishaps, and drew from the reverend Father strong encomiums upon their merits; and after a brief delay we resumed our road, but at a much more orderly and becoming pace than before.

Charles Lever, *Jack Hinton* [9]

We have seen some unedifying examples of the hunting parson, but Jack Russell seems to belong with the eccentrics rather than the bad. Although his activities would not escape official censure today, he did not totally neglect his duties and was generous and kind-hearted. Like Froude and the fictional Chowne, he was a West Country man.

Much has been said of the active service which Russell expected from his curates in the hunting-field, when parochial duties did not absolutely require their attendance at home; but the figure of hyperbole could scarcely be more strained than by some of the stories told in that respect One, for instance, describes him as testing the voices of two rival applicants aspiring to become his curate, by making them give 'view-holloas', and then accepting the one whose voice sounded the most penetrating and most sonorous – a capital story, no doubt, for those who cultivate charity by believing and circulating such tales; but, as a matter of fact, it is one which rests on as baseless a fabric as the fleecy clouds that float through the sky.

That he never objected to the company and help of his curate in the hunting-field is quite true, provided always that the parochial duty, for which he was responsible, was first attended to and duly fulfilled; nay, if his curate had a taste for hunting, Russell would even encourage him to enjoy the pastime, maintaining, with Dr Watts, that Satan would find him something worse to do, if he remained idle at home.

The following anecdote, however, is, beyond all doubt, a true one, and shall be given in the very words of an ear-witness, the late Rev. William Hocker, vicar of Buckerell, who related it to the writer of this memoir soon after the incident occurred. Mr Hocker was standing at a shop-door in Barnstaple on a market-day, when Will Chapple, the parish clerk of Swymbridge, entered the shop, and while his business was being attended to, the grocer thus interrogated him.

'Well, Mr Chapple, and have'ee got a coorate yet for Swymbridge?'

'Not yet, sir – master's nation partic'ler; 'tisn't this man nor 'tisn't that as'll suit un; but here's his advertisement' (pulling out a copy of the *North Devon Journal*), 'so I reckon he'll get one now: "Wanted, a curate for Swymbridge; must be a gentleman of moderate and orthodox views".'

'Orthodox! Mr Chapple, what doth he mean by that?' inquired the grocer.

'Well,' said the clerk, in some perplexity, knowing the double nature of the curate's work, secular as well as sacred, 'I can't exactly say; but I reckon 'tis a man as can *ride* pretty well.'

E. W. L. Davies, *A Memoir of the Rev. John Russell*[10]

Joshua Brookes had little opportunity for hunting when he was chaplain of the Manchester Collegiate Church (which later became Manchester Cathedral) at the beginning of the nineteenth century, but he was equal to any of the hunting parsons for unorthodox ways.

Some of the stories about him are very ludicrous. Once he was expelled from the chapter house on account of some fiery and hasty speech, and was not allowed to return until he made an apology. This he refused to do, but he put on his surplice in an adjoining chapel of the church, and then, standing outside the chapter-house door, exclaimed to all the persons who were passing on to attend the service, 'They won't let me in; they say I can't behave myself.' Sometimes he would during service box the ears of a chorister for coming late; and once he clouted a boy who was singing the Kyrie after the Fifth Commandment, saying, 'Hold thy noise, lad; what hast thou to do with the Fifth Commandment? Thou'st got neither father nor mother.' [...]

When reading the Burial Service he would break off in the middle, go to a neighbouring confectioner's shop, procure a supply of horehound drops, and then return to his neglected duties and conclude the service. Easter Monday was the great day for weddings at the old church, and large numbers flocked to be married, and with so many couples it was rather difficult to get them properly sorted, as one reading of the service sufficed for all. It was on one of these occasions that some of the bridegrooms got married to the wrong brides and the parson shouted out, 'Sort yourselves when you go out.' It was a Lancashire custom for the bridegroom to kiss the bride directly the marriage knot was tied, and if he did not perform this duty quickly some other person might seize the opportunity. On one occasion a bridegroom attempted to kiss his neigh-bour's bride. The chaplain, however, was angry and pushed him back, uttering the well-known Lancashire proverb, 'Friend, dip in thy own treacle.'

P. H. Ditchfield, *The Old-Time Parson*[11]

Richard Whately (1787–1863) went from the Provostship of Oriel College, Oxford to be Anglican Archbishop of Dublin. He was noted for his caustic wit and showed a regard for other denominational churches which was, regrettably, unusual for his time.

Whately never wasted a thought upon his dignity. If he had, the dignity would have been an unwelcome weight; but, without any intentional arrogance, he was accustomed to assume the intellectual dictatorship of every company in which he found himself. There could be no greater mistake than to infer from this that there was any tincture in him of ecclesiastical intolerance. He was in reality intolerant of intolerance, and of not many things beside. He lived upon easy terms with the young men about the Viceregal Court, and one of them, a young nobleman who was Aide-de-camp to the Lord-Lieutenant, made a little mistake in assuming that a scoff at the Roman Catholic Bishops would be acceptable: 'My Lord Archbishop', said the Aide-de-camp, 'do you know what is the difference between a Roman Catholic Bishop and a donkey?' 'No', said the Archbishop. 'The one has a cross on his breast and the other on his back,' said the Aide-de-camp. 'Ha!' said the Archbishop, 'do you know the difference between an Aide-de-camp and a donkey?' 'No', said the Aide-de-camp. 'Neither do I', said the Archbishop.

Henry Taylor, *Autobiography*[12]

Another Archbishop of Dublin, Richard Chevenix Trench (1807–86), was a noted philologist and a man of much learning. He was, however, prone to be absent-minded.

The late Archbishop Trench, a man of singularly vague and dreamy habits, resigned the see of Dublin on account of advancing years, and settled in London. He once went back to pay a visit to his successor, Lord Plunket. Finding himself back again in his old palace, sitting at his old dinner-table, and gazing across it at his old wife, he lapsed in memory to the days when he was master of the house, and gently remarked to Mrs Trench, 'I am afraid, my love, that we must put this cook down among our failures.'

G. W. E. Russell, *Collections and Recollections*[13]

Samuel Wilberforce (1805–73), successively Bishop of Oxford and Winchester, has been rather unfairly remembered as 'Soapy Sam' and as coming off worst in a debate with T. H. Huxley about the theory of evolution. He was in fact one of the more intelligent and reasonable Victorian bishops, with a quick wit of which these are a few examples.

Some clergyman had introduced Gregorian chants into his church. Now Gregorian music is, doubtless, very fine and grand when chanted by a strong choir, led by a powerful organ; but when village choirs essay to sing these chants the result is often most painful. Bishop Wilberforce found it so, and after a somewhat prolonged and dreary dose of Gregorians, he ventured to suggest to the rector of the parish that perhaps they were a little unsuited to a country choir. The rector prided himself on the music, and said: 'David sang his psalms to Gregorian melodies'. 'Then I don't wonder Saul cast his javelin at him,' replied the bishop. On another occasion he visited a church where there was an oldfashioned service with a choir led by several musical instruments, the vicar and musicians rather priding themselves on their abilities. The vicar asked him afterwards 'What did you think of our choir?' 'Well,' replied the bishop, 'the singers go before, and the minstrels follow after.' On one occasion he was trying to move the generosity of some rich but stingy magnate, and to get him to subscribe to the diocesan funds. The rich but stingy person, in answer to his appeal, said: 'I shall be happy to give my mite.' 'I always thought there were two,' quickly retorted the bishop.

P. H. Ditchfield, *The Old-Time Parson*[14]

A. H. Stanton has already been included among the ranks of the good clergy (p. 11). His virtues did not extinguish his sense of humour.

On questions of Church ritual Stanton was always ready-witted with dull and pompous critics. Once a visitor to St Alban's suggested that the use of incense and processions and lights was not wise, and Stanton answered immediately, 'My dear fellow, not wise! Why, there are only two sorts of people called "wise" in the Gospels – the "wise" men who offered incense, and the "wise" virgins who carried processional lights.'

Another visitor objected to the *smell* of incense. 'Well,' said Stanton, 'there are only two stinks in the next world: incense and brimstone; and you've got to choose between them.'

Once at Woolwich, when Stanton and Dolling were passing down a street together, a private soldier called out to a friend: 'Look at those two – Popes!' Stanton turned round, and said, in mild, reproachful tones: 'Now, you shouldn't call us "Popes"; it's not at all a kind thing to say. Why, we are respectable Protestant clergymen belonging to the Established Church.' The soldier was staggered, and became one of Stanton's friends.

One August day in London I met Stanton accidentally outside a Tube station, and he got talking about the Feast of the Assumption of Our Lady. 'What I don't understand,' said Stanton, 'is this: all good Protestants say their own mothers have been assumpted into heaven, and yet they won't have it that Christ's own Blessed Mother has been taken up.'

When asked what authority there was for keeping this Feast of the Assumption of the Blessed Virgin Mary, Stanton replied: 'Why, the authority of the City Temple, of course. Didn't Dr Parker give out (when Mrs Parker died) that Mary had gone to heaven? You wouldn't have the assumption of Mrs Parker kept at the City Temple, without the Assumption of the Blessed Virgin Mary being kept at St Alban's?'

Joseph Clayton, *Father Stanton*[15]

Dom Aelred Carlyle (1874–1955) must come among the eccentrics, though he could also be numbered with the monks. In 1906 he founded an Anglican Benedictine abbey on Caldey Island, off the south-west coast of Wales. After seven years, most of the community moved into the Roman Catholic Church and later left for Prinknash in Gloucestershire. His biographer tells of his later years, after describing some of his lively and boyish antics during recreation periods.

He could be just as much of a naughty boy when vested as a prelate, singing pontifical High Mass or Vespers and seated on his throne. It was quite frequent that the assistants were reduced to helpless giggles by his audible jokes.

On the other hand Dom Aelred was so much of the prelate that he never took his breakfast or tea in the refectory with the Community. A dainty repast, usually consisting of crisp toast and fruit, with a silver tea or coffee pot, was carried to his reception room on a tray by a young novice or alumnus, known as the abbatial *familiarius*. The tea or coffee pot contained maté, otherwise Paraguay tea, because our Abbot maintained that it was more digestive.

It was impossible to forget that he was the Lord of the Manor as well as the Lord Abbot of Caldey. Visitors would meet him on a showery day, dressed in an all-white ensemble – sou-wester, mackintosh, and rubber boots, with a gun under his arm and his pet spaniel at his heels, going off pheasant shooting. Or they would be confronted by him striding through the farm or gardens, brandishing a shooting-stick, with his white habit tucked up into his leather belt, revealing bare knees, white stockings and scarlet garters.

His moods were as changeable as the climate of Caldey. One was never sure which of the many Aelreds one would find. When one expected him to be serious he would insist on playing the fool. When one took it for granted that he would be in one of his lighter moods, he would be the most pontifical of prelates, or else the mystic in quest of solitude. There were still many people who found him a most helpful spiritual director, and who consulted him on the difficult problems of the interior life. Sometimes one would find him quite alone in his private chapel, kneeling before the altar, rapt in prayer.

Journeys to London and other parts of England were still fairly frequent. He would be seen embarking for the mainland wearing well-polished black leather shoes with silver buckles, a long black cloak or *douilette* over his habit, and a wide brimmed furry hat with tassels – every inch a prelate. The Lord Abbot of Caldey always travelled *en grande luxe*, with expensive looking suitcases, and first-class sleepers to and from London. More often than not in those last years he engaged a private suite at the Paddington Hotel. This was obviously convenient for business and interviews, but it was difficult for those who knew of it to believe that the Caldey community was as always on the verge of bankruptcy.

Peter Anson, *Abbot Extraordinary*[16]

Lest they should take themselves too seriously, clergy should remember that there may at any time be a satirical eye and ear in the congregation. Here the response of a boy is used to emphasize the thin line between solemnity and absurdity.

The minister gave out the hymn, and read it through with a relish, in a particular style which was much admired in that part of the country. His voice began on a medium key, and climbed steadily up till it reached a certain point, where it bore with strong emphasis upon the topmost word and then plunged down as if from a spring-board:

Shall I be carried to the skies, on flow'ry *beds*
of ease,
While others fought to win the prize, and sailed thro' *blood-*
-y seas?

He was regarded as a wonderful reader. At church 'sociables' he was always called upon to read poetry; and when he was through, the ladies would lift up their hands and let them fall helplessly in their laps, and 'wall' their eyes, and shake their heads, as much as to say, 'Words cannot express it; it is too beautiful, *too* beautiful for this mortal earth.'

After the hymn had been sung, the Rev. Mr Sprague turned himself into a bulletin board and read off 'notices' of meetings and societies and things till it seemed that the list would stretch out to the crack of doom – a queer custom which is still kept up in America, even in cities, away here in this age of abundant newspapers. Often, the less there is to justify a traditional custom, the harder it is to get rid of it.

And now the minister prayed. A good, generous prayer, it was, and went into details: it pleaded for the church, and the little children of the church; for the other churches of the village; for the village itself; for the county; for the State; for the State officers; for the United States; for the churches of the United States; for Congress; for the President; for the officers of the government; for poor sailors, tossed by stormy seas; for the oppressed millions groaning under the heel of European monarchies and Oriental despotisms; for such as have the light and the good tidings, and yet have not eyes to see nor ears to hear withal; for the heathen in the far islands of the sea; and closed with a supplication that the words he was about to speak might find grace and favor, and be as seed in fertile ground, yielding in time a grateful harvest of good. Amen.

There was a rustling of dresses, and the standing congregation sat down. The boy whose history this book relates did not enjoy the prayer, he only endured it – if he even did that much. He was restive, all through it; he kept tally of the details of the prayer, unconsciously – for he was not listening, but he knew the ground of old, and the clergyman's regular route over it – and when a little trifle of new matter was interlarded, his ear detected it and his whole nature resented it; he considered additions unfair, and scoundrelly [...]

The minister gave out his text and droned along monotonously through an argument that was so prosy that many a head by and by began to nod – and yet it was an argument that dealt in limitless fire and brimstone and thinned the predestined elect down to a company so small as to be hardly worth the saving. Tom counted the pages of the sermon; after church he always knew how many pages there had been, but he seldom knew anything else about the discourse. However, this time he was really interested for a little while. The minister made a grand and moving picture of the assembling together of the world's hosts at the millennium when the lion and the lamb should lie down together and a little child should lead them. But the pathos, the lesson, the moral of the great spectacle was lost upon the boy; he only thought of the conspicuousness of the principal character before the onlooking nations; his face lit with the thought, and he said to himself that he wished he could be that child, if it was a tame lion.

Mark Twain, *The Adventures of Tom Sawyer*[17]

In real life, the most unusual English parson of the twentieth century was probably Harold Davidson, Rector of Stiffkey in Norfolk. As well as being an undischarged bankrupt, he came to be known as 'the prostitutes' padre' from his habit of leaving his parish during the week and going to London, ostensibly to do reclamation work among prostitutes. It was alleged that his journeys were in fact made for his own gratification and immoral practices. When he was eventually called before a consistory court, he said that his popular sobriquet was 'the proudest title that a true priest of Christ can hold'. The court disagreed, and although an appeal went as far as the Privy Council, he was found guilty of immorality and defrocked. For the remainder of his life he indulged in various forms of public display, including sitting in a barrel on the promenade in Blackpool. He was killed when he got too close to a lioness at the amusement park in Skegness, Lincolnshire, in 1937. He was clearly a very unsatisfactory member of the clergy, but somehow his colourful life and vivid death seem to make it right to put him among the eccentric rather than the bad.

There are many stories and sayings which circulate without any clear ascription. Here are a few, but promising no certificate of authenticity in every case.

Most of the Victorian bishops were unsympathetic to the revival of cere-monial in the Church of England. When a priest appealed to the example of St Ambrose, Bishop Blomfield replied, 'Sir, St Ambrose was not Bishop of London, and I am. Yours truly, William Londin.'

Mandell Creigton, Bishop of London (1897–1901), told an incumbent who was using incense and who remarked that he had 'the cure of ten thous-and souls' – 'Well, you needn't cure them with smoke as if they were so many kippers.'

The saintly Edward King, Bishop of Lincoln (1885–1910), having some diffi-culty in rising from a park bench, was helped by a little girl. When he praised her strength, she replied, 'Oh, I've often helped my Dad when he was much drunker than what you are.'

W. A. Spooner (1844–1930), Warden of New College, Oxford, was famous for the confusion of initial consonants, which came to be known as 'spoonerisms'. Many of these are entirely apocryphal; it is doubtful that he ever proposed a toast to 'our queer dean' instead of 'our dear Queen' or told an undergraduate that 'You have hissed all my mystery lectures and you will leave by the town drain.' He certainly sometimes became muddled about names, and on one occasion, when leaving the pulpit, he returned and said, 'When I have referred to Aristotle in my sermon this morning, I should have said the Apostle Paul.'

W. R. Inge (1860–1954) was known as 'the gloomy Dean' when he was Dean of St Paul's Cathedral. He was notable for his scepticism towards most con-temporary events and attitudes, and for his resistance to current clerical enthusiasms. When asked if he was interested in liturgy, he replied, 'No – neither do I collect stamps.'

Henry Montgomery Campbell, Bishop of London (1956–61), was visited by a young curate with a load of pious reasons why he felt called to seek a move. Campbell cut him short. 'Why don't you say you don't like your Vicar? Neither do I.'

When he knocked on the door of St Paul's Cathedral for his formal admission as Bishop, there was some delay in opening it. He turned to his chaplain and said, 'Do you think we've come to the right place?' When it was at last opened, he looked at the assembled dignitaries inside and said, 'Ah, the See gives up its dead.'

After his retirement as Archbishop of Canterbury in 1961, Geoffrey Fisher remarked, 'I am a kind of extinct volcano, still able to erupt from time to time in a private and unofficial way.'

When the famous Methodist Minister Donald Soper was made a peer, he said, 'I will try to keep those bishops in order.'

When Soper was asked if Christians could dance, he replied, 'Some can, some can't. I don't think there is any danger to our morals – it's too much like violent exercise nowadays.'

Chapter 11

In Sundry Places

While the majority of clergy have served in their native country, some have gone out to find new places for their ministry. The Church began as a missionary enterprise: the Acts of the Apostles is a missionary journal. After the first spreading of the faith across Europe and North Africa, the long centuries of Christendom saw comparatively little missionary activity, but the opening of the New World in the sixteenth century brought new fields for conversion. Men and women from all the churches went out into the world to tell others of the good news which they believed. The nineteenth century saw the greatest expansion of missionary work going out from Britain, with the founding of missionary societies, sometimes at odds with each other. There was great heroism, suffering, persecution and sometimes martyrdom. There was also, as Imperial power increased, occasionally a regrettable confusion of political and religious aims, and insensitivity to the native cultures. But on the whole it is a proud record and deserves to be remembered with respect and affection, at a time when it is often from the former dependent territories that the West is reminded of orthodox faith and morals. Missionaries who have spread the gospel and chaplains who have served the armed forces and the new settlements are here recorded. Like those who have stayed at home, most are shown as faithful and courageous, some well-meaning but inadequate, only a few seeking their own advantage.

In 1735 John Wesley went to Georgia as a missionary sponsored by the Society for the Propagation of the Gospel. He had hopes of converting some of the Native Americans, but, like many other missionaries, found that his fellow believers gave him enough problems of their own, and he returned to England in 1737. These excerpts from his journal show at the same time his inexperience, his loving care for souls and his fearless zeal. In the second entry there is a hint of the 'Class System' which was to become a feature of Methodism.

(1736) Sunday 7 March. I entered upon my ministry at Savannah, by preaching on the epistle for the day, being the thirteenth of the first of Corinthians. In the second lesson (Luke xviii) was our Lord's prediction of the treatment which He Himself (and consequently His followers) was to meet with from the world, and His gracious promises to those who are content *nudi nudum Christum sequi* [*naked to follow the naked Christ*].

Saturday 17 April. Not finding, as yet, any door open for the pursuing our main design, we considered in what manner we might be most useful to the little flock at Savannah. And we agreed: 1. To advise the more serious among them to form themselves into a sort of little society, and to meet once or twice a week, in order to reprove, instruct, and exhort one another. 2. To select out of these a smaller number for a more intimate union with each other, which might be forwarded, partly by our conversing singly with each, and partly by inviting them all together to our house; and this, accordingly, we determined to do every Sunday in the afternoon.

Monday 10 May. I began visiting my parishioners in order, from house to house; for which I set apart the time when they cannot work, because of the heat, viz. from twelve till three in the afternoon.

Tuesday 23 November. Mr Oglethorpe sailed for England, leaving Mr Ingham, Mr Delamotte, and me, at Savannah; but with less prospect of preaching to the Indians than we had the first day we set foot in America. Whenever I mentioned it, it was immediately replied, 'You cannot leave Savannah without a minister.'

To this indeed my plain answer was, 'I know not that I am under any obligation to the contrary. I never promised to stay here one month. I openly declared both before, at, and ever since my coming hither, that I neither would nor could take charge of the English any longer than till I could go among the Indians.' But though I had no other obligation not to leave Savannah now, yet that of love I could not break through. I could not resist the importunate request of the more serious parishioners, 'to watch over their souls yet a little longer, till someone came who might supply my place.' And this I the more willingly did, because the time was not come to preach the gospel of peace to the heathens; all their nations being in a ferment.

(1737) Monday 4 April. I began learning Spanish, in order to converse with my Jewish parishioners; some of whom seem nearer the mind that was in Christ than many of those who call Him Lord.

Sunday 3 July. Immediately after the holy communion, I mentioned to Mrs Williamson (Mr Causton's niece) some things which I thought reprovable in her behaviour. At this she appeared extremely angry; said she did not expect such usage from me; and at the turn of the street through which we were walking home, went abruptly away. The next day Mrs Causton endeavoured to excuse her; told me she was exceedingly grieved for what had passed the day before, and desired me to tell her in writing what I disliked; which I accordingly did the day following.

Sunday 7 August. I repelled Mrs Williamson from the holy communion. [*What provoked this clerical censure is not known, but the aggrieved family were influential enough to get Wesley into trouble with the local law, charged with defamation. He was acquitted by a Grand Jury, but his patience was running out.*]

Friday 7 October. I consulted my friends, whether God did not call me to return to England. The reason for which I left it had now no force; there being no possibility, as yet, of instructing the Indians; neither had I as yet, found or heard of any Indians on the continent of America who had the least desire of being instructed. And as to Savannah, having never engaged myself, either by word or letter, to stay there a day longer than I should judge convenient, nor ever taken charge of the people any otherwise than as in my passage to the heathens, I looked upon myself to be fully discharged herefrom, by the vacating of that design. Besides there was a probability of doing more service to that unhappy people in England, than I could do in Georgia, by representing, without fear or favour, to the trustees the real state the colony was in. After deeply considering these beings, they were unanimous, 'that I ought to go; but not yet.' So I laid the thoughts of it aside for the present; being persuaded, that when the time was come, God would 'make the way plain before my face.'

Thursday 3 November. I again consulted my friends, who agreed with me, that the time we looked for was now come. And the next morning, calling on Mr Causton, I told him, I designed to set out for England immediately. I set up an advertisement in the Great Square to the same effect and quietly prepared for my journey.

Thursday 22 December. I took my leave of America (though if it please God, not for ever) going on board the *Samuel*, Captain Percy.

The Journal of John Wesley[1]

Clergy of the Established Church were sometimes unflattering about early missionary work – partly perhaps because it was largely, though by no means exclusively, based on Nonconformist initiative. They were also suspicious of the desire of some missionaries to win more freedom for native colonial people. Sydney Smith did not like what he heard about the Indian missions.

The plan, it seems, is this: we are to educate India in Christianity, as a parent does his child; and, when it is perfect in its catechism, then to pack up, quit it entirely, and leave it to its own management. This is the evangelical project for separating a colony from the parent country. They see nothing of the bloodshed, and massacres, and devastations, nor of the speeches in Parliament, squandered millions, fruitless expeditions, jobs and pensions, with which the loss of our Indian possessions would necessarily be accompanied; nor will they see that these consequences could arise from the attempt, and not from the completion, of their scheme of conversion. We should be swept from the peninsula by Pagan zealots; and should lose, among other things, all chance of ever really converting them [...] Prove to us that they are fit men, doing a fit thing, and we are ready to praise the missionaries; but it gives us no pleasure to hear that a man has walked a thousand miles with peas in his shoes, unless we know why and wherefore, and to what good purpose he has done it [...] The missionaries complain of intolerance. A weasel might as well complain of intolerance when he is throttled for sucking eggs.

The Wit and Wisdom of the Rev. Sydney Smith[2]

Charles Kingsley, vigorous in attacking many things that he disliked, gives a cruel picture of a dissenting missionary. The radical tailor Alton Locke remembers his childhood experience when, just after he had decided that he himself wanted to become a missionary, a returned missionary came to visit his mother, together with a minister of gentler disposition. The greed and verbose piety depicted are reminiscent of Dickens' treatment of Stiggins (p. 33) and of Chadband in Bleak House.

You may guess then my delight when, a few days afterwards, I heard that a real live missionary was coming to take tea with us. A man who had actually been in New Zealand! – the thought was rapture. I painted him to myself over and over again; and when, after the first burst of fancy, I recollected that he might possibly not have adopted the native costume of that island, or, if he had, that perhaps it would look too strange for him to wear it about London, I settled within myself that he was to be a tall, venerable-looking man, like the portraits of old Puritan divines which adorned our day-room [...]

Well, they came. My heart was in my mouth as I opened the door to them, and sank back again to the very lowest depths of my inner man when my eyes fell on the face and figure of the missionary – a squat, red-faced, pig-eyed, low-browed man, with great soft lips that opened back to his very ears: sensuality, conceit, and cunning marked on every feature – an innate vulgarity, from which the artisan and the child recoil with an instinct as true, perhaps truer, then that of the courtier, showing itself in every tone and motion – I shrank into a corner, so crestfallen that I could not even exert myself to hand round the bread and butter, for which I got duly scolded afterwards. Oh! that man! – how he bawled and contradicted, and laid down the law, and spoke to my mother in a fondling, patronising way, which made me, I knew not why, boil over with jealousy and indignation. How he filled his teacup half full of the white sugar to buy which my mother had curtailed her yesterday's dinner – how he drained the few remaining drops of the three-penny-worth of cream, with which Susan was stealing off to keep it as an unexpected treat for my mother at breakfast the next morning – how he talked of the natives, not as St Paul might of his converts, but as a planter might of his slaves; overlaying all his unintentional confessions of his own greed and prosperity, with cant, flimsy enough for even a boy to see through, while his eyes were not blinded with the superstition that a man must be pious who sufficiently interlards his speech with a jumble of old English picked out of our translation of the New Testament. Such was the man I saw. I don't deny that all are not like him. I believe there are noble men of all denominations, doing their best according to their light, all over the world; but such was the one I saw – and the men who were sent home to plead the missionary cause, whatever the men may be like who stay behind and work, are, from my small experience, too often such. It appears to me to be the rule that many of those who go abroad as missionaries, go simply because they are men of such inferior powers and attainments that if they stayed in England they would starve.

Three parts of his conversation, after all, was made up of abuse of the missionaries of the Church of England, not for doing nothing, but for being so much more successful than his own sect; accusing them, in the same breath, of being just of the inferior type of which he was himself, and also of being mere University fine gentlemen. Really, I do not wonder, upon his own showing, at the savages preferring them to him; and I was pleased to hear the old white-headed minister gently interpose at the end of one of his tirades – 'We must not be jealous, my brother, if the Establishment has discovered what we, I hope, shall find out some day, that it is not wise to draft our missionaries from the offscouring of the ministry, and serve God with that which costs us nothing except the expense of providing for them beyond seas.'

Charles Kingsley, Alton Locke[3]

The heroism and perseverance of missionaries is rightly celebrated. If there were some who found the going too hard, it does not spoil a noble record. This fictional story reflects what happened in some cases. It is told through the news received by the young woman hoping one day to marry Owen Sandbrook, who has gone as a missionary to those now more properly known as Native Americans. The prejudiced attitude towards North America, shared by Dickens and Frances Trollope among others, is also sadly apparent.

Such was the change in Honora's outward life. How was it with that inmost shrine where dwelt her heart and soul? A copious letter writer, Owen Sandbrook's correspondence never failed to find its way to her, though they did not stand on such terms as to write to one another; and in those letters she lived, doing her day's work with cheerful brightness, and seldom seeming preoccupied, but imagination, heart, and soul were with his mission.

Very indignant was she when the authorities, instead of sending him to the interesting children of the forests, thought proper to waste him on mere colonists, some of them Yankee, some Presbyterian Scots. He was asked insolent, nasal questions, his goods were coolly treated as common property, and it was intimated to him on all hands that as an Englishman he was little in their eyes, as clergyman less, as gentleman least of all. Was this what he had sacrificed everything for?

By dint of strong complaints and entreaties, after he had quarrelled with most of his flock, he accomplished an exchange into a district where red men formed the chief of his charge; and Honora was happy, and watched for histories of noble braves, gallant hunters, and meek-eyed squaws. Slowly, slowly she gathered that the picturesque deer-skins had become dirty blankets, and that the diseased, filthy, sophisticated savages were among the worst of the pitiable specimens of the effect of contact with the most evil side of civilization. To them, as Owen wrote, a missionary was only a white man who gave no brandy, and the rest of his parishioners were their obdurate, greedy, trading tempters! It had been a shame to send him to such a hopeless set, when there were others on whom his toils would not be thrown away. However, he should do his best.

And Honora went on expecting the wonders his best would work, only the more struck with admiration by hearing that the locality was a swamp of luxuriant vegetation, and equally luxuriant fever and ague; and the letter he wrote thence to her mother on the news of their loss [*her father's death*] did her more good than all Humfrey's considerate kindness.

Next he had had the ague and had gone to Toronto for change of air. Report spoke of Mr Sandbrook as the most popular preacher who had appeared in Toronto for years, attracting numbers to his pulpit, and sending them away enraptured by his power of language. How beautiful that a man of such talents, always so much stimulated by appreciation, should give up all this most congenial scene and devote himself to his obscure mission.

Report said more, but Honora gave it no credit till old Mr Sandbrook called one morning in Woolstone-lane, by his nephew's desire, to announce to his friends that he had formed an engagement with Miss Charteris, the daughter of a general officer there in command.

Charlotte M. Yonge, *Hopes and Fears*[4]

James Chalmers (1841–1901) was a man of a very different type, and not guilty of the charges often made against missionaries. A Congregationalist minister, he devoted his life to work in New Guinea, where he respected the customs and the dress of the native inhabitants. His own dress caused some consternation when he landed at Navapo.

I landed at Navapo in my whaleboat. As we neared the beach I stood on the bow, and sprang ashore; the boat was then backed into deep water. The beach swarmed with natives, but they gave me a wide berth as I walked up to the nearest house. I was dressed in white except my boots, which were black. The natives kept at a good distance from me, and discussed me. Some thought it better to get their spears and clubs, and many of these were in the long grass close by. My clothing bothered them, and the black feet frightened them. One came and touched and tested the shirt, and found that it was all right; it was cloth. Then the trousers were tried, and also pronounced right. The brave ones who came to try returned to the others to discuss the position; but no one had yet had the pluck to touch my feet. At last one old woman could stand the uncertainty no longer, and she came slowly up, tears rolling down her cheeks, and covering her heart with her arm, lest I should see how excited she was, she tried first the shirt, then the trousers. She then looked piteously up at me, and I nodded, as I knew well what she was going to do. She then placed her hand on my left boot and was feeling it. I picked my right foot up and drew off my boot. Poor woman, she screamed and rushed away, and with her the whole crowd, helter-skelter into the bush, and I saw no more of them. In after visits to the Bay we became capital friends, and teachers were settled among them.

[*However, he was not afraid to oppose the common opinion about changing native costumes.*]

I fear I shall shock many of my friends and a large number of Christians in what I am now going to propose. The natives of New Guinea now under British rule do not wear much clothing, and it is desirable they should be encouraged to use only a very little. The women in many parts are clothed enough, and in others, where their clothing is scant, they should be encouraged to take to the petticoats and nothing more. Nowhere do the men want more than a loincloth, and every effort should be used to discourage anything more. Too little attention has been paid to the effect clothing has had hitherto on native races. Syphilis and strong drink have received the blame for the deterioration and extinction of native races, but I think the introduction of clothing has done much in this direction. A great mistake has hitherto been made in missionary work; the missionaries have reported 'respectably clothed natives who once were naked savages', and the churches have applauded in the conversion of the savages. These clothed natives are, I believe, only hurrying along an easy and respectable road to the grave. To swathe their limbs in European clothing spoils them, deteriorates them, and, I fear, hurries them to premature death. Put excessive clothing with syphilis and strong drink, and, I think, we shall be nearer the truth. Retain native customs as much as possible – only those which are very objectionable should be forbidden – and leave it to the influence of education to raise them to purer and more civilized customs.

Richard Levett, *James Chalmers*[5]

Some missionaries were less sympathetic to their new environment, there were failures of communication long after the nineteenth century. Nathan Price is a Baptist missionary in the Congo in the 1960s. His daughter narrates his confrontation with the local Chief after his congregation have voted against accepting Christianity. Political and theological choices are regarded differently by the two men.

Father spoke slowly, as if to a half-wit, 'Elections are good, and Christianity is good. Both are good.' We in his family recognized the danger in his extremely calm speech, and the rising color creeping toward his hairline. 'You are right. In America we honor both these traditions. But we make our decisions about them in different houses.'

'Then you may do so in America,' said Tata Ndu. 'I will not say you are unwise. But in Kilanga we can use the same house for many things.'

Father blew up. 'Man, you understand *nothing! You* are applying the logic of children in a display of childish ignorance.' He slammed his fist down on the pulpit, which caused all the dried-up palm fronds to shift suddenly sideways and begin falling forward, one at a time. Father kicked them angrily out of the way and strode toward Tata Ndu, but stopped a few feet short of his mark. Tata Ndu is much heavier than my father, with very large arms, and at that moment seemed more imposing in general.

Father pointed his finger like a gun at Tata Ndu, then swung it around to accuse the whole congregation. 'You haven't even learned to run your own pitiful country! Your children are dying of a hundred different diseases! You don't have a pot to piss in! And you're presuming you can take or leave the benevolence of our Lord Jesus Christ!'[...]

Tata Ndu seemed calm and unsurprised by anything that had happened. 'A, Tata Price,' he said, in his deep, sighing voice. 'You believe we are *mwana*, your children, who knew nothing until you came here. Tata Price, I am an old man who learned from other old men. I could tell you the name of the great chief who instructed my father, and all the ones before him, but you would have to know how to sit down and listen. There are one hundred twenty-two. Since the time of our *mankulu* we have made our laws without help from white men.'

Barbara Kingsolver, The Poisonwood Bible[6]

J. C. Patteson (1827–71) founded the Melanesian Mission and became the first Bishop of Melanesia. He was killed by some islanders, who supposed him to be one of the European traders who had preyed on native labour. His great contribution was to train native clergy to share in the work of mission. This account of Christmas Day on Norfolk Island in 1871 may raise a smile by the observance of British customs, but its warmth and joy are unmistakable. The Book of Praise *was a hymnal edited by Roundell Palmer, published in 1863. It included seven hymns by John Keble.*

My dear Sisters – What a happy, happy day! At 12.5 a.m. I was awoke by a party of some twenty Melanesians, headed by Mr Brice, singing Christmas carols at my bedroom door. It is a glass window, opening on to the verandah. How delightful it was! I had gone to bed with the Book of Praise by my side and Mr Keble's hymn in my mind; and now the Mota versions, already familiar to us, of the Angels' Song and of the 'Light to lighten the Gentiles', sung too by some of our heathen scholars, took up as it were the strain. Their voices sounded so fresh and clear in the still midnight, the perfectly clear sky, the calm moon, the warm genial climate.

I lay awake afterwards, thinking on the blessed change wrought in their minds, thinking of my happy, happy lot, of how utterly undeserved it was and is, and (as is natural) losing myself in thoughts of God's goodness and mercy and love.

When at 4.45 a.m. I got up, a little later perhaps than usual, Codrington and Brooke were very soon at work finishing the decorations in the Chapel; branches of Norfolk Island pines, divers evergreens, pomegranates and oleanders and lilies (in handfuls) and large snow-white arums; on the altar-table arums above, and below lilies and evergreens. Oleanders and pomegranates marked the chancel arch. The rugs looked very handsome, the whole floor at the east end is covered with a red baize to match the curtains.

7 a.m. Holy Communion. Six clergymen in surplices and fifteen other communicants. At 10 a.m. a short, very bright, joyful service, the regular Morning Prayers, Psalms xcv, xix, cx, all chanted. Proper Lessons, two Christmas hymns.

Then games, cricket, prisoner's base, running races. Beef, pork, plum-puddings.

Now we shall soon have evening Chapel, a great deal of singing, a few short words from me; then merry, innocent evening, native dances, coffee, biscuit, and snapdragons to finish with.

If you had been here to-day, you would indeed have been filled with surprise and thankfulness.

Charlotte M. Yonge, *Life of John Coleridge Patteson*[7]

A very different kind of colonial bishop is celebrated in this ballad. It is a sequel to an earlier account of him; and if it is not strictly politically correct, it is surely hard to be offended by anything that W. S. Gilbert wrote. The 'Synod, called Pan-Anglican' may be taken as referring to the Lambeth Conference of Anglican Bishops, which met for the first time in 1867.

I often wonder whether you
Think sometimes of that Bishop, who
From black but balmy Rum-ti-foo
    Last summer twelvemonth came.

Unto your mind I p'raps may bring
Remembrance of the man I sing
To-day, by simply mentioning
   That PETER was his name.

Remember how that holy man
Came with the great Colonial clan
To Synod, called Pan-Anglican;
   And kindly recollect
How, having crossed the ocean wide,
To please his flock all means he tried
Consistent with a proper pride
   And manly self-respect.

He only of the reverend pack
Who minister to Christians black
Brought any useful knowledge back
   To his Colonial fold.
In consequence a place I claim
For 'PETER' on the scroll of Fame
(For PETER was that Bishop's name,
   As I've already told).

He carried Art, he often said,
To places where that timid maid
(Save by Colonial Bishops' aid)
   Could never hope to roam.
The Payne-cum-Lauri feat he taught
As he had learnt it; for he thought
The choicest fruits of Progress ought
   To bless the Negro's home,

And he had other work to do,
For, while he tossed upon the blue,
The islanders of Rurn-ti-foo
   Forgot their kindly friend.
Their decent clothes they learnt to tear –
They learnt to say, 'I do not care,'

Though they, of course, were well aware
  How folks, who say so, end.

Some sailors whom he did not know,
Had landed there not long ago,
And taught them 'Bother!' also, 'Blow!'
  (Of wickedness the germs.)
No need to use a casuist's pen
To prove that they were merchantmen;
No sailor of the Royal N.
  Would use such awful terms.

And so, when Bishop PETER came
(That was the kindly Bishop's name),
He heard these dreadful oaths with shame,
  And chid their want of dress.
(Except a shell – a bangle rare –
A feather here – a feather there –
The South Pacific negroes wear
  Their native nothingness.)

He taught them that a Bishop loathes
To listen to unseemly oaths,
He gave them all his left-off clothes –
  They bent them to his will.
The Bishop's gift spreads quickly round;
In PETER'S left-off clothes they bound
(His three-and-twenty suits they found
  In fair condition still).

The Bishop's eyes with water fill,
Quite overjoyed to find them still
Obedient to his sovereign will,
  And said, 'Good Rum-ti-foo!
Half-way I'll meet you, I declare:
And fasten feathers in my hair,
And dance the Cutch-chi-boo!'

And to conciliate his see
He married PICCADILLILLEE,
The youngest of his twenty-three,
   Tall – neither fat nor thin.
(And though the dress he made her don
Looks awkwardly a girl upon,
It was a great improvement on
   The one he found her in.)

W. S. Gilbert, 'The Bishop of Rum-Ti-Foo Again'[8]

The presence of returned missionaries at church gatherings could inspire respect and excitement instead of mirth. Even into the twentieth century there was a certain romance about the mission field, as a priest well known for his social and economic concern recalls. We have already met Bishop Patteson (p. 209), whose martyrdom is here commemorated.

Ah! And it was very real, this romance. As we looked at those men among us then, we recalled Archdeacon Johnson, blind and worn in Nyassa: and the body of Chancey Maples under the lake water: and Bishop Hannington, dying under the malarian tyranny: and the white body of Patteson floating out in the lone boat, with the martyr-palms laid by those who killed him, crossed on his breast. And many a lonely grave of those well known to us, hidden away in far corners of African jungles, came back on the imagination. Here was adventure: here was romance [...]

And the odd, and the comforting thing is this – that these returning heroes of ours – these, our braves – looked, after all, very like us. You could not tell us apart. These Bishops, who have swum their way across the foaming floods, 'in faerie lands forlorn,' might any one of them have been sitting in a comfy Palace in a Midland Diocese. When they mixed in Processions, or mingled with Fulham Garden Parties, you had to ask which was which. 'Can you tell me if that is the Bishop of London?' 'No! That is the Bishop of Natal.' 'Really! Thank you! I should not have thought it!' That was the way that conversation ran. You found yourself listening to breathless tales from someone who was just as ordinary-looking as you are.

I always remember the shock of a most proper looking parson, straight from Cambridge, a 'Varsity oar, in his long black coat and stiff starched collar, telling us quite simply of the three separate occasions on which he had just escaped being eaten by cannibals in the New Hebrides. We kept wondering – would they have eaten the coat, too, and swallowed the collar? It was as astonishing to hear them talk as it would be, if the Ancient Mariner, as he held you with his glittering eye, were to wear gaiters and buttons; or as if a portly gentleman, in a shovel hat and apron, were to appear with a dead albatross slung round his neck.

Now, this was comforting; because their romance, in this way, began to infect us. If they were so like us, might not we be rather like them? Why should our gaiters and buttons matter more than theirs? Might not our own Home Diocesans swim rivers, and shoot bears, and dive ashore through the surf in the Solomon Islands, as well as any?

Henry Scott Holland, A Bundle of Memories[9]

Not exactly a missionary journey, but an interesting record of foreign tra-vel in what, even in the latter part of the nineteenth century, seemed very exotic territory, is given by Mary Sumner. She is well remembered in her own right as the founder of the Mothers' Union, but here she writes as the wife of George Sumner, Bishop of Guildford. He went to North Africa to recover from illness and they both set off intrepidly for further exploration.

On March 9th the Bishop and his wife, with her maid, left Algiers in the early morning, driving across the plains under the spurs of the Atlas Mountains, and through cork forests and fields of asphodels, *en route* to Biskra. They slept at Setif, 3500 feet high on tableland, and the next day they entered the Sahara Desert, through the striking defile of El Kan-tarah, and reached Biskra in the evening. It is in a great oasis in the waste of red earth, with stony hills, sparkling in an ocean of golden light, that seem as if they were giant waves that had turned into stone in their attempt to break into the endless desert, stretching to the blue horizon. There are, in the Sahara, 360 oases belonging to the French, and it is said that Biskra has 160,000 date palms in its oasis, besides 6000 olive trees.

The size of the town rather surprised the travellers, with its 1100 Europeans, a large population of natives, and a French garrison of 600 or 800, and the comfort of the hotel was also unexpected. We were much interested in the animal life at Biskra. Great lizards, two feet long, and smaller palm lizards with spiked tails, are to be seen alive, or stuffed by hundreds in the bazaars. Scorpions and centipedes abound, and one of our party was alarmed at finding on her pillow one night a centipede as large as her hand, crawling uncomfortably near, and evidently intending to remain. Locusts are also very common, and in the springtime occ- asionally stop the trains by their multitudes.

Of birds there are many – eagles, buzzards, hoopoes, flamingos, and turtle doves, and the climate is most delightful and invigorating. The first day we spent at Biskra was a Sunday, and Mr Morton (the Chaplain) held a service – Morning Prayer and Holy Communion – in a large salon of the hotel. The congregation consisted of a number of English and American visitors. The afternoon walk to a wooded part of the oasis, under palms, olive, orange and lemon trees, and by streams of water, was delightful.

During our stay at Biskra the Bishop and I visited some native abodes – mud huts, with goats on the roof and dark dwelling rooms below – the manners of these Arab people were singularly courteous, and they welcomed us to their homes very graciously. It is wonderful to see the great flocks of camels, sheep, and goats leaving the town in the early morning to pasture on the scant vegetation of the desert wilderness. The face of a camel is a curious study: he wears an abiding expression of supercilious contempt and dignified suffering which appeals to one very strongly, and may be the result of long centuries of unsympathis- ing treatment.

Mary Sumner, *Memoir of George Henry Sumner*[10]

Missionaries were faced with the same practical problems as explorers with more secular purpose. One of the first missionaries sent out by the Uni- versities Mission to Central Africa, founded after a call by David Livingstone in 1857, tells of his journey in the company of C. F. Mackenzie, the first Bishop of South Africa.

The mission had twenty-one porters at its command. Then came the allocation of burdens, and then for the first time we experienced the traveller's difficulty. Some of the burdens were larger than others, some lighter, and the clamour and contention before each man was satisfied with his particular load was amusing. With the expedition party there was no such disputing; the Makololo and the Sena men did just as they were bidden, and were out of the ship and on to the other side of the river before we were ready to follow. When all was settled and we had got our fellows on to the island, they discovered that they had left their bows and arrows behind. Miserable discovery! for they would not go without them. I laughed at them, I coaxed them, I punched them good-humouredly, I did all that Mr Paymaster Jones himself could have done, in order to get them to enter the boat; but they would have their weapons of war, nobody but slaves went without, and so off they went to the village again, I and William going with them to ensure their return. When once in the village they were in no hurry to leave it, they rushed to their huts and began smoking, and looked as though they did not intend to leave again for a week to come. It was a great trial of patience, but it was no use getting angry: so I kept my temper, and having persuaded one fellow to put down his pipe, I went down to the boat with him trusting the others like sheep would follow. And so they did, with the exception of one man, and his place was well supplied, for nine others stepped forward and offered their services. I chose one to supply the place of him who held back, told the others to await my return, and went off with those to whom burdens were already apportioned. I found the Bishop had gone on ahead, but we soon overtook him with the rest of the mission party. Mr Waller returned with me in order to equip the other porters, and the Bishop went onwards with his detachment – pastoral staff in one hand, and a gun in the other. This pastoral staff was given to him by some of the clergy at Cape Town. The Bishop thought that as it must go up at some time to the place where we should halt, it had better go up at once, and that no person was so fitted by office to carry it is himself. So he set forward. It was a puzzle to the natives; they were afraid of the staff, and thought it was a new kind of gun. Said one –

'Mfuti?' (a gun?)

'Aye mfuti ikuri!' (a great gun) said another.

Henry Rowley, The Story of the Universities Mission to Central Africa[11]

Many missionaries were accompanied by their wives, but there were also women who were missionaries in their own right. Unable to be ordained at that time, they deserve a place in the clerical saga. Edgar Wallace (1875–1932) is best remembered for his crime stories, but he also wrote about the doings of Sanders, a District Commissioner in West Africa in colonial days. He is distinctly cynical about a society woman sent out by a missionary organization.

The missionary was on the point of making one of his long tours in the forest, and would be away with his wife for three months. He placed his pleasant little house at Cynthia's disposal, together with lay workers and interpreters. To Cynthia he sent a long epistle full of words beginning with capitals, such as Faith, Sacrifice, Grace, and Glory. Cynthia read the letter twice to discover whether there was a bath-room in the house [...]

Cynthia did not like her new home, though the novelty of the surroundings was delightful. She spent two days photographing the village, and had herself photographed by a native lay preacher, surrounded by little children who wore no clothes and smelt queerly.

The nights were the worst. In the daytime she could amuse herself with the camera and read the lessons in the thatched church, but the nights were awfully dark and still, and the Christian girl in the next room snored and talked in her sleep about her lover – one M'gara, the Akasava fisherman. Happily, Cynthia did not understand Bomongo and never knew that the scandals of Mayfair have a strong family likeness to the scandals of the Isisi River. For M'gara was a married man and no gentleman.

Then came a new interest in life, for, just as she was getting very bored, Cynthia made a notable convert – Osaku, son of a great witch-doctor, and himself skilled in the arts of magic and necromancy. He was a tall man. 'A noble-looking savage', Cynthia described him in her first letter home. 'And so awfully nice. I gave him a cake of soap – one of those we bought at Pinier's in Paris – and now he simply haunts the place.'

Edgar Wallace, *Sanders*[12]

Christian missionaries were sometimes accused of imposing an alien cultural pattern on converts. But there were many who learned how to distinguish between essentials and local customs. A missionary priest in China has come upon a village where Christian worship has long been celebrated, led by Liu-Chi, a local priest whose usage is unexpected.

Speaking slowly, to make himself understood, Liu-Chi said: 'We welcome you with joy, Father. Come to my house and rest a little before prayer.'

He led the way to the largest house, built on a stone foundation next the church, and showed Father Chisholm, with courteous urbanity, into a low cool room. At the end of the room stood a mahogany spinet and a Portuguese wheel clock. Bewildered, lost in wonder, Francis stared at the clock. The brass dial was engraved: *Lisbon 1632*. He had no time for closer inspection, Liu-Chi was addressing him again. 'Is it your wish to offer mass, Father? Or shall I?' As in a dream Father Chisholm nodded his head towards the other. Something within him answered: 'You … please!' He was groping in a great confusion. He knew he could not rudely break this mystery with speech. He must penetrate it graciously, in patience, with his eyes.

Half an hour later they were all within the church. Though small it had been built with taste in a style that showed the Moorish influence on the Renaissance. There were three simple arcades, beautifully fluted. The doorway and the windows were supported by flat pilasters. On the walls, partly incomplete, free mosaics had been traced. He sat in the front row of an attentive congregation. Every one had ceremonially washed his hands before entering. Most of the men and a few of the women wore praying caps upon their heads. Suddenly a tongueless bell was struck and Liu-Chi approached the altar, wearing a faded yellow alb and supported by two young men. Turning, he bowed ceremoniously to Father Chisholm and the congregation. Then the service began. Father Chisholm watched, kneeling erect, spellbound, like a man beholding the slow enactment of a dream. He saw now that the ceremony was a strange survival, a touching relic of the mass. Liu-Chi must know no Latin, for he prayed in Chinese. First came the confiteor, then the creed. When he ascended the altar and opened the parchment missal on its wooden rest, Francis clearly heard a portion of the gospel solemnly intoned in the native tongue. An original translation … He drew a quick breath of awe.

The whole congregation advanced to take communion. Even children at the breast were carried to the altar steps. Liu-Chi descended, bearing a chalice of rice wine. Moistening his forefinger he placed a drop upon the lips of each. Before leaving the church, the congregation gathered at the Statue of the Saviour, placing lighted joss-sticks on the heavy candelabrum before the feet. Then each person made three prostrations and reverently withdrew. Father Chisholm remained behind, his eyes moist, his heart wrung by the simple childish piety – the same piety, the same simplicity he had so often witnessed in peasant Spain. Of course the ceremony was not valid – he smiled faintly, visualising Father Tarrant's horror at the spectacle – but he had no doubt it was pleasing to God Almighty none the less.

A. J. Cronin, *The Keys of the Kingdom*[13]

A less pleasant aspect of service overseas in the nineteenth century was performed by clergy who went as chaplains to the penal settlements. At a convict station in Australia, North is the chaplain about to be replaced by a newcomer. He is sensitive and compassionate towards the prisoners, but an alcoholic who sometimes fails in his duties. His replacement, Meekin, is a different type. P.-J. de Béranger (1780–1857) was a French poet, popular and much translated in Britain and the United States. Sancho Panza's fantasy island appears in Don Quixote.

'You will find this a terrible place, Mr Meekin,' said North to his supplanter, as they walked across to the Commandant's to dinner. 'It has made me heart-sick.'

'I thought it was a little paradise,' said Meekin. 'Captain Frere says that the scenery is delightful.'

'So it is,' returned North, looking askance; 'but the prisoners are not delightful.'

'Poor, abandoned wretches,' said Meekin, 'I suppose not. How sweet the moonlight sleeps upon that bank! Eh!'

'Abandoned, indeed, by God and man – almost.'

'Mr North, Providence never abandons the most unworthy of His servants. Never have I seen the righteous forsaken, nor his seed begging their bread. In the valley of the shadow of death He is with us. His staff, you know, Mr North. Really, the Commandant's house is charmingly situated!'

Mr North sighed again. 'You have not been long in the colony, Mr Meekin. I doubt – forgive me for expressing myself so freely – if you quite know our convict system.'

'An admirable one! A most admirable one!' said Meekin. 'There were a few matters I noticed in Hobart Town that did not quite please me –

the frequent use of profane language for instance – but on the whole I was delighted with the scheme. It is so complete.'

North pursed up his lips. 'Yes, it is very complete,' he said; 'almost too complete. But I am always in a minority when I discuss the question, so we will drop it, if you please.'

'If you please,' said Meekin, gravely. He had heard from the Bishop that Mr North was an ill-conditioned sort of person, who smoked clay pipes, had been detected in drinking beer out of a pewter pot, and had been heard to state that white neck-cloths were of no consequence.

The dinner went off successfully. Burgess – desirous, perhaps, of favourably impressing the chaplain whom the Bishop delighted to honour – shut off his blasphemy for a while, and was urbane enough. 'You'll find us rough, Mr Meekin,' he said, 'but you'll find us "all there" when we're wanted. This is a little kingdom in itself.'

'Like Béranger's?' asked Meekin, with a smile. Captain Burgess had never heard of Béranger, but he smiled as if he had learnt his words by heart.

'Or like Sancho Panza's island,' said North. 'You remember how justice was administered there?'

'Not at this moment, sir,' said Burgess, with dignity. He had been often oppressed by the notion that the Reverend Mr North 'chaffed' him. 'Pray, help yourself to wine.'

'Thank you, none,' said North, filling a tumbler with water. 'I have a headache.'

His manner of speech and action was so awkward that a silence fell upon the party, caused by each one wondering why Mr North should grow confused, and drum his fingers on the table, and stare everywhere but at the decanter.

Marcus Clarke, *For the Term of his Natural Life*[14]

In 1820, and not in the world of fiction, William Bedford became chaplain to the penal colony in Van Diemans Land – later Tasmania. He decided that the authorities needed reforming even more than the convicts.

He wept, he raged, he prayed. Indignation got the better of his sympathy. His righteous excitement was kindled, not against the poor outcast prisoner, but against the authorities in office. These were seen to live shamelessly in sin. Against these he thundered with a Knox-like zeal in the church which they were forced in etiquette to attend. He denounced their guilt in the language of the old seers, and uttered warnings and judgements with the energy of an Elijah.

He rested not here. To purify the land he appealed to the executive. If a change of heart could not be secured, at least the outward shame of sin might be removed. It would be idle for him to enforce the seventh commandment upon the convicts, when they saw its open violation by their superiors.

He found an able seconder of his schemes of reformation in Governor Arthur, then recently appointed. A Government order was issued, commanding all officers, on pain of dismissal from public service, to amend their lives, and to be united in matrimony with those with whom they had been publicly living in shame, and by whom, in many instances, they had a family. This struck terror into the community of officials. They wished to retain their position, but not to be fettered by the marriage tie. They conjured and they blustered, they presented memorials and they condemned the tyranny; but all in vain. The law was intended for obedience.

Then the malcontents turned upon the real author of this invasion of the rights of their domestic institutions. They sought to cajole him in private, they insulted him in public. They appealed to his generosity at one time, to his fears at another. Prayers, bribes, and threats were all in vain. The fighting Chaplain was not to be driven from his entrenchments nor from his duty.

Gradually and sulkily the discomfited chiefs gave in. Their mistresses were made wives, and their children were legitimatised in the eyes of the law. Then, and not till then, did the champion of virtue attack those of lesser name, and bring his influence to bear upon their public conduct.

The good man fought and conquered. Commencing his warfare almost single-handed, he soon gathered around him useful auxiliaries in the field, who performed valiant service for truth under his captainship. It may be that he struck hard blows with sharp weapons; but it was because he saw that the battle must be real and the struggle be sharp. It was not that his nature was all sternness. We know, from personal acquaintance, that the man was full of human sympathies, and that he combined the love of John with the fire of Peter.

He has since gone to his rest. The colonial lovers of virtue will never cease to recognise with gratitude the labours of the Rev. Dr Bedford, the venerable Chaplain of Hobart Town.

James Bickford, *Christian Work in Australasia*[15]

There have been chaplains in the Royal Navy for many centuries, men – and now women – of sterling quality. It was not always considered so worthwhile a ministry, as Roderick Random, a surgeon's mate in the eighteenth century, discovers when he is ill and visited by the ship's chaplain. 'Bumbo' was a rum punch.

The parson having felt my pulse, inquired into the nature of my complaints, hemmed a little, and began thus: 'Mr Random, God out of his infinite mercy hath been pleased to visit you with a dreadful distemper, the issue of which no man knows. You may be permitted to recover, and live many days on the face of the earth; and, which is more probable, you maybe taken away and cut off in the flower of your youth. It is incumbent on you, therefore, to prepare for the great change, by repenting sincerely of your sins; of this there cannot be a greater sign, than an ingenuous confession, which I conjure you to make, without hesitation or mental reservation; and when I am convinced of your sincerity, I will then give you such comfort as the situation of your soul will admit of. Without doubt, you have been guilty of numberless transgressions to which youth is subject, as swearing, drunkenness, whoredom, and adultery; tell me, therefore, without reserve, the particulars of each, especially the last, that I may be acquainted with the true state of your conscience: for no physician will prescribe for his patient until he knows the circumstances of his disease.' As I was not under any apprehensions of death, I could not help smiling at the chaplain's inquisitive remonstrance, which I told him savoured more of the Roman than of the Protestant church, in recommending auricular confession; a thing, in my opinion, not at all necessary to salvation, and which, for that reason, I declined.

This reply disconcerted him a little; however he explained away his meaning, in making learned distinctions between what was absolutely necessary, and what was only convenient; then proceeded to ask what religion I professed. I answered, that I had not as yet considered the difference of religions, consequently, had not fixed on any one in particular, but that I was bred a presbyterian. At this word the chaplain expressed great astonishment, and said he could not apprehend how a presbyterian was entitled to any post under the English government. Then he asked if I had ever received the sacrament, or taken the oaths; to which questions I replying in the negative, he held up his hands, assured me he could do me no service, wished I might not be in a state of reprobation, and returned to his messmates, who were making merry in the ward-room, round a table well stored with bumbo and wine.

Tobias Smollett, *Roderick Random*[16]

Chaplains to all arms of the services have a fine reputation. Their heroism and self-sacrifice is attested through many wars. William Swayne, Bishop of Lincoln (1920–33), recalls with some amusement his time as a chaplain in the Boer War.

My orders were that the first Sunday after my arrival it was the turn of Touws River to have a Parade Service, and that in the afternoon I should go to Verkeerdevlei for a Parade Service there. I was provided with a Cape cart to drive the twelve miles over the veldt. After Parade Service at Touws River I made my way to Verkeerdevlei and reached it about 1 p.m. The little camp lay at the beginning of the foothills basking in the sun. Everybody seemed to be asleep. Presently a man, aged about forty, who looked as if he might be an officer, came to the door of a tent. He was in his shirt-sleeves. He said, 'Who are you?' I explained that I was from Touws River, and that I had relieved Price. 'What do you want?' he inquired. I replied that I understood that it was their Sunday for a Parade Service. He gazed at me, and then shouted, 'Sergeant! Here is a chaplain who says it is Sunday. Is it Sunday?' A sergeant came out from a tent, also in his shirt-sleeves. 'It is Sunday right enough, sir', he said. 'But we have had no orders for a Parade Service.' I explained that I had only arrived at Touws River the previous day, that I had my orders and understood that the previous chaplain had made the necessary arrangements. 'Well', said Lieutenant Fraser, 'now that you are here we must see what can be done about it, but the men who have been on night patrol are asleep. Others are out with the horses at pasture on the veldt. There are very few left in camp, but I am just going to have my lunch. I always have the same as the men. Will that do for you?' I told him that I had bread and cheese in my haversack, but that I rather thought that the tin of stew being taken into his tent smelled good, and that if he had a ration to spare I would lunch with him. We had a pleasant lunch together. [...] After an interval the sergeant came and reported that he had fallen the men in for Parade Service. It was a hot afternoon. I found a parade of about twelve men, looking thoroughly sulky. They had been dozing in their tents after their dinner and had been suddenly called upon to smarten themselves up for parade. Probably, like Fraser, they had forgotten that it was Sunday. Certainly they had not had a Parade Service for seven weeks. They did not look lovingly at me. Directly we faced the men one of them said, 'May I fall out, sir? I am an atheist.' Fraser turned to the sergeant: 'What religion did Private Cox register when he was recruited?' 'Church of England, sir', said the sergeant. Fraser said: 'Private Cox, you are Church of England until the end of the war. Then you can become an atheist. Fall in. It won't hurt you.'

I distributed my hymn-papers and said, 'We will begin with "Rock of Ages", you can all sing that. I will do the praying and preaching, but you must help with the singing. I am not a songster.'

I started with the first line of 'Rock of Ages'. Not a sound from the men. They gazed stolidly at me. I could not keep it up. I broke down. 'Fair play, men', I said; 'I told you I could not sing'. Fraser said, 'Come, men, raise a song'. Then to me, 'Try again'. I made another effort, and one or two joined in. By the end of the second verse they were all singing. After that the service went perfectly well. There were two more hymns which they sang heartily. I was careful that the service should not be too long, as we were all standing in the sun. After the service I went to the men's tents and had a chat with some of them.

W. S. Swayne, *Parson's Pleasure*[17]

Studdert Kennedy was an army chaplain in the Great War who was much loved by the troops, who nicknamed him 'Woodbine Willie' from his habit of giving out cigarettes. He wrote a number of poems, and although he was not a Wilfred Owen or a Siegfried Sassoon, his love and sincerity break through the language. It is good to remember the heroism shown by many of the chaplains, and not to forget the horror of that and all wars.

There's a broken, battered village
   Somewhere up behind the line,
There's a dug-out and a bunk there
   That I used to say were mine.

I remember how I reached them
   Dripping wet and all forlorn,
In the dun and dreary twilight
   Of a weeping summer morn.

All that week I'd buried brothers,
   In one bitter battle slain,
In one grave I laid two hundred.
   God! What sorrow and what rain!

And that night I'd been in trenches,
   Seeking out the sodden dead,
And just dropping them in shell-holes,
   With a service swiftly said.

For the bullets rattled round me,
   But I couldn't leave them there,
Water-soaked in flooded shell-holes,
   Reft of common Christian prayer.

So I crawled round on my belly,
   And I listened to the roar
Of the guns that hammered Thiepval,
   Like big breakers on the shore.

Then there spoke a dripping sergeant,
  When the time was growing late,
'Would you please to bury this one,
  'Cause 'e used to be my mate?'

So we groped our way in darkness
  To a body lying there,
Just a blacker lump of blackness,
  With a red blotch on his hair.

Though we turned him gently over,
  Yet I still can hear the thud,
As the body fell face forward,
  And then settled in the mud.

We went down upon our faces,
  And I said the service through,
From 'I am the Resurrection'
  To the last, the great 'adieu'.

We stood up to give the Blessing,
  And commend him to the Lord,
When a sudden light shot soaring
  Silver swift and like a sword.

At a stroke it slew the darkness,
  Flashed its glory on the mud,
And I saw the sergeant staring
  At a crimson clot of blood.

There are many kinds of sorrow
  In this world of Love and Hate,
But there is no sterner sorrow
  Than a soldier's for his mate.

    G. A. Studdert Kennedy, 'His Mate'[18]

Chapter 12

All Sorts and Conditions

Make any categories that you will, of any group of the human race, and there will be many who do not come under any precise heading. There have been, and always will be, clergy who do not fit into any special category but are interesting in their own right. Here is a miscellany, selected from the wide range of the clerical order, some at their work, some going about their own lives in their own way.

The three parties to this conversation are a young clergyman, his father, and an older priest called Harrison – 'the doctor'. It is the morning after they have had a disagreeable encounter with some young men who showed little respect for the Cloth. It is a revealing glimpse of the hawks and doves in the Church, still sometimes at odds when clergy talk together. The argument perhaps also tells us something about youthful impatience and elderly moderation as broader human traits. The closing remarks remind us that still, as in the eighteenth century, the clergy are under the strain of being expected always to be 'good'.

The next morning, when the doctor and his two friends were at breakfast, the young clergyman, in whose mind the injurious treatment he had received the evening before was very deeply impressed, renewed the conversation on that subject.

'It is a scandal,' said he, 'to the government, that they do not preserve more respect to the clergy, by punishing all rudeness to them with the utmost severity. It was very justly observed of you, sir,' said he to the doctor, 'that the lowest clergyman in England is in real dignity superior to the highest nobleman. What then can be so shocking as to see that gown, which ought to entitle us to the veneration of all we meet, treated with contempt and ridicule? Are we not, in fact, ambassadors from heaven to the world? And do they not, therefore, in denying us our due respect, deny it in reality to Him that sent us?'

'If that be the case,' says the doctor, 'it behoves them to look to themselves; for He who sent us is able to exact most severe vengeance for the ill treatment of his ministers.'

'Very true, sir,' cries the young one; and I heartily hope He will; but those punishments are at too great a distance to infuse terror into wicked minds. The government ought to interfere with its immediate censures. Fines and imprisonments and corporal punishments operate more forcibly on the human mind than all the fears of damnation.'

'Do you think so?' cries the doctor; 'then I am afraid men are very little in earnest in those fears.'

'Most justly observed,' says the old gentleman. 'Indeed, I am afraid that is too much the case.'

'In that,' said the son, 'the government is to blame. Are not books of infidelity, treating our holy religion as a mere imposture, nay, sometimes as a mere jest, published daily, and spread abroad amongst the people with perfect impunity?'

'You are certainly in the right,' says the doctor; 'there is a most blameable remissness with regard to these matters; but the whole blame doth not lie there; some little share of the fault is, I am afraid, to be imputed to the clergy themselves.'

'Indeed, sir,' cries the young one, 'I did not expect that charge from a gentleman of your cloth. Do the clergy give any encouragement to such books? Do they not, on the contrary, cry loudly out against the suffering them? This is the invidious aspersion of the laity; and I did not expect to hear it confirmed by one of our own cloth.'

'Be not too impatient, young gentleman,' said the doctor. 'I do not absolutely confirm the charge of the laity; it is much too general and too severe; but even the laity themselves do not attack them in that part to which you have applied your defence. They are not supposed such fools as to attack that religion to which they owe their temporal welfare. They are not taxed with giving any other support to infidelity than what it draws from the ill examples of their lives; I mean of the lives of some of them. Here too the laity carry their censures too far; for there are very few or none of the clergy whose lives, if compared with those of the laity, can be called profligate; but such, indeed, is the perfect purity of our religion, such is the innocence and virtue which it exacts to entitle us to its glorious rewards and to screen us from its dreadful punishments, that he must be a very good man indeed who lives up to it. Thus then these persons argue. This man is educated in a perfect knowledge of religion, is learned in its laws, and is by his profession obliged, in a manner, to have them always before his eyes. The rewards which it promises to the obedience of these laws are so great, and the punishments threatened on disobedience so dreadful, that it is impossible but all men must tearfully fly from the one, and as eagerly pursue the other. If, therefore, such a person lives in direct opposition to, and in a constant breach of, these laws, the inference is obvious.'

Henry Fielding, *Amelia*[1]

Several clerical diarists have been quoted. The most famous and the most endearing in James Woodforde (1740–1803), Rector of Weston Longeville, Norfolk, from 1774. His diary tells of his social life, his home affairs where his niece Nancy was his housekeeper, many details of his food and drink, but also his pastoral concern that belies the bad image of the careless eighteenth-century parson. A few extracts give the essence of the man, beginning with the traditional dinner which he gave to farmers who came to pay their tithes. Such hospitality was intended to soften the imposition; Woodforde seems to have been more successful than some of his contemporaries.

December 3 [1776]. My Frolic for my People to pay Tithe to me was this day. I gave them a good dinner, sirloin of Beef roasted, a Leg of Mutton boiled and plumb Puddings in plenty. Rec⟨eive⟩d to-day only for Tithe and Glebe of them ⟨£⟩236.2. They all broke up about 10 at night. Dinner at 2. Every Person well pleased, and were very happy indeed. They had to drink Wine, Punch, and Ale as much as they pleased; they drank of wine 6 Bottles, of Rum 1 gallon and half, and I know not what ale […] We had many droll songs from some of them.

[*A few years later, he records one of his evenings out.*]
June 10 [1784]. About 3 o'clock this Afternoon Mr and Mrs Custance called on us, took us into their Coach and carried us to Mr Micklethwaite's where we dined and spent the remaining part of the Afternoon and part of the Evening […] We had a very genteel Dinner, Soles and Lobster Sauce, Spring Chicken boiled and a Tongue, a Piece of roast Beef, Soup, a Fillet of Veal roasted with Morells and Truffles, and Pigeon Pie for the first Course: Sweet-breads, a green Goose and Peas, Apricot

Pie, Cheese-cakes, Stewed Mushrooms and Trifle. The Ladies and Gentlemen very genteely dressed. Mr Micklethwaite had in his Shoes a Pair of Silver Buckles which cost between 7 and 8 Pounds. Miles Branthwaite had a pair that cost 5 guineas.

[*But here is another aspect of this country parson.*]
June 9 [*1787*]. I went and read Prayers again this morning to Mrs Leggatt and administered also the H⟨oly⟩ Sacrament to her – she was very weak indeed and but just alive. She was sensible and showed marks of great satisfaction after receiving the H⟨oly⟩ Sacrament. She never received it before. Pray God bless her.

June 12. Our Archdeacon Mr Younge and Morphew junr. breakfasted with us this Morning at 9 o'clock. After breakfast I walked with them to our Church to see the same, as the Archdeacon is going round to survey the Churches of this Deanery. And there I took my leave of them for the present. We had Tea and Coffee for breakfast. Nancy likes the Archdeacon much, he is a very cheerful merry little Man and sensible, and came out of Devonshire some few Years ago.

[*News travelled slowly. The Bastille fell on 14 July 1789 and Woodforde made a laconic note of it ten days later.*]
July 24 [*1789*]. Friday I breakfasted, dined &c. again at Cole. To a Fisherman for a fine Crab, 4 p⟨oun⟩d, p⟨ai⟩d 1 s⟨hilling⟩. Very great Rebellion in France by the Papers. The Bath Paper (the only Paper taken in here) comes every Friday Morning. Mr Robert Clarke of Castle-Cary spent the Aft⟨ernoon⟩. with us. He was drove in the Rain, as he was going to Bruton, and stayed till the Evening, he did not go to Bruton.

[*During the Napoleonic Wars, days of national penance and fasting were sometimes declared. Woodforde responded conscientiously to his duty, but the last entry for the day rather lets down the observance of the fast.*]
April 19 [*1793*]. Friday, Fast-Day. This being a Day appointed to be observed as a publick Fast in these seditious times and France (the avowed Disturbers of all Peace in Europe) having declared War against us, unprovoked, I walked to Church about 11 o'clock and read Prayers provided on the occasion at Weston Church this Morning, a large Congregation attended Divine Service which I was very glad to meet on the Occasion. Pray God our Prayers may be accepted, the Hearts of all the

Enemies to Peace converted, and a happy and general restoration to Peace, good Order and Government re-established to all the different Powers of Europe concerned. I found it very cold to Church and back again rough N.E. Wind with Hail and Snow &c. Dinner to day roast Loin of Pork &c.

[*Although later polemicists made much of the neglect of the Eucharist at this period, here is more evidence of the importance which Woodforde attached to this part of his ministry.*]

May 8 [*1796*]. By particular desire of Billy Gunton, & which I promised him on Friday last, as this day to administer the H⟨oly⟩ Sacrament to him, himself with his Mistress Mrs Michael Andrews, came to my House about 11 o'clock this Morning and I then had them into the Parlour and there administered the H⟨oly⟩ Sacrament to them and which I hope will be attended with due effects both to him, Mrs Andrews & myself. I put on my Gown and Band on the Occasion. Mrs Andrews appeared to pay as much Attention to Billy Gunton, tho' her Servant, as if it was really her own Son – very good of her. It gave me great pleasure, tho' far from well, in doing what I did, as it will ever give me pleasure to do any thing in my power, that may give any satisfaction or ease to any person whatever, especially to the distressed. No Service at Church this Afternoon, the Church not being fit. Next Sunday I hope there will. Dinner today, Leg of Mutton roasted &c.

James Woodforde, *The Diary of a Country Parson*[2]

Parish ministry has never been without its problems. John Skinner, a Somerset rector in the early nineteenth century, took the funeral of a man who had died suddenly by a fall from his horse, and of whose way of life he did not approve. His diary records his trials both in church and with an odd collection of personal opponents.

July 28 [*1821*]. I was up early, and commenced writing the sermon I have for some time been reflecting on, respecting the awful departure of Charles Dando, on the text 'Let us eat and drink for tomorrow we die.' I had ever made a point during the whole of my Ministry, not to be personal in my sermons, and therefore should not mention any names or particulars, but I conceived it my duty not to let slip this solemn opportunity of impressing the necessity of reformation, lest we should be cut off suddenly, and it be too late.

July 29. I preached to a crowded audience, so great indeed, the Church could not contain them. They were for the most part attentive to the discourse, which spoke of Death and Immortality. I must say, I was not a little hurt at the total want of all propriety in the people after the Service was concluded, since instead of returning quietly to their respective homes in order to reflect on the subject I had taken so much pains to impress on their minds, and which had so fully occupied my own, they banish at once all serious reflection by a merry peal! This barbarous interruption to self communion however, I soon put a stop to in person, and gave orders to the Clerk to bring the Key of the Church in future to the Parsonage, as soon as the service was concluded. Alas! my labours in the Vineyard, I feel more and more convinced are of no avail: when I look for good fruit the grapes still continue to tart, they set my teeth on edge. Truly may it be said Society is now out of joint; what with Methodists, Catholics, Colliers, Servants and Attornies, all domestic comfort is estranged: may better prospects brighten upon me.

Journal of a Somerset Rector[3]

Among all the changes in the ministry of the churches, personal appearance is not to be forgotten. E. B. Ellman (1815–1906) remembers controversy about beards.

Nowadays many clergymen wear hair on their faces – I, myself, in my old age, have given up shaving – and few people would know the commotion a beard on a clergyman's face made a few years ago. The Rev. C. Bradford, once Vicar of Arlington, on returning to England after several years' absence, requested permission of Bishop Gilbert to officiate occasionally in the Diocese, at the same time he mentioned that by the advice of a Servian doctor he had given up shaving. At that time it was most peculiar for an officiating clergyman not to be clean-shaven. Shortly afterwards, Mr Bradford appeared in the reading-desk at St Mary's, Brighton, to take the prayers, whereupon as soon as the service began, one of the congregation immediately left the church (or chapel as it was then called), went home, and wrote a letter to the Bishop. His letter said that he was sure his lordship would not approve of anyone with an unshaven face officiating in the Diocese. It was a fact which he himself had been witness to in St Mary's. He added that he could not stop to the service, as he felt it his duty to show his disapprobation, and at once to inform his lordship. My informant was the Rev. Henry Browne, the Bishop's Chaplain. He said it was amusing to see the Bishop's eyes twinkling as he told him of the letter he had received, mentioning that he himself had given to Mr Bradford permission to officiate in the Diocese, 'with an unshaven face,' and adding, 'What could I say, when I look at the portraits of these, my predecessors', pointing as he spoke to the unshaven faces of the Bishops who adorn the wall of the dining-room at the palace.

E. B. Ellman, *Recollections of a Sussex Parson*[4]

The Presbyterian Church of Scotland suffered division and disruption in the eighteenth century after the Patronage Act of 1712 seemed to infringe the right of local congregations to choose their own ministers. John Galt (1779–1839) created the Revd Michael Balwhidder, who tells of his troubles and pleasures as a minister in Ayrshire from 1760 to 1810. He begins with a lively account of his tumultuous induction as an unpopular patron's choice.

It was a great affair; for I was put in by the patron and the people knew nothing whatsoever of me, and their hearts were stirred into strife on the occasion, and they did all that lay within the compass of their power to keep me out, insomuch, that there was obliged to be a guard of soldiers to protect the presbytery; and it was a thing that made my heart grieve when I heard the drum beating and the fife playing as we were going to the kirk. The people were really mad and vicious, and flung dirt upon us as we passed, and reviled us all, and held out the finger of scorn at me; but I endured it with a resigned spirit, compassionating their wilfulness and blindness. Poor old Mr Kilfuddy of the Braehill got such a dash of glar [*mud*] on the side of his face, that his eye was almost extinguished.

When we got to the kirk door, it was found to be nailed up, so as by no possibility to be opened. The serjeant of the soldiers wanted to break it, but I was afraid that the heritors would grudge and complain of the expense of a new door, and I supplicated him to let it be as it was; we were, therefore, obligated to go in by a window, and the crowd followed us, in the most unreverent manner, making the Lord's house like an inn on a fair day, with their grievous yellyhooing. During the time of the psalm and the sermon, they behaved themselves better, but when the induction came on, their clamour was dreadful; and Thomas Thorl the weaver, a pious zealot in that time, he got up and protested, and said, 'Verily, verily, I say unto you, he that entereth not by the door into the sheepfold, but climbeth up some other way, the same is a thief and a robber.' And I thought I would have a hard and sore time of it with such an outstrapolous people. Mr Given, that was then the minister of Lugton, was a jocose man, and would have his joke even at a solemnity. When the laying of the hands upon me was a-doing, he could not get near enough to put on his, but he stretched out his staff and touched my head, and said, to the great diversion of the rest, 'This will do well enough, timber to timber;' but it was an unfriendly saying of Mr Given, considering the time and the place, and the temper of my people.

After the ceremony, we then got out at the window, and it was a heavy day to me, but we went to the manse, and there we had an excellent dinner, which Mrs Watts of the new inns of Irvilles prepared at my request, and sent her chaise-driver to serve, for he was likewise her waiter, she not having but the one chaise, and that not often called for.

John Galt, *Annals of the Parish*[5]

Yet some clergy have known greater distress than unresponsive congrega-tions. Arthur Dimmesdale is one of the best-known tormented fictional clergymen. Highly respected by his New England flock, he is the father of the illegitimate child for whom Hester Prynne has been put to public shame. He lives with a secret that he is afraid to confess openly.

To the high mountain-peaks of faith and sanctity he would have climbed, had not the tendency been thwarted by the burden, whatever it might be, of crime or anguish, beneath which it was his doom to totter. It kept him down on a level with the lowest; him, the man of ethereal attributes, whose voice the angels might else have listened to and answered! But this very burden it was that gave him sympathies so intimate with the sinful brotherhood of mankind; so that his heart vibrated in unison with theirs, and received their pain into itself, and sent its own throb of pain through a thousand other hearts, in gushes of sad, persuasive eloquence. Oftenest persuasive, but sometimes terrible! The people knew not the power that moved them thus. They deemed the young clergyman a miracle of holiness. They fancied him the mouthpiece of Heaven's messages of wisdom, and rebuke, and love. In their eyes, the very ground on which he trod was sanctified. The virgins of his church grew pale around him, victims of a passion so imbued with religious sentiment, that they imagined it to be all religion, and brought it openly, in their white bosoms, as their most acceptable sacrifice before the altar. The aged members of his flock, beholding Mr Dimmesdale's frame so feeble, while they were themselves so rugged in their infirmity, believed that he would go heavenward before them, and enjoined it upon their children that their old bones should be buried close to their young pastor's holy grave. And all this time, perchance, when poor Mr Dimmesdale was thinking of his grave, he questioned with himself whether the grass would ever grow on it, because an accursed thing must there be buried!

It is inconceivable, the agony with which this public veneration tortured him. It was his genuine impulse to adore the truth, and to reckon all things shadow-like, and utterly devoid of weight or value, that had not its divine essence as the life within their life. Then what was he? – a substance? – or the dimmest of all shadows? He longed to speak out from his own pulpit at the full height of his voice, and tell the people what he was. 'I, whom you behold in these black garments of the priesthood – I, who ascend the sacred desk, and turn my pale face heavenward, taking upon myself to hold communion in your behalf with the Most High Omniscience – I, in whose daily life you discern the sanctity of Enoch – I, whose footsteps, as you suppose, leave a gleam along my earthly track, whereby the pilgrims that shall come after me may be guided to the regions of the blest – I, who have laid the hand of baptism upon your children – I, who have breathed the parting prayer over your dying friends, to whom the Amen sounded faintly from a world which they had quitted – I, your pastor, whom you so reverence and trust, am utterly a pollution and a lie!'

Nathaniel Hawthorne, *The Scarlet Letter*[6]

Perhaps self-satisfaction and narrow perception are even worse afflictions than guilt, because they are not recognized by the one who suffers from them. Loyalty to denomination above all else was immortalized by Henry Fielding in the words of Parson Thwackum.

When I mention religion, I mean the Christian religion; and not only the Christian religion, but the Protestant religion; And not only the Protestant religion, but the Church of England.

Henry Fielding, Tom Jones[7]

The same fault appears in every generation. Harriet Beecher Stowe is too often thought of as the author of one novel, but she was a prolific writer. After the success of Uncle Tom's Cabin *she returned to the attack on slavery in* Dred, *in which the clergy who supported slavery with various degrees of conviction are pilloried. Dr Calker is an heir to the tradition of Thwackum.*

Dr Calker was a man of powerful though narrow mind, of great energy and efficiency, and of that capability of abstract devotion which makes the soldier or the statesman. He was earnestly and sincerely devout, as he understood devotion. He began with loving the church for God's sake, and ended with loving her better than God. And, by the church, he meant the organization of the Presbyterian church in the United States of America. Her cause, in his eyes, was God's cause; her glory, God's glory; her success, the indispensable condition of the millennium; her defeat, the defeat of all that was good for the human race. His devotion to her was honest and unselfish.

Of course Dr Calker estimated all interests by their influence on the Presbyterian church. He weighed every cause in the balance of her sanctuary. What promised extension and power to her, *that* he supported. What threatened defeat or impediment, that he was ready to sacrifice. He would, at any day, sacrifice himself and all his interests to that cause, and he felt equally willing to sacrifice others and their interests. The anti-slavery cause he regarded with a simple eye to this question. It was a disturbing force, weakening the harmony among brethren, threatening disruption and disunion. He regarded it, therefore, with distrust and aversion. He would read no facts on that side of the question. And when the discussion of zealous brethren would bring frightful and appalling statements into the general assembly, he was too busy in seeking what could be said to ward off their force, to allow them to have much influence on his own mind. Gradually he came to view the whole subject with dislike, as a pertinacious intruder in the path of the Presbyterian church. That the whole train of cars, laden with the interests of the world for all time, should be stopped by a ragged, manacled slave across the track, was to him an impertinence and absurdity. What was he, that the Presbyterian church should be divided and hindered for him? So thought the exultant thousands who followed Christ, once, when the blind beggar raised his importunate clamor, and they bade him hold his peace. So thought not HE, who stopped the tide of triumphant success, that he might call the neglected one to himself, and lay his hands upon him.

Dr Calker had from year to year opposed the agitation of the slavery question in the general assembly of the Presbyterian church, knowing well that it threatened disunion. When, in spite of all his efforts, disunion came, he bent his energies to the task of reuniting and he was the most important character in the present caucus.

Harriet Beecher Stowe, *Dred* [8]

Gerard Manley Hopkins (1844–89) stopped writing poetry when he entered the Jesuit Order but began again with the permission, and indeed the encouragement, of his Superior. In one of his finest poems he records an episode in the life of a Roman Catholic priest ministering to the sick and dying. The relationship which he describes will be familiar to priests and ministers of all denominations.

Felix Randal the farrier, O he is dead then? my duty all ended,
Who have watched his mould of man, big-boned and hardy-
    handsome
Pining, pining, till time when reason rambled in it and some
Fatal four disorders, fleshed there, all contended?
Sickness broke him. Impatient he cursed at first, but mended
Being anointed and all; though a heavenlier heart began some
Months earlier, since I had our sweet reprieve and ransom
Tendered to him. Ah well, God rest him all road ever he offended!

This seeing the sick endears them to us, us too it endears.
My tongue had taught thee comfort, touch had quenched thy tears,
Thy tears that touched my heart, child, Felix, poor Felix Randal,
How far from then forethought of, all thy more boisterous years,
When thou at the random grim forge, powerful amidst peers,
Didst fettle for the great grey drayhorse his bright and battering
    sandal!

G. M. Hopkins, 'Felix Randal'⁹

Sometimes the priest is lonely and is not the type to seek refuge in extro-version.

The priest picks his way
Through the parish. Eyes watch him
From windows, from the farms
Hearts wanting him to come near
The flesh rejects him.

Women, pouring from the black kettle
Stir up the whirling tea-grounds
Of their thoughts; offer him a dark
Filling in their smiling sandwich.

Priests have a long way to go.
The people wait for them to come
To them over the broken glass
Of their vows, making them pay
With their sweat's coinage for their correction.

He goes up a green lane
Through growing birches; lambs cushion
His vision. He comes slowly down
In the dark, feeling the cross warp
In his hands; hanging on it his thought's icicles.

'Crippled soul', do you say? looking at him
From the mind's height; 'limping through life

On his prayers. There are other people
In the world, sitting at table
Contented, though the broken body
And the shed blood are not on the menu.'

'Let it be so,' I say. 'Amen and amen.'

R. S. Thomas, 'The Priest'[10]

Whether or not this next priest is a dream-figure, he stands for the faithful continuance of priestly service when no one notices or seems to care.

Sadly the dead leaves rustle in the whistling wind,
Around the weather-worn, grey church, low down the vale:
The Saints in golden vesture shake before the gale;
The glorious windows shake, where still they dwell enshrined;
Old Saints by long-dead, shrivelled hands, long since designed:
There still, although the world autumnal be, and pale,
Still in their golden vesture the old Saints prevail;
Alone with Christ, desolate else, left by mankind.

Only one ancient Priest offers the Sacrifice,
Murmuring holy Latin immemorial:
Swaying with tremulous hands the old censer full of spice,
In grey, sweet incense clouds; blue, sweet clouds mystical:
To him, in place of men, for he is old, suffice
Melancholy remembrances and vesperal.

Lionel Johnson, 'The Church of a Dream'[11]

Conscience and the rules of the Church can add to the burdens of the clergy, already in the spotlight of lay observation. This is a revealing and moving idea of how priests need and find mutual support. In late nineteenth-century Ireland Father Tom, badly in need of money for the repair of his church, has refused to marry a young couple until they can produce the proper fee, and finds that they have apparently spent the night together. He goes to consult his clerical uncle, Father John, who speaks first.

'But have you refused to marry anyone because they couldn't pay you your dues?'

'Listen, the church is falling.'

'My dear Tom, you shouldn't have refused to marry them,' he said, as soon as his soul-stricken curate had laid the matter before him.

'Nothing can justify my action in refusing to marry them,' said Father Tom, 'nothing. Uncle John, I know that you can extenuate, that you are kind, but I don't see it is possible to look at it from any other side.'

'My dear Tom, you are not sure they remained together; the only knowledge you have of the circumstances you obtained from that old woman, Biddy M'Hale, who cannot tell a story properly. An old gossip, who manufactures stories out of the slightest materials ... but who sells excellent eggs; her eggs are always fresh. I had two this morning.'

'Uncle John, I did not come here to he laughed at.'

'I am not laughing at you, my dear Tom; but really you know very little about this matter.'

'I know well enough that they remained together last night. I examined the old woman carefully, and she had just met Kate Kavanagh on the road. There can be no doubt about it,' he said.

'But,' said Father John, 'they intended to be married; the intention was there.'

'Yes, but the intention is no use. We aren't living in a country where the edicts of the Council of Trent haven't been promulgated.'

'That's true,' said Father John. 'But how can I help you? What am I to do?'

'Are you feeling well enough for a walk this morning? Could you come up to Kilmore?'

'But it is two miles – I really –'

'The walk will do you good. If you do this for me, Uncle John –'

'My dear Tom, I am, as you say, not feeling very well this morning, but –'

He looked at his nephew, and seeing that he was suffering, he said: 'I know what these scruples of conscience are; they are worse than physical suffering.'

But before he decided to go with his nephew to seek the sinners out, he could not help reading him a little lecture.

'I don't feel as sure as you do that a sin has been committed; but admitting that a sin has been committed, I think you ought to admit that you set your face against the pleasure of these poor people too resolutely.'

'Pleasure,' said Father Tom. 'Drinking and dancing, hugging and kissing each other about the lanes.'

'You said dancing – now, I can see no harm in it.'

'There's no harm in dancing, but it leads to harm. If they only went back with their parents after the dance, but they linger in the lanes.'

'It was raining the other night, and I felt sorry, and I said, "Well, the boys and girls will have to stop at home to-night, there will he no courting to-night." If you don't let them walk about the lanes and make their own marriages, they marry for money. These walks at eventide represent all the aspiration that may come into their lives. After they get married, the work of the world grinds all the poetry out of them.'

'Walking under the moon,' said Father Tom, 'with their arms round each other's waists, sitting for hours saying stupid things to each other – that isn't my idea of poetry. The Irish find poetry in other things than sex.'

'Mankind,' said Father John, 'is the same all the world over. The Irish aren't different from other races; do not think it. Woman represents all the poetry that the ordinary man is capable of appreciating.'

'And what about ourselves?'

'We're different. We have put this interest aside. I have never regretted it, and you have not regretted it either.'

'Celibacy has never been a trouble to me.'

'But Tom, your own temperament should not prevent you from sympathy with others. You aren't the whole of human nature; you should try to get a little outside yourself.'

George Moore, 'Patchwork'[12]

The Parochial Church Council (PCC) in Church of England parishes, and its equivalent in other churches, can be a great support to the clergy. Unfortunately, meetings are not always entirely irenical. Here a PCC meeting is divided over a controversial letting of the curate's house and vandalism in the churchyard. Then another issue, one familiar in a previous chapter and not quite forgotten in recent times, causes further disruption. The fact that the Vicar is murdered later in the novel does not arise from these sad disagreements.

The two rows of cane-bottomed chain creaked in disharmony like the members of a mutinous orchestra. The old clergyman sitting at bay behind the table facing them blew his nose and added a thunderous crescendo. As if in mockery of his catarrh, rain dripped down the windows and carried a stream of North London dirt to swell the flow of water and dead leaves into the churchyard next door. The parish room was cheerless enough to suggest a slight alleviation of the November night rather than a shelter from it. Modified cold and not real warmth came from the iron stove at the wrong end of the room, occasionally adding a puff of smoke to the stale air. The Church of England, scorned by her enemies as a prosperous bastion of the Establishment, offered to her friends only a thorough mortification of the flesh and a touch of holy poverty. In a mood suitable to the night, the Parochial Church Council was assembled [...]

'It's a judgement on the Popish practices that are tolerated in this parish.'

A sigh ran through the small assembly, and heads turned with a movement of resignation rather than from any need to find out who had spoken. A woman of about forty was standing up in the middle of the second row of chairs, clutching her large black handbag as if she intended to use it as a weapon if she were given any more provocation. She herself, though clearly human in all normal respects, gave the impression of being somehow wrought out of the same black leather. She was thinnish yet seemed to be stuffed until shiny and threadbare with the material for denunciation. Her mouth was a tight clasp, now snapped open for an exodus of tumbling words.

'Ever since I came to live in this parish', she said, 'I have watched with sorrow the Protestant church of this land being profaned and degraded. I have sat on this Council and tried to add my voice to the cause of pure religion, in the face of those who are Roman Catholics in all but name. After four hundred years of freedom from superstition and priestcraft, we are being made to bow down before the idols of incense, vestments – and now we hear a word like *aumbry* being used freely in an open meeting.'

'Aumbries are all right, you know, Miss Mason,' the Vicar said gently and more cheerfully. 'Of course it depends on what authority you attach to the 1928 Book. And please let me assure you that nobody is expected to bow down to things which are but the traditional externals of Catholic worship.'

'Catholic!' said Miss Mason with horrified scorn.

'We so confess ourselves in the Creed,' said the Vicar.

'This is just playing with words. I say, look at reality and see where all these practices have brought us. First of all we are held up to public ridicule because of this affair of the parish house, and now we get hooligans treating us with contempt and desecrating the church.'

'Our level of churchmanship has nothing to do with the first affair, and I fail to see how it can be affected by the second.'

'When people know that a church is riddled with superstition, they see it as a ground for any kind of wickedness. It's as plain as the nose on your face.'

The Vicar wiped his sore and insulted nose tenderly and shook his head.

Simon Nash, *Unhallowed Murder*[13]

A clergyman who prefers to remain anonymous has versified some possible experiences of parish ministry.

They told me in my training all the things I ought to do:
How to read the lessons clearly, and to give the hymns out too,
They said that every sermon the listeners should enthral,
With three clear points of doctrine and no long words at all.
I must never fall asleep if the PCC should be a bore,
And if I did, be very, very careful not to snore.
As for marriage preparation, I had the answers pat,
And I thought the job would work out just like that.

Very soon, with my new collar, and a Bible in my hand,
I made a point of visiting one of our faithful band –
A very nice old lady, though she had a lot to say,
And I found that she was having a rather nasty day.
'My chest is something cruel, there's a swelling on my knee,
And my back's all red and swollen – oh, would you like to see?'

'No, I really couldn't help, I'm not a doctor, where's my hat?'
I didn't think the job would be like that.

I needed some refreshment, so I made another call
On a regular church member, once a colonel in Bengal.
He made me very welcome, and to put me at my ease
Showed me photographs of tigers, and men with guns in trees
'Now I think a drop of whisky would be just the thing for me.
I know you won't touch it, Padre, but do have a cup of tea –
And then we can continue with our cosy little chat.'
I didn't think the job would be like that.

The Sunday School seemed easy – each a charming little mite,
If I told some Bible stories, it would fill them with delight.
'What team did Samson play for?' asked a cheeky sort of lad.
'Johnny's been and stole my pencil', said another. 'Oh, that's bad.
You must not pull Susan's pigtails, it isn't very nice.
Yes, we love all living creatures, but you can't bring your white mice.
No, we haven't room for skateboards, Oh, be quiet, you horrid brat!'
I didn't think the job would be like that.

I went into the vestry just to get a bit of quiet.
When the verger, said, 'Come quickly, you've got to stop a riot.
Two ladies here are fighting about where to put the flowers,
And the bellringers would like to ring a peal for sixteen hours.
The chancel roof is leaking, the boiler will not light,
The Archdeacon says he wants a word with you tomorrow night,
And a piece from off the tower, has just killed a neighbour's cat.'
I didn't think the job would be like that!

Anonymous *(unpublished)*

What of the Christian groups who have declined to have an ordained ministry? Those who have led them, often against much opposition from the mainstream churches, deserve their place in the record.

George Fox, the founder of the Society of Friends, was one of the most courageous men in the history of British Christianity. He suffered much persecution and was never one to shrink from declaring himself. Here is what an admiring Victorian biographer calls 'one of the most extravagant manifestations of folly that he ever exhibited', though the present age, perhaps more tolerant of maverick behaviour, may read it with greater sympathy. Fox was moving through the English Midlands, preaching.

I shall relate it exactly as he relates it himself in his own journal. Were it told by anyone else, we should of necessity suppose that there must be some exaggeration in the account. As he was walking along, he says, with several friends, he lifted up his head, and saw three steeple-house spires, which, as he expresses it, struck at his life. He asked his companions what place that was, and they told him Lichfield; and immediately the word came to him that he must go thither. He said nothing to his friends, however, of his intention to do so, but went with them to a house where they were to stop, and as soon as he saw them fairly lodged, stole away from them, and scampered in a straight line over hedges and ditches till he came to a field within a mile of Lichfield, where there were some shepherds keeping sheep. 'There' says he, 'I was commanded by the Lord to pull off my shoes; and I stood still, for it was winter, and the word of the Lord was like a fire in me. So I put off my shoes, and left them with the shepherds, and the poor shepherds trembled and were astonished. Then I walked on about a mile till I came into the city, and as soon as I got within the city, the word of the Lord came to me again, saying, "Cry, Woe unto the bloody city of Lichfield!" So I went up and down the streets, crying with a loud voice, "Woe to the bloody city of Lichfield!" And, it being market-day, I went into the market-place and to and fro in the several parts of it, and made stands, crying as before, "Woe to the bloody city of Lichfield!" And no one laid hands on me; but as I went thus crying through the streets, there seemed to me, to be a channel of blood running down the streets, and the market-place appeared like a pool of blood. Now when I had declared what was upon me, and felt myself clear, I went out of the town in peace, and, returning to the shepherds, gave them some money, and took my shoes of them again. But the fire of the Lord was so in my feet, and all over me, that I did not matter to put on my shoes any more, and was at a stand whether I should or no till I felt freedom from the Lord so to do; and then, after I had washed my feet, I put on my shoes again.'

[*Reflecting on the reason for what he had done, Fox discovered that, as well as more recent persecutions, there had been a great slaughter of Christians at Lichfield in the time of Diocletian.*]

J. S. Watson, *Life of George Fox*[14]

George Fox was on the whole not typical of the Society of Friends which he founded. A gentler and less eccentric manner was, and is, generally found among them. John Woolman (1720–72) was an American Quaker, born in New Jersey, who came to England to win support for his work for the abolition of slavery, a cause in which later members of the Society were to be prominent. This eulogy is part of a Testimony issued after his death by the Meeting in the town of his birth.

His Concern for the Poor and those in Affliction was evident by his Visits to them; whom he frequently relieved by his Assistance and Charity. He was for many Years deeply exercised on Account of the poor enslaved Africans, whose Cause, as he sometimes mentioned, lay almost continually upon him, and to obtain Liberty to those Captives, he laboured both in public and private; and was favoured to see his Endeavours crowned with considerable Success. He was particularly desirous that Friends should not be instrumental to lay Burthens on this oppressed People, but remember the Days of suffering from which they had been providentially delivered; that, if Times of Trouble should return, no Injustice dealt to those in Slavery might rise in judgment against us, but, being clear, we might on such Occasions address the Almighty with a degree of Confidence, for his Interposition and Relief; being particularly careful, as to himself, not to countenance Slavery even by the Use of those Conveniences of Life which were furnished by their Labour.

He was desirous to have his own, and the Minds of others, redeemed from the Pleasures and immoderate Profits of this World, and to fix them on those joys which fade not away; his principal Care being after a Life of Purity, endeavouring to avoid not only the grosser Pollutions, but those also which, appearing in a more refined Dress, are not sufficiently guarded against by some well-disposed People. In the latter Part of his Life he was remarkable for the Plainness and Simplicity of his Dress, and, as much as possible, avoided the Use of Plate, costly Furniture, and feasting; thereby endeavouring to become an Example of Temperance and Self-denial, which he believed himself called unto, and was favoured with Peace therein, although it carried the Appearance of great Austerity in the View of some. He was very moderate in his Charges in the Way of Business, and in his Desires after Gain; and, though a Man of Industry, avoided, and strove much to lead others out of extreme Labour and Anxiousness after perishable Things; being desirous that the Strength of our Bodies might not be spent in Procuring Things unprofitable, and that we might use Moderation and Kindness to the brute Animals under our Care, to prize the Use of them as a great Favour, and by no Means abuse them; that the Gifts of Providence should be thankfully received and applied to the Uses they were designed for.

He several Times opened a School at Mount-Holly, for the Instruction of poor Friends' Children and others, being concerned for their Help and Improvement therein: His Love and Care for the rising Youth among us were truly great, recommending to Parents and those who have the Charge of them, to choose conscientious and pious Tutors, saying, 'It is a lovely Sight to behold innocent Children' and that 'to labour for their Help against that which would mar the Beauty of their Minds, is a Debt we owe them.'

The Journal and Other Writings of John Woolman[15]

The Plymouth Brethren took their name from the establishment of their first English congregation in that city, but their real origin was in Dublin, where a group of like-minded Evangelical Christians had started coming together for worship. Their founder, J. N. Darby, is described with great respect by an anonymous later member of the Brethren, though the final comment has a strong reservation about one aspect of his work.

Meanwhile, from Dublin, the little company of worshippers had extended itself to other towns. The expansion was largely due to the untiring efforts of J. N. Darby. His was a very remarkable and powerful personality. Born in 1800, he became a high church clergyman in Wicklow, where his intense devotion, asceticism and zeal made a deep impression on the simple country folk, but he lost sympathy with the Church on account of its subservience to the State instead of to the supreme Head, the Lord Jesus Christ. At this time he was introduced […] to the little gatherings in Dublin, and he was led to publish a tract on the nature and unity of the Church, as comprising no one sect, but all

true believers who walked in the light. He resigned his curacy in 1828
[…] It was mainly owing to Mr Darby's influence that these principles
spread far and wide, and that an informal fellowship developed, linking
together those who held them. He was a man of tremendous force of
character and determination, with a most uncommon power of in-
fluencing the minds of others, not only of weaklings, but of strong men
and learned theologians. He was a deep student of the Word, and read
scarcely anything else. Possessed of private means, and able to speak
fluently in several languages, he was one of those important men who
think in terms, not of parishes, but of continents. He travelled everywhere, staying a few months at a time in each place, and either found or
founded gatherings of earnest Christians, in many cases the pick and
flower of the Churches, who rejoiced in the truths he had to teach, and
in the prospect of returning to the days of the apostles. He extended his
labours to Canton Vaud and elsewhere in French Switzerland, where he
reaped a very large accession of members […] It was naturally thrown
up against Mr Darby that he detached Christians from their own
Churches, which was true, but as a matter of fact very many were converted under his ministry. The power of his preaching and the freshness
and comprehensiveness of his teaching can scarcely be gauged from his
writings, which are often wretchedly composed.

'A Younger Brother'[16]

*William Booth, who founded the Salvation Army in 1878, is remembered by
his son, who succeeded him as General.*

One picture among the many that I cherish of my father I should like to
place at the very beginning of what I have to say of him here. It explains
a certain new development in the history of The Army, but it also gives
a glimpse of the deep fires that burned in the personality of William
Booth. One morning, away back in the eighties, I was an early caller at
his house in Clapton. Here I found him in his dressing-room, completing his toilet with ferocious energy. The hair-brushes which he held
in either hand were being wielded with quite eloquent vigour upon a
mane that was more refractory than usual, and his braces were flying like
the wings of Pegasus. No good-morning-how-do-you-do here!
 'Bramwell!', he cried, when he caught sight of me, 'did you know that

men slept out all night on the bridges?' He had arrived in London very late the night before from some town in the south of England, and had to cross the city to reach his home. What he had seen on that midnight return accounted for this morning tornado. Did I know that men slept out all night on the Bridges?

'Well, yes,' I replied, 'a lot of poor fellows, I suppose, do that.'

'Then you ought to be ashamed of yourself to have known it and to have done nothing for them,' he went on, vehemently.

I began to speak of the difficulties, burdened, as we were already, of taking up all sorts of Poor Law work, and so forth. My father stopped me with a peremptory wave of the brushes. 'Go and do something!' he said. 'We must do something.'

'What can we do?'

'Get them a shelter.'

'That will cost money.'

'Well, that is your affair. Something must be done. Get hold of a warehouse and warm it, and find something to cover them. But mind, Bramwell, no coddling!'

That was the beginning of The Salvation Army Shelters, the earliest and most typical institutions connected with our now world-wide Social Work. But it also throws a ray of light on the characteristic benevolence of The Army's Founder. Benevolence, which is a languid quality in many men, with him was passionate. I should be disposed to place his benevolence first among his characteristics. I write of him here, as far as it is possible to do so, aside from what I humbly acknowledge to have been the great determining force of his life – namely, the uplifting and guiding influence of the Spirit of God. This apart, his benevolence was the first quality to light up. The governing influence of his life was good will to his fellows. I am not saying that he never thought of himself. His saintship was not after the pattern of Francis d'Assisi, at least as described by Paul Sabatier. Nor can I say that he was always at the same level of self-denial and self-effacement in order to give practical expression to his benevolent impulse. But I do say, looking at his life as I saw it over a great span of years, not only in workday association as his comrade and principal helper, but in the still closer intimacy of a son, that his benevolence was the leading feature of his character. He really set out to do good to all men – an object which, no doubt, often seemed hopeless, but not on that account to be less sought after. The horizon of his soul was not limited by human hope – it reached out to Divine Power and Love. His heart was a bottomless well of compassion, and it was for this reason principally that, although perhaps more widely and persistently abused than any other figure of his time, he was even more widely and tenaciously loved.

Bramwell Booth, *Echoes and Memories*[17]

William Cooper was Pastor of the Strict Baptist chapel at Lakenheath, Suffolk for nearly forty years until his death in 1940. Independent of any central ecclesiastical authority, the local minister can still have his problems. He relates one of them, with the mingled love and severity which appears all through his autobiography.

I found there was some chaff in the place that needed to he winnowed out, and which created a great dust. Previously, they had let a man into the church with a fair tongue, but found he wanted to remodel the church. His tongue was very buttery to me, and they soon proved they had made a mistake, as he had great visions about things. He used to go into the desk before I came, saying the old deacons were antiquated, and the church needed fresh blood. Alas! there are such about to-day, who think they can improve the old truths our fathers lived out and died on. This man went so far as to conclude that the church should he disbanded by him and another formed. He had arranged who was to lead the singing, and who the deacons should be, but all this was revealed to me by one of his party who had been misled by him. This poor man was smitten down by the affliction of dropsy, and sent to the infirmary to finish his days. On his dying bed he told me all the plot, but I felt the Lord had forgiven him, and I believe he went home to glory. He asked me to bury him, and wished me to have his garden tools (a nice lot), which I needed, and they are still in use after thirty-four years.

The troubler in Israel had to be withdrawn from, and, finally, because I would not bear his part, he used to shout in the village after me in contempt, and also to some of the timid sheep of Christ's flock. On Sunday he would come, make all the noise he could, and throw the hymnbook along the seat when the hymn was given out, with a contemptible 'Ah, ah!' Some suggested calling the policeman, but I had the words, 'Let him alone;' though once in the pulpit I felt my nature rise, as if to say: 'Put him out, you men.' I was on the point of saying so when the thought of Christ in the garden of Gethsemane came so solemnly to me that I was taken right away from the man. He left the village after some months, and I don't think there was one who regretted it, either professor or profane.

W. S. Cooper, *Goodness and Mercy*[18]

The custom of offering thanks before a meal is one which has unhappily declined and is to be encouraged. Nevertheless, it can become counter-productive.

I once drank tea in company with two Methodist divines of different persuasions, whom it was my fortune to introduce to each other for the first time that evening. Before the first cup was handed round, one of these reverend gentlemen put it to the other, with all due solemnity, whether he chose to *say anything*. It seems it is the custom with some sectaries to put up a short prayer before this meal also. His reverend brother did not at first quite apprehend him, but upon an explanation, with little less importance he made answer that it was not a custom known in his church: in which courteous evasion the other acquiescing for good manners' sake, or in compliance with a weak brother, the supplementary or tea grace was waived altogether. With what spirit might not Lucian have painted two priests, of *his* religion, playing into each other's hands the compliment of performing or omitting a sacrifice, – the hungry God meantime, doubtful of his incense, with expectant nostrils hovering over the two flamens, and (as between two stools) going away in the end without his supper. A short form upon these occasions is felt to want reverence; a long one, I am afraid, cannot escape the charge of impertinence.

Charles Lamb, 'Grace Before Meat'[19]

And, in happy conclusion …

Really the people are very fond of their parson. They know that in him they have a friend to whom they can always go when they are in trouble or perplexity, or when they want 'a character.' If he is ill, or suffering some grievous sorrow, he knows that he has the affectionate sympathy of every one in the village. His virtues are especially dwelt upon, stories told of his charity, his sympathy, his kindliness of heart, and his sermons pronounced miracles of oratory, directly he dies or removes to another parish. There is a large amount of *post-mortem* kindness in the world. His parishioners always take a keen interest in everything he does or says. His words are reported, magnified, transmogrified, so that he hardly recognises his original utterances when again they reach his ears. His people know far more of his concerns than he knows himself. They know the hour he breakfasts, the time at which he seeks his couch. No king's movements are so closely watched and recorded as are those of the parson.

P. H. Ditchfield, *The Old-Time Parson*[20]

Sources

Chapter 1: Godly, Righteous and Sober

1. From *Ecclesiastical Sonnets*, 1822.
2. General Prologue, lines 477–528 (editor's translation).
3. 1665. Bell, 1884, pp. 229–30.
4. 1670. Bell, 1884, pp. 308–9.
5. *Selections from the Poetical Works of Bishop Ken*, Hamilton Adams, 1857, pp. 47–8.
6. 1770.
7. 1857. Dent, 1906, pp. 211, 213.
8. Parker, 1869, pp. 558–9.
9. Wells, Gardener, Darton, 1913, pp. 127–9.
10. SPCK, 1896, pp. 66–7.
11. 1891. Macmillan, 1985, pp. 170–72.
12. 1909.
13. John Murray, 1926, p. 28.
14. Cassell, 1892, pp. 23–5.
15. Foulis, 1914, pp. 204–7.
16. In *Prose, Poems and Parodies of Percy French*, Talbot Press, Dublin, 1929, pp. 141–3.
17. 1656. Epworth Press, 1950, pp. 72–3.

Chapter 2: Erred and Strayed

1. 1637.
2. 1663, Part 1, Canto 3.
3. 1785, Book 2, 'The Timepiece'.
4. 1813, Chs 15 and 18.
5. 1857, Ch. 4.
6. 1837, Chs 27 and 45.
7. 1847, Ch. 4.

8. Bentley, 1838, Vol. 2, pp. 132–4.
9. 1872. Blackwood, 1879, pp. 166–8.
10. Methuen, 1890, pp. 152–3.
11. 1820, Vol. 1. Newnes, 1902, p. 136.
12. From *Poetical Works*, Reeves and Turner, 1859, p. 229.
13. From *Poems*, Benjamin Mussey, Boston, 1850, pp. 145–6.

Chapter 3: *Divers Orders*

1. Dent, n.d., pp. 139–40.
2. Longmans, Brown, Green, 1869, pp. 99–100.
3. Act IV, Scene 1, lines 429–58.
4. Skeffington, 1898, pp. 60–61.
5. In *Collected Poems, Epistles and Satires*, Dent, 1944, p. 391.
6. Constable, 1931, pp. 34–5.
7. Brentano's, 1929, pp. 247–9.
8. Longmans, Green, 1886, pp. 148, 325.
9. Lines 395–431.
10. 1918. Penguin, 1948, pp. 212–13.
11. Skeffington, 1912, p. 174.
12. Dent, 1917, p. 165.

Chapter 4: *To Instruct the People*

1. In *Five Hundred Points of Good Husbandry* (1557), Lackington, 1812, p. 317.
2. Ed. E. F. Rimbault. Reeves and Turner, 1890, pp. 128–9.
3. 1845. Routledge, 1863, p. 16.
4. 1796. Routledge and Kegan Paul, 1971, pp. 31–2.
5. From *Essays of Elia*, Odhams, n.d., pp. 38–40.
6. July 1878, pp. 27–8.
7. Macmillan, 1900, pp. 48–50.
8. 1860, Book 2, Ch. 1.
9. Fellowes, 1858, Vol. 2, pp. 132–4.
10. Part 1, Ch. 8.
11. Macmillan, 1898, p. 65.
12. Longmans, Green, 1930, pp. 68–9.

Chapter 5: *Then Shall Follow the Sermon*

1. 1628. Harding, 1811, pp. 4–8.
2. 1711, No. 106.
3. 1742, Book 1, Ch. 16.
4. Bell, 1906, pp. 427–8.
5. 1792. Clarendon Press, 1914, pp. 108–9.
6. 1759–67. Oxford University Press, 1903, pp. 391–2.
7. 1790, Vol. 3, pp. 11–12.
8. 1859, Ch. 2.
9. 1825. Collins, 1969, p. 71.
10. 1857. Routledge, 1910, pp. 54–5.
11. T. Fisher Unwin, 1899, pp. 76–8.
12. In *Discourses in America*, Macmillan, 1885, pp. 139–42.
13. Vol. 15, p. 195.
14. Skeffington, 1898, pp. 60–61.
15. 1871. Houghton Mifflin, 1913, p. ix.
16. 1895.
17. Ed. James Gibson, Macmillan, 1976, p. 416.
18. Ed. T. H. Johnston, Faber, 1970, p. 533.

Chapter 6: *Such Things as He Possesseth*

1. 1631. *Works*, Clarendon Press, 1938, Vol. 1, p. 516.
2. 1597. *Collected Poems*, Liverpool University Press, 1940, p. 29.
3. From *Poems*, Edward Arnold, 1989, pp. 38–40.
4. Ackermann, 1838, pp. 61–4.
5. Longmans, Green, 1886, p. 143.
6. Joseph Masters, 1856, p. 73.
7. 1861. Dent, 1961, pp. 139–40.
8. 1855. Oxford University Press, 1961, Ch. 8, pp. 96–7.
9. 1865. *Complete Works*, Routledge, 1883, Vol. 5, pp. 216–17.
10. 1903. Collins, n.d., pp. 143–5.
11. Bentley, 1838, Vol. 2, p. 166.
12. 1857. John Murray, 1914, pp. 51–5.
13. Oxford University Press, 1943, pp. 47–8.
14. From *Poetical Works*, Oxford University Press, 1963, p. 169.
15. From *Collected Poems*, ed. James Gibson, Macmillan, 1976, p. 713.

16. Nicholson, 1862, pp. 5–6.
17. 1913. Penguin, 1961, pp. 46–7.
18. 1734, The *Gentlemans Magazine*

Chapter 7: *Forsaking All Worldly and Carnal Affections*

1. Trans. J. A. Giles, Lumley, 1840, pp. 232–3.
2. General Prologue, lines 118–62, editor's translation.
3. 1843, Book 2, Ch. 15.
4. Jackson, Walford and Hodder, 1867, pp. 509, 511–12.
5. 1594. *Dramatic Works*, Pickering, 1873, Vol. 1, p. 152.
6. Act 4, Scene 3.
7. Mowbray, 1907, pp. 99–100.
8. 1881. Macmillan, 1883, pp. 52–3.
9. From *New Poems*, Macmillan, 1900, pp. 30–32.
10. In Lennox Robinson, ed., *A Golden Treasury of Irish Verse*, Macmillan, 1927.
11. From *Poems*, Oxford University Press, 1944, p. 8.
12. 1897. Swan Sonnenschein, 1899, pp. 170–71.
13. In *Some Eminent Women of our Time*, Macmillan, 1889, p. 195.
14. Joseph Masters, 1856, pp. 217–18.
15. 1882, pp. 157–8.
16. Jonathan Cape, 1940.
17. Hutchinson, 1909, pp. 163–5.
18. Sheldon Press, 1975, pp. 392–3.

Chapter 8: *An Honourable Estate*

1. Hurst and Blackett, 1870, pp. 257, 269.
2. 1665. Bell, 1884, pp. 186–8.
3. 1652. Clarendon Press, 1941, p. 239.
4. Mowbray, 1907, pp. 94–5.
5. 1766, Ch. 4.
6. 1814, Book 8.
7. 1848, Ch. 11.
8. Edited by his wife. Kegan, Paul and Trench, 1883, Vol. 2, pp. 34–5.
9. 1903, Ch. 16.
10. 1857, Chs 3 and 11.
11. 1844. Longmans, Green, 1896, p. 66.

12. 1871, Ch. 20.

13. 1873. Macmillan, 1907, Vol. 1, pp. 4–5.

14. Hurst and Blackett, 1870, pp. 333–4.

15. Jonathan Cape, 1953, pp. 148–50.

16. 1870, Ch. 10.

Chapter 9: Factious, Peevish and Perverse

1. 1835. T. Werner Laurie, 1942, pp. 50–51.

2. 1848. Macmillan, 1879, pp. 238–9.

3. 1858.

4. *Edinburgh Review*, Vol. 98, 1853, p. 31.

5. 1903, Chs 51 and 56.

6. Jonathan Cape, 1940, pp. 318–20.

7. 1892. Nelson, 1908, pp. 169–70.

8. Macmillan, 1894, pp. 71–2.

9. 1854, in *Mark Twain's Library of Humor*. Chatto and Windus, 1888, pp. 38–41.

10. Nelson, n.d., pp. 368–70.

11. 1877. Chatto and Windus, 1895, pp. 95–6.

12. 1887. Cape, 1927, pp. 307–9.

13. 1848. Longmans, Green, 1893, pp. 391–2.

14. 1836, pp. 74–6.

15. Chapman and Hall, 1863, Vol 1., pp. 120–22.

16. Hodder and Stoughton, 1906, pp. 14–15.

17. In *Literary Remains*, Macmillan, 1905, pp. 373–4.

Chapter 10: Joyful in the Lord

1. 1640. Bell, 1884, pp. 74–5.

2. Methuen, 1912, pp. 237–8.

3. Pickering, 1838, pp. 4–5, 7.

4. 1831. Hamish Hamilton, 1947, pp. 158–61.

5. 1899. Methuen, 1913, pp. 77–8.

6. From *Scenes of Clerical Life*, 1858. Blackwood, n.d., pp. 73–4.

7. Longmans, Green, 1886, pp. 149–50.

8. 1848. Macmillan, 1879, pp, 161–2.

9. 1843. Routledge, n.d., pp. 230–32.

10. Bentley, 1878, pp. 243–5.

11. Methuen, 1910, pp. 178–9.

12. 1885, Vol. 1, p. 322.
13. P. 289.
14. Methuen, 1910, p. 70.
15. Wells, Gardener, Darton, 1913, pp. 126–7.
16. Faith Press, 1958, pp. 211–12.
17. 1876. The Library of America, 1987, pp. 38–40.

Chapter 11: *In Sundry Places*

1. SCM Press, 1955, pp. 15–17, 21–3.
2. Longmans, Green, 1886, p. 68.
3. 1850. Walter Scott, n.d., pp. 9–11.
4. 1860. Macmillan, 1889, pp. 14–15.
5. Religious Tract Society, 1912, pp. 155–6, 257.
6. Faber, 1998, pp. 378–9
7. Macmillan, 1874, pp. 344–5.
8. From *The Bab Ballads*, Routledge, 1877, pp. 189–93.
9. Wells, Gardner, Darton, 1916, pp. 234–5.
10. Warren & Son, 1910, pp. 95–6.
11. Sanders Otley, 1867, pp. 99–100.
12. Hodder & Stoughton, 1926, pp. 146–8.
13. Gollancz, 1942, pp. 121–3.
14. 1874. Bentley, 1897, pp. 271–2.
15. Wesleyan Conference Office, 1878, pp. 243–4.
16. 1748. Folio Society, 1961, p. 214.
17. Blackwood, 1934, pp. 171–3.
18. In *The Unutterable Beauty*, Hodder & Stoughton.

Chapter 12: *All Sorts and Conditions*

1. 1752, Ch. 10.
2. Oxford University Press, 1935.
3. John Murray, 1930, p. 167.
4. Skeffington, 1912, pp. 186–7.
5. 1821. Oxford University Press, 1967, pp. 5–6.
6. 1850. Nelson, n.d., pp. 157–8.
7. 1749, Book 1, Ch. 3.
8. 1856. Ryburn, 1992, pp. 526–7.
9. In *Poems*, Oxford University Press, 1944, p. 48.
10. In *Collected Poems*, Dent, 1993.

11. In Lennox Robinson, ed., *A Golden Treasury of Irish Verse*, Macmillan, 1927.
12. In *The Untilled Field*, 1903. Heinemann, 1915, pp. 76–9.
13. Geoffrey Bles, 1966, pp. 7, 15–16.
14. Saunders, Otley, 1860, pp. 85–7.
15. 1774. Dent, n.d., pp. 10–11.
16. In *The Principles of Christians Called 'Open Brethren'*, Pickering & Inglis, 1913, pp. 89–91.
17. Hodder & Stoughton, 1925, pp. 1–2.
18. Farncombe, 1943, pp. 97–8.
19. In *Essays of Elia*, Odhams, n.d., p. 136.
20. Methuen, 1910, p. 2.

Acknowledgements

Permission to include the following copyright material is gratefully acknowledged:

From *The Keys of the Kingdom* by A. J. Cronin. Reprinted by kind permission of Victor Gollancz Ltd (a division of the Orion Publishing Group Ltd).

From *Candleford Green* by Flora Thompson. Reprinted by kind permission of Oxford University Press.

From *Seven-Story Mountain* by Thomas Merton. Reprinted by kind permission of Sheldon Press/SPCK.

From *Jane and Prudence* by Barbara Pym, published by Jonathan Cape. Reprinted by kind permission of the Random House Group Ltd.

'The Priest' by R. S. Thomas from *Collected Poems*. Reprinted by kind permission of J. M. Dent.

From *The Poisonwood Bible* by Barbara Kingsolver. Reprinted by kind permission of Faber and Faber.

Attempts have been made to trace all copyright holders. Any errors or omissions, if notified, will be corrected in any future edition.

Index of Authors Quoted

Index of Clergy

(Fact and fiction together, with appropriate title alone – Mr, Dr, Fr – where no Christian name is recorded.)